Storied Revelations

DISTINGUISHED DISSERTATIONS IN CHRISTIAN THEOLOGY

Series Foreword

We are living in a vibrant season for academic Christian theology. After a hiatus of some decades, a real flowering of excellent systematic and moral theology has emerged. This situation calls for a series that showcases the contributions of newcomers to this ongoing and lively conversation. The journal *Word & World: Theology for Christian Ministry* and the academic society Christian Theological Research Fellowship (CTRF) are happy to cosponsor this series together with our publisher Pickwick Publications (an imprint of Wipf and Stock Publishers). Both the CTRF and *Word & World* are interested in excellence in academics but also in scholarship oriented toward Christ and the Church. The volumes in this series are distinguished for their combination of academic excellence with sensitivity to the primary context of Christian learning. We are happy to present the work of these young scholars to the wider world and are grateful to Luther Seminary for the support that helped make it possible.

Alan G. Padgett
Professor of Systematic Theology
Luther Seminary

Beth Felker Jones
Assistant Professor of Theology
Wheaton College

www.ctrf.info
www.luthersem.edu/word&world

Storied Revelations
*Parables, Imagination
and George MacDonald's Christian Fiction*

GISELA H. KREGLINGER

FOREWORD BY
EUGENE H. PETERSON

☙PICKWICK *Publications* · Eugene, Oregon

STORIED REVELATIONS
Parables, Imagination and George MacDonald's Christian Fiction

Distinguished Dissertations in Christian Theology 9

Copyright © 2013 Gisela H. Kreglinger. All rights reserved. Except for brief quotations in critical publications or reviews, no part of this book may be reproduced in any manner without prior written permission from the publisher. Write: Permissions, Wipf and Stock Publishers, 199 W. 8th Ave., Suite 3, Eugene, OR 97401.

Pickwick Publications
An Imprint of Wipf and Stock Publishers
199 W. 8th Ave., Suite 3
Eugene, OR 97401

www.wipfandstock.com

ISBN 13: 978-1-62032-533-9

Cataloguing-in-Publication data:

Kreglinger, Gisela H.

Storied revelations : parables, imagination and George MacDonald's Christian fiction / Gisela H. Kreglinger, with a foreword by Eugene H. Peterson.

Distinguished Dissertations in Christian Theology 9

xiv + 220 pp. ; 23 cm. Includes bibliographical references and indices.

ISBN 13: 978-1-62032-533-9

1. MacDonald, George, 1824–1905—Criticism, interpretation, etc. 2. Imagination. 3. Parables. 4. Christian Fiction. I. Title.

PR4969 K77 2013

Manufactured in the U.S.A.

For
Rosa and Peter Kreglinger

"What do you mean by *a parable*, Mr. Henry?" interrupted Mrs. Cathcart. "It sounds rather profane to me."

"I mean a picture in words, where more is meant than meets the ear."

"But why call it a parable?"

"Because it is one."

"Why not speak in plain words then?"

"Because a good parable is plainer than the plainest words. You remember what Tennyson says—that

'truth embodied in a tale
Shall enter in at lowly doors'?"

"Goethe," said the curate, "has a little parable about poems, which is equally true about parables—

'Poems are painted window-panes.
If one looks from the square into the church,
Dusk and dimness are his gains—
Sir Philistine is left in the lurch.
The sight, so seen, may well enrage him,
Nor any words hence forth assuage him.

But come just inside what conceals;
Cross the holy threshold quite—
All at once, 'tis rainbow-bright;
Device and story flash to light;
A gracious splendour truth reveals.
This, to God's children, is full measure;
It edifies and gives them pleasure.'"

—George MacDonald, *Adela Cathcart*, 272.

Contents

Foreword by Eugene H. Peterson| ix

Acknowledgments | xiii

Introduction | 1

1 George MacDonald: Poet and Theologian | 4

2 Patterns of Subversion and Promise: Jesus' Parables | 14

3 Patterns of Subversion and Promise: Romanticism | 60

4 George MacDonald's Theological Rationale for Story and the "Parabolic" | 102

5 Patterns of Subversion and Promise: *Lilith* | 168

Conclusion | 207

Bibliography | 213

Author Index | 223

Scripture Index | 227

Subject Index | 231

Foreword

THIS IS A MOST timely book. Timely, because the lives of Americans are increasingly distracted, and diverted—hijacked by the computer into cyberspace where it is possible to live without relationships, without grounding, without connection, without commitments, without ritual, without worship. A great number of wise and insightful observers for several decades now have been calling our attention to the resulting cultural, political, and spiritual poverty.

One of the great storytellers in the Christian tradition is George MacDonald, whose storytelling has entered into the Christian mind as a bulwark against the scourge of meaninglessness. MacDonald was a Scottish pastor who turned his writing desk into a pulpit. In addition to sermons, he wrote novels formed out of a penetrating theological imagination. He wrote novels for children and the young, novels for adults. His stories and poems provide his readers with ways to reclaim as their own a world fragmented by secularism and devastated by the "acids of modernity" as fundamentally a world loved by God, a world of grace and salvation.

The Victorian Age (the nineteenth century) provided the setting in which MacDonald did his work. It was the century in which the Christian community was required to think through and reimagine much of what it had grown up with, not unlike the times in which we are now living. Two major events transpired in that century. One, the rise of higher criticism beginning with David Strauss's *Life of Jesus*, which in effect eliminated the supernatural from its understanding of Jesus' life—a Jesus without God. As momentum gathered around this publication, the faith of many was shaken. The second event was the advent of the new science of geology that provided evidence that the age of the earth was much older than the traditional seven-day creation had it. This was followed by the publication of Charles Darwin's *Origin of the Species* that called into question the divine creation of Adam and Eve. The combination of higher criticism questioning the authority of Scripture followed by the evolutionary challenge to divine creation produced a "perfect storm" of doubt and skepticism in both academy and church.

This is the world in which MacDonald wrote. It anticipated the conditions now exacerbated in our times, a depersonalized cyberspace world in which science and religion are so frequently at odds. In the name of the Lord of language MacDonald rescues language from being debased into argument and polemic. He provides us with access to an imagination that cannot be at the service of science alone or religion alone. We need his voice still.

Dr. Gisela Kreglinger has a written a study of George MacDonald that brings his voice back into circulation in a fresh way. Using story laced with poetry and parable and metaphor, MacDonald builds within us the imaginative capacity to comprehend the detailed richness of a world penetrated in every dimension by Father, Son, and Holy Ghost.

As we give ourselves to the power of story, we are moved from the position of a spectator into a life of active participation. This world and the people in it are not here to be explained or argued with; it is a world in which we have been created as participants in relationship with other participants. We are in a *story*—a story that is overall a story of Jesus Christ. And in this Jesus story, in MacDonald's words, "a thousand truths, unknown and yet active, which, embodied in theory, and dissociated from the living mind that was in Christ, will as certainly breed worms as any omer (jar) of hoarded manna."

It has always seemed a great irony to me that people who put such a high value on Scripture, the moment they begin to write and talk about Scripture characteristically depart radically from the way Scripture itself is written. Scripture is primarily written as story, a story chock full of metaphors, and as poetry. How does it happen that abstract propositions, impersonal definitions, and explanations become the stock in trade for so many in the Christian community? If they do tell a story, it is debased to the level of anecdote or illustration. But if we trust the Bible so thoroughly why don't we trust the way the Bible is written? Why this long ingrained habit of reducing these intricately crafted stories to moral lessons, these wild and exuberant metaphors to doctrinal explanations?

Stories and poems have always and continue to be the best verbal way we have to train our imaginations to see and embrace the particularity of place and person, *hereness* and *nowness*, the endless complexity of souls, the glorious diversities of place. It is the best verbal way we have for defending our understanding of God and the world around us against oversimplification and reduction, of preserving the ambiguity and mystery inherent in all of life, an ambiguity and mystery even more pronounced when life is understood under the auspices of God and salvation.

The Christian life, as revealed in our Scriptures and proclaimed in our churches in Word and Sacrament, everywhere and always is a matter of flesh and blood, named persons, places you can locate on a map, personal conversations. The centerpiece of this revelation is the Word made flesh, Jesus born in Bethlehem, raised in Nazareth, walking the roads of Galilee, killed in Jerusalem, and resurrection-alive in the most unexpected places. The Word that is Jesus, and all the words leading up to and deriving from this Word that is Jesus are embodied words, words that are given to us in the form of stories and poems that comprise people, time, and place.

The Devil, according to many who think hard about these things, is incapable of taking on flesh. The Word that saves us became incarnate, took on flesh in Jesus—and, if we will, in us. The Devil who would damn us is disincarnate, incapable of flesh. This Devil's characteristic work is to disincarnate words—turn them into abstractions and generalities, cut them loose from history, from the here and now, and distill them down into a "truth" or "doctrine" or "moral," which we can then use without bothering with the *way* we use them and quite apart from people whose names we know or the local conditions in which we have responsibilities. These de-historicized words can then be wrenched out of the storied context where we first learned them, manipulated at will, used to seduce and make war, arbitrarily stuck here and there, cut and pasted, depersonalized into slogans and ideas, truths and causes quite apart from person and place and time, quite apart from the biblically contextualized word of God. Wonderful truths but without feet-on-the-ground relationships. The Devil is a great intellectual; he loves getting us discussing ideas about God, *especially* ideas about God. He does some of his best work when he gets us so deeply involved in ideas about God that we are hardly aware that while we are reading or talking about God, God is actually present to us and the people whom he has placed in our lives to love, placed right there in front of us. It is the Devil's own work to suggest an inspiring spirituality without the inconvenience of keeping company with Jesus on his way to Jerusalem and the cross. The Devil loves being involved in our Bible studies, diverting our attention from the story itself to figuring out the meaning of this or that word so we can use it in an argument, or carry it around as a kind of talisman. He knows there is no harm in letting us read the Bible if he can just get us excited about the basic truths and inspiring passages, "make them our own" as we say, and forget about the world of listening prayer and the Spirit's presence in everything and everyone all around us. Once he has gotten us in the habit of disincarnating words—turning them into truths or definitions or morals or dogma—he is well on the way to disincarnating *us*, furnishing us with a storyless Christian role, a storyless Christian function. The Devil doesn't tell stories.

George MacDonald continues to be a strong and intelligent presence among us for keeping us alert and participatory in language that derives from the Word made flesh. Dr. Kreglinger has provided us with a magnificent orientation in this Christ-infused theological imagination.

MacDonald referred to stiffly literal and non-relational uses of language as "mummies." Whenever I come across that metaphor, I think of Jesus calling Lazarus from the tomb with "his hands and feet bound" and telling his disciples "Unbind him and let him go." George MacDonald is the disciple who has done that for many of us, and hopefully for many more as you read this book.

Eugene H. Peterson
Professor Emeritus of Spiritual Theology
Regent College, Vancouver, B. C.

Acknowledgments

IT WAS DURING MY studies at Regent College, Vancouver that the idea of this interdisciplinary project was born. Thank you in particular to Mary Ruth Wilkinson for sparking my interest in George MacDonald and Eugene Peterson for his insistence that spiritual theology must avoid as much as possible the tendency toward abstraction and seek to be grounded in actual places, dealing with real people in specific times. He convinced me that story is indeed an important way by which to pursue theology.

I am deeply grateful for the community at St Mary's College, University of St. Andrews. Professor Trevor Hart and Professor Richard Bauckham, as my supervisors, merit special mention for having directed me in this interdisciplinary project. In attempting to bridge the study of theology and literature, the path was often dimly lit and it took special care in placing one step in front of the other. For their guidance and support, I am particularly grateful. Conversations with Thomas Gerold, Carolyn Kelly, and Kirstin Jeffrey Johnson have focused and enriched my thinking about George MacDonald as a theological thinker. Thank you for your encouragement. It is impossible to name everyone here and express in words the gratitude that I feel toward all my housemates, officemates, prayer group members, and the community at All Saint's Episcopal church, St. Andrews.

I thank particularly Poul Guttesen, Ivan and Julie Khovacs, and Dave and Chelle Sterns, Susan and Victor Reynolds, and Hilary and Geoffrey Bridge for their support, hospitality, and friendship. You truly stood by me.

The Gladstone Foundation and St. Deiniol's Library were generous in providing scholarships to study and write in the beautiful setting of

St. Deiniol's library, Hawarden. My teaching assistant Rebecca Poe Hays helped edit the final manuscript. Joshua Hays helped with the indexing. Thank you, Rebecca and Joshua.

I am particularly grateful to Eugene and Jan Peterson for their friendship, hospitality, and generous support.

My family and friends in Germany, and my parents Rosa and Peter Kreglinger in particular, have extended their hospitality to me even when I was not at home. Your annual allotments of wine have followed me even to northern Scotland. Thank you. And yes, there is some *in vino veritas*.

Introduction

"Jesus told the crowds all these things in parables; without parables he told them nothing. This was to fulfill what had been spoken through the prophet: 'I will open my mouth to speak in parables; I will proclaim what has been hidden from the foundation of the world.'" Matt 13:34–35, quoting Ps 78:2

"[I]n the realm of parable writing no one went further than MacDonald in the whole of the nineteenth century."[1]

PARABLES—USED BY JESUS TO reveal to us the Kingdom of God, used to move us from being bystanders to active recipients of God's work of revelation—are constantly at risk of being buried into "mummies of prose" as George MacDonald puts it. We become so familiar with the language of Scripture and are so far removed from the context in which these parables had their meaning that Jesus' parables no longer work on us in this revelatory and transforming way. Each new generation must recover the vibrant, often shocking dimension of Jesus' parables and create a new context in which the gospel is able to recover its piercing truth about the nature of Christian discipleship.

George MacDonald, the Victorian poet and theologian, observed this very process at work in Victorian society. It was a culture *saturated* with Christian jargon but often *void* of a profound understanding of the gospel for its own time and culture. The language of Scripture no longer penetrated people's hearts, thoughts, and attitudes; it no longer transformed people's lives. MacDonald, called to be a pastor, turned to story and more specifically the "parabolic" as a means of spiritual awakening. He created

---

1. MacNeice, *Varieties of Parable*, 95.

fictive worlds in which the language of Jesus would find a new home and regain its revelatory power for his particular Victorian audience.

The following chapters explore the interface between the Bible and George MacDonald's fiction. The way Jesus uses language in the parables sheds light on our understanding of MacDonald's careful use of language in his fiction. Further still, many of MacDonald's stories are infused with the language of the Bible, often in rather surprising ways. While MacDonald was inspired by and well versed in the great Western literary tradition including Dante, Shakespeare, Herbert, Milton, and Goethe, the Romantics were the ones who challenged MacDonald to think more carefully about poetics and the imagination and their respective roles in Christian formation. He found great inspiration in the writings of Novalis, whose reflections on the priest as poet helped elicit MacDonald's own calling as a poet and theologian. Coleridge in turn challenged MacDonald to think about the far-reaching role of the imagination in human cognition, poetic creativity, and spiritual formation, albeit from a much stronger theological perspective.

In light of these influences, MacDonald developed a profoundly *theological rationale* for employing story pastorally that was based on his understanding of Scripture, language, creation, the imagination, and how Christ reveals the Father in and through creation. The purpose of this book is to consider MacDonald's theological rationale for writing Christian fiction and the ways in which his fiction might be invested with parabolic patterns reminiscent of Jesus' parables and the Romantic idea of the priest as poet. Once explicated in light of his theological rationale, *Lilith*, MacDonald's most complex and disputed work of fiction, is a fascinating theological reflection on the theme of participation in Christ's death and resurrection and its importance for Christian formation.

George MacDonald is *not* usually thought of as a theologian. He is most known for his far-reaching influence on C. S. Lewis and the Inklings. *Phantastes* played an important role in Lewis' conversion to Christianity. J. R. R. Tolkien read *The Princess and the Goblin* and *The Princess and Curdie* as a child, and resonances of these stories are found throughout *The Lord of the Rings*.[2] The profoundly theological nature of MacDonald's fiction, however, has too often gone unnoticed and eclipsed MacDonald's pastoral concern to recover Scripture's transformative power for his time. The first chapter introduces the reader to George MacDonald as a poet *and*

---

2. See Kreglinger, "MacDonald."

theologian. What led MacDonald to consider story and the imagination as such central elements in spiritual formation when he grew up in a Scottish reformed tradition that tended to draw on a rather rigid theological system, focusing on the utter depravity of humanity and penal substitution as the primary metaphor for understanding the atonement? The second chapter immerses us in the world of Jesus' parables and discerns a decidedly biblical understanding of parable. What actually is a parable and how do metaphor and allegory work together in parable? These explorations shall provide us with some answers to the question of why Jesus spoke so prominently in parable and the importance of the "parabolic" for spiritual formation. Chapter 3 will then take us to consider the influence of German and English Romanticism on George MacDonald. Novalis, the early German Romantic poet, inspired MacDonald to think carefully about the role of poetry in drawing the believer more fully into the mystery of Christ's death and resurrection. Coleridge became an important conversation partner as MacDonald sought to come to terms with the imagination and human cognition. Coleridge sought to blend Idealism with Christian theology, but MacDonald went in a different direction.

In chapter 4 MacDonald's theological rationale for writing Christian fiction will be explored. MacDonald's perceptive response to the Victorian crisis of faith in light of scientific advancement and the encroachment of historical criticism upon the Victorian mindset sets the stage. It becomes apparent that he refused to embrace historical criticism with its naïve belief that historical investigation can provide direct access to reality. Instead, he points to Christ as the one who reveals the Father in and through creation. Jesus' use of symbols from creation becomes a primary inspiration for MacDonald's use of symbols in his stories and his understanding of the "parabolic." The final chapter offers a decidedly theological interpretation of *Lilith*, one of MacDonald's most complex and disputed works of fiction. MacDonald is far more than a writer of Christian fiction. The volume concludes by considering George MacDonald as a spiritual theologian whose holistic and creative view of spiritual formation in and through story offers a rich fountain from which to draw.

I

George MacDonald
Poet and Theologian

MACDONALD IS PRIMARILY A theological thinker and writer. This seems surprising to many as he is mostly known today for his fiction and fairy-tales and his influence on the famous Inklings, especially C. S. Lewis and J. R. R. Tolkien. This book explores MacDonald's theological rationale for writing Christian fiction, arguing that it is precisely in his less overt theological works of fiction that one finds some of his most profound thinking on the lived dimension of Christian faith. When MacDonald has been considered as a serious theologian (as is the case in two of the most recent important works on MacDonald), his theology, and especially his theological understanding of the imagination, is not brought to bear upon his intentional creation of Christian fiction for expressing his theology.[1] Only when one considers both the form and the content of his works of fiction as theology does one come to a deeper understanding of his particular theology, a theology that aims at the participation and transformation of his literary audience. Many went before MacDonald and shaped him in profound ways, but the greatest influence upon MacDonald always remained Scripture. His imaginative engagement with the world, Scripture, and literature made him a unique voice within

---

1. It was Kerry Dearborn's groundbreaking doctorial dissertation that ushered in a new era in MacDonald scholarship from a theological perspective. See Dearborn, "Prophetic or Heretic." Her published work focuses on the theological importance of the imagination: Dearborn, *Baptized Imagination*. Thomas Gerold's published PhD dissertation focuses on MacDonald's theological anthropology. Gerold, *Gotteskindschaft*. Both of these works are immense contributions to understanding George MacDonald as a theological thinker and writer.

his Victorian context, where story became a primary way to express his theology—a kinship that is ancient but often forgotten in our time, especially in theological circles. Today we would call George MacDonald a spiritual theologian because his primary interest was in the lived dimension of the Christian faith. All of his writings give witness to this pastoral concern, but his fiction does so in a unique way.

MacDonald employed a wide range of genres for his writing. Realistic fiction, mostly set in Scotland and England, make up the largest part of the MacDonald corpus. These novels are significant theologically, as MacDonald addresses many theological issues of his time in these novels, often employing the Aberdeenshire dialect Doric for his most important discussions.[2] MacDonald also wrote poetry and essays on literature, the imagination, and human development. He translated significant literary works from German, Latin, and Italian, including works by Novalis, Schiller, Goethe, Heine, Luther, and Milton.[3] He wrote and preached sermons throughout his life, and these sermons are an important key to understanding his theology. In what follows, we shall provide a brief introduction to George MacDonald that focuses on his Scottish theological background, his emerging interest in literature, and his call to pastoral ministry.[4]

MacDonald's Scottish Background

George MacDonald was born in Huntly, Aberdeenshire, Scotland in 1824 to a financially struggling family, deeply steeped in rural culture with strong roots in Scottish reformed Protestantism. Like his mother, George MacDonald struggled with tuberculosis for most of his life but lived to the

---

2. Dearborn, for example, draws heavily on these novels for tracing MacDonald's theology. Dearborn, "Prophet or Heretic."

3. In *England's Antiphon* he discusses the history of English religious poetry. *Rampolli* contains many of MacDonald's translations.

4. Both Dearborn and Gerold provide careful introductions to his theological and literary background, though I shall offer some different perspectives to the Romantic influences in what follows. Due to the parameters of this book, we will not be able provide a complete biography of MacDonald's life. Important biographies include Hein, *Victorian Mythmaker*; Greville MacDonald, *MacDonald and Wife*; Raeper, *George MacDonald*. Raeper's biography is the most helpful introduction. Greville MacDonald's biography is important as he offers a wealth of information, but must be read with caution. His close relationship with his father makes him less critical, and at times one cannot be certain whether his writing reflects his or his father's opinions. Rolland Hein's biography is important because his access to unpublished MacDonald letters adds some helpful information on MacDonald's life.

age of eighty-one and died in 1905. While MacDonald's maternal grandparents were Catholic, the primary spiritual influence came from his paternal grandparents and his father, who were Protestant. MacDonald's mother died when he was only nine. His grandmother left the mainstream Presbyterian church to attend an independent church called "The Missionar Kirk," which split off from the mainstream Reformed church as a result of the Secession. The family ran a bleaching business but was financially burdened due to a family scandal. MacDonald's uncle Charles had fled the country after accumulating a high amount of debt in illegal financial affairs, and MacDonald's family was held responsible to pay back the debt. George MacDonald's grandmother, a strong and religiously fervent woman, believed that it was Charles's violin lessons that lured him into Satan's snares and resulted in his scandalous behavior. Not uncommon among Secession churches, she burned his violin, believing that music had a bad influence on her children.[5] We mention this particular incident as it shows that MacDonald grew up in a religious context that had at least a skeptical but sometimes even hostile attitude towards the arts. The novel *Robert Falconer* contains autobiographical references to this incident. Greville, George MacDonald's son, mentions that Secession churches on the Isle of Lewis burned pipes and fiddles. How was it possible that such a seemingly narrow religious context would produce one of the most creative and prolific spiritual theologians of the Victorian period?

MacDonald's Theological Background: Scottish Calvinism

MacDonald grew up in a reformed Scottish church that was deeply steeped in scholastic Calvinism of the time. A one-sided emphasis on the sovereignty of God, double predestination, the wrath and judgment of God, and a highly mechanical, impersonal, and legal/contractual understanding of the atonement with a focus on humanity's utter depravity provided the seedbed for a spirituality that was fueled by fear and great uncertainty of one's election into God's kingdom. It also eclipsed God's great love and compassion for his creation. Good works were seen as a sign of God's sovereign election of the believer, and this belief developed into a severe and rigid from of legalism. Kerry Dearborn in particular

---

5. Greville MacDonald, *MacDonald and Wife*, 27–29; Raeper, *George MacDonald*, 19–20; Hein, *Victorian Mythmaker*, 30–31.

has gone to great lengths to show the kind of theory of atonement that MacDonald sought to critique and move away from.[6]

The character of Annie Anderson, an orphan child in MacDonald's adult novel *Alec Forbes of Howglen*, personifies the kind of terror a child would have felt by being continually exposed to this particular teaching. MacDonald provides a careful account of the preaching of Annie's local Missionar Kirk and her response to it. It is worth quoting MacDonald here at some length in order to demonstrate the pastoral impact of this particular teaching:

> He chose for his text these words of the Psalmist: 'The wicked shall be turned into hell, and all the nations that forget God.' His sermon . . . consisted simply of answers to the two questions: 'Who are the wicked?' and 'What is their fate?' The answer to the former question was, 'The wicked are those that forget God;' the answer to the latter, 'The torments of everlasting fire.' Upon Annie the sermon produced the immediate conviction that she was one of the wicked, and that she was in danger of hell-fire . . . A spiritual terror was seated on the throne of the universe, and was called God—and to whom should she pray against it? Amidst the darkness, a deeper darkness fell. She knelt by her bedside, but she could not lift up her heart; for was she not one of them that forget God? And was she not therefore wicked? And was not God angry with her every day? Was not the fact that she could not pray a certain proof that she was out of God's favour, and counted unworthy of his notice? But there was Jesus Christ: she would cry to him. But did she believe in him? She tried hard to convince herself that she did; but at last she laid her weary head on the bed, and groaned in her young despair.[7]

MacDonald's theological and pastoral response to this one-sided and at times distorted theological perspective of this particular scholastic Calvinism was a nuanced one. He continued to affirm the sovereignty of God, rejected double predestination, and focused on the love rather than the wrath of God as the primary motivation of God's redemptive work. He developed a strong emphasis on Jesus, the atoner himself, and his work of reconciling his creation to a loving and forgiving Father. Annie's discovery of the Parable of the Prodigal Son later in the novel gives expression to

---

6. Dearborn, "Prophet or Heretic," 100–129; idem, *Baptized Imagination*, 10–14. For a helpful introduction to the development of Calvin's thought into scholastic Calvinism of MacDonald's time, see Hart, "Reformed Theology."

7. George MacDonald, *Alec Forbes*, 114–16.

MacDonald's theological and pastoral emphasis: it is the love and compassion of God the Father that motivates him to redeem his creation in and through Jesus Christ.[8] Thomas Gerold's careful systematic study of George MacDonald's theology highlights and explores this important emphasis.[9] Surely MacDonald's strong and loving relationship with his own father was a major influence and inspiration in this regard, as well as other contemporary theologians like Thomas Erskine (1788–1870), John McLeod Campbell (1800–1872), and F. D. Maurice (1805–1872).[10]

MacDonald also never lost his love and concern for the physically and spiritually poor, another important heritage of his Scottish Calvinist upbringing. His social consciousness continued to develop under the influence of the Christian Socialist Movement, a movement that found its beginning within the Church of England in the mid-nineteenth century pioneered by such figures as J. M. Ludlow, F. D. Maurice, and Charles Kingsley, the two latter ones personally known by George MacDonald.[11] Industrialization brought with it an urbanization of society and incredible poverty amongst the working class masses in the cities. Peter Jones bemoans the "social complacency" of much of Victorian religious society, and it was a complacency that MacDonald found intolerable and in contradiction to his understanding of the gospel of Jesus Christ.[12]

For MacDonald the gospel must reach into all spheres of life, including the social dimensions, and F. D. Maurice was a great inspiration for him in this regard. This dual emphasis on personal formation and social concern for the poor was an important corrective to a spirituality that tended to emphasize the perfection of the individual, especially popular in the Evangelical party of the Church of England that had been strongly influenced by the Puritan teachings on holiness.[13] An important way the Christian Socialists sought to help the working class was through providing education. Mac-

---

8. Ibid., 361.

9. Gerold, *Gotteskindschaft*.

10. See here especially Horrocks, *Laws*. For the influence of F. M. Maurice on George MacDonald, see Dearborn, *Baptized Imagination*, 48–65. For MacDonald's relationship with his father see the many personal correspondences in Sadler, *Expression of Character*.

11. Jones, *Christian Socialist Revival*.

12. Ibid., 7.

13. Woodworth, *Christian Socialism*, 17–18. George MacDonald's adult novel *Robert Falconer* is a profound reflection on this important dual emphasis in Christian spirituality.

Donald became involved with Bedford College, London teaching English literature, the first British institution to offer higher education for women. MacDonald's affirmation of and concern for women is not rooted in his Scottish heritage but seems to have emerged out of his own understanding of a personal God who has both masculine and feminine attributes and the many female characters that play significant roles in the Bible.[14] MacDonald did not believe that women were the weaker sex, and his choice of female figures for personification of divine attributes in many of his novels and fiction expresses this conviction.[15] The great-grandmother Irene in *The Princess and the Goblin* and *The Princess and Curdie* is surely one of the most powerful and beautiful examples: exuberant in femininity, gentleness of spirit, strength, wisdom, and truth.

George MacDonald, Scripture, and the Parables: Some Introductory Notes

A profound impact on MacDonald's life was his daily exposure to and profound knowledge of Scripture. Raised in a rural Scottish village with a family deeply committed to the Christian faith, his growing up years were marked by daily readings of the Bible. At the age of forty-two, he writes that he has studied the Gospels more than any other book.[16] MacDonald's theological training further contributed to his knowledge of Scripture.[17] In several adult novels MacDonald depicts the importance and centrality of Scripture in the rural Scottish Presbyterian tradition of his day. Janet and David Elginbrod in *David Elginbrod* (1863), Janet Grant in *Sir Gibbie* (1879), and John McLear in *Salted with Fire* (1897)

---

14. Dearborn, *Baptized Imagination*, 113–14. Surely his study of women in the Bible was a major inspiration. See his collections of poems on "Gospel Women" in George MacDonald, *Poetical Works*, 1:221–47.

15. It is obvious in the short story "The Day Boy and the Night Girl" that the girl Nycteris has a stronger character than the boy Photogen. See George MacDonald, *Fairytales*, 304–41.

16. As one would expect of someone who reads the Bible throughout life, MacDonald not only enjoyed reading Scripture but also wrestled with its content. See his various comments on this subject matter in his letters in Sadler, *Expression of Character*, 17, 22, 59, 62, 153–54, 156, 170–71, 179, 275–78, 284, 292, 301. MacDonald read both the NT in Greek and the Septuagint, the Greek translation of the Jewish Scriptures.

17. To what extent this was so, we cannot say as there are no records available on his time spent at Highbury College. Raeper, *George MacDonald*, 63–64; Greville MacDonald, *MacDonald and Wife*, 118.

are all characters that exemplify this deep commitment to reading and knowing Scripture within the family context. MacDonald's many sermons also show his careful engagement with the Bible, focusing primarily on the New Testament (NT).

The parables of Jesus play significant roles in MacDonald's adult fiction and in the spiritual development of his characters. The Parable of the Prodigal Son features prominently in *Robert Falconer*, and Robert and Janet Grant read the Parable of the Prodigal Son to Sir Gibbie in *Sir Gibbie*. Hearing this parable provides a turning point in Annie Anderson's life in *Alec Forbes of Howglen*. Dearborn argues that the Parable of the Prodigal Son is the most important parable in the MacDonald corpus and shaped his theology in considerable ways.[18] MacDonald's short story "The Castle: A Parable" bears significant similarities to the Parable of the Wicked Tenants (Mark 12:1–12 par). Rector Wingfold in *There and Back* reverts to the model of parable speaking in seeking to imitate his Lord. In *Adela Cathcart* the curate Ralf Armstrong employs parable speaking. MacDonald's careful engagement with the Bible can also be seen in the many Scriptural references and allusions that are woven into his fairytales and fantasy novels. This aspect of MacDonald's writing is often neglected by MacDonald scholarship, but we shall pay special attention to it in our discussion of *Lilith*.

Literary Influences and the Shaping of MacDonald's Pastoral Imagination

Another important influence upon MacDonald is his interest in and knowledge of literature in general and the German and English Romantic tradition, with its emphasis on aesthetics and poetics as a way to approach mystery, in particular. It is remarkable that MacDonald, despite the prevalent suspicion towards art in his own tradition, began thinking about the importance of poetry and the imagination at an early age. Surely his exposure to the Bible (King James Version) with its poetic aspects and the Celtic tradition in childhood paved the way for a more conscious engagement with poetics at a later stage in his life. George MacDonald's maternal uncle George MacKay was a Celtic scholar and a friend of Sir Walter Scott. Due to his ill health in childhood, George MacDonald spent

---

18. Dearborn, *Baptized Imagination*, 113.

many a summer holiday with his uncle's family by the coast.[19] MacDonald started reading German literature some time during his college years at King's College in Aberdeen and must have taught himself to read it.[20] At the age of twenty-six, he was able to give an impressive translation of Novalis' "Spiritual Songs," taking his introductory notes from Tieck's writings on Novalis. It was of importance for MacDonald to keep "the rhythm and rhyme of the original" as much as possible.[21] This is remarkable because MacDonald never took a degree in literature or German, and yet his grasp of the German language with its poetic nuances is impressive. To this day, his translations of Luther's hymns are the choice translations used in the American Edition of *Luther's Works* because they capture the rhythm and rhyme of the original so well.[22]

MacDonald's studies at King's College Aberdeen included classical languages (Latin and Greek) and the sciences (mathematics, physics, and chemistry). In preparation for becoming a pastor, he went to study theology at Highbury Theological College, London. It was during this time that he was exposed to lectures on literature by A. J. Scott at Marylebone Institute.[23] It was most likely Scott's passion for both theology and literature and his wide range of interests in general that shaped MacDonald's journey in a significant way.[24] Scott was friends with Thomas Erskine, F. D. Maurice, and John Ruskin, and he opened many doors for MacDonald. Under the influence of Scott, MacDonald also turned to lecturing on literature as early as 1853, and his talks included lectures on Dante,

---

19. On Macdonald's celtic roots see Greville MacDonald, *MacDonald and Wife*, 38, 44, 46–47. Dearborn, *Baptized Imagination*, 14–17. Hein, *Victorian Mythmaker*, 39.

20. Greville suggests that MacDonald came across a whole range of romances and German classics while cataloguing a library in the north of Scotland during his summer break in 1842. Greville MacDonald, *MacDonald and Wife*, 72–73.

21. George MacDonald, *Spiritual Songs*, vi.

22. Leupould, *Luther's Works*, 189–94.

23. Raeper, *George MacDonald*, 43, 67–68.

24. MacDonald dedicated his novel *Robert Falconer* to Scott and writes: "To the memory of the man who stands highest in the oratory of my memory, Alexander John Scott." Thomas Erskine, a close friend of Scott's, writes about Scott in the preface to one of Scott's books: "I often wondered . . . at the number and variety of matters in which he took interest, and which he had made himself master of; and yet I always felt that he never lost sight of the relation of each department to the great whole, the place which it held in the hierarchy of things." Scott, *Discourses*, xvii. See also MacDonald's many comments on and letters to A. J. Scott in Sadler, *Expression of Character*. For a sample of Scott's lectures on literature see Scott, *Vernacular Literature*.

Shakespeare, Milton, Robert Burns, Sir Walter Scott, Tennyson, Wordsworth, and Shelley.[25]

The Call to Pastoral Ministry

Another shaping force was MacDonald's strong sense of call to pastoral ministry. His first intention was not to become a writer. He had set his heart on becoming a minister, and his official training had prepared him for this vocation. His employment as a congregational minister in Arundel, a small town south of London, did not, however, last very long. Soon his orthodoxy was questioned, as MacDonald believed that animals would go to heaven and that "heathens" would be given another chance in the afterlife. He was also accused of being "tainted with German theology," which was probably related to MacDonald's recent private publication of Novalis' "Spiritual Songs." He was forced to resign his office in 1853 after being a minister to this congregation for less than three years.[26]

What is significant at this point of MacDonald's life is that he had no intention to lay down his calling as a preacher of the gospel. In March 1853 he writes to his brother: "My desire from God is that he would give me a place to speak freely and work freely in." Similarly, he writes to his father the same year: "Do not think I intend giving up preaching—but I shall be very happy not to be dependent on it—if so it pleases God. Preaching I think is in part my mission in this world and I shall try to fulfil it."[27] The writing life that unfolded before MacDonald, sometimes under the most painful circumstances of vocational uncertainly, physical suffering, financial poverty, and the loss of many loved ones, became the context in which he was able to speak and write freely. The pen, as Kirstin Jeffrey Johnson puts it, became his pulpit.[28] Ronald MacDonald, MacDonald's son, asserts that

> Because his religion was his life, he could no more divide the religious from the secular than a fish separate swimming from water . . . I have heard of men whose whole lives were coloured by religion. But George MacDonald's life *was* religion . . . his

---

25. Amell, *Art of God*. Amell introduces this collection with a helpful essay on MacDonald's development as a lecturer under the influence of Scott.

26. Raeper, *George MacDonald*, 90–95. Greville MacDonald, *MacDonald and Wife*, 177–80.

27. Raeper, *George MacDonald*, 94. Sadler, *Expression of Character*, 67.

28. Johnson, "Sacred Story," 35.

imaginative faculty was a prism, falling through which the Great White Light was disparted into seventy times seven hues of human delight.[29]

While MacDonald scholarship is in consensus that this might be true for his adult novels, poems, and written sermons, there is less agreement about his fantasy and fairytales and to what extent these are theological and were written in the service of the gospel. By looking at George MacDonald within the parabolic tradition of the NT and the subversive poetics of the Romantics, we seek to shed new light on this very important question and reconsider whether Ronald MacDonald's assessment that MacDonald could not "divide the religious from the secular" is indeed correct.

In the following chapter we shall look at the parables of Jesus. There is considerable confusion over what parables actually are and how they function. Drawing on the philosophy of language will shall explore the nature of the parables of Jesus. This discussion will become very important for understanding MacDonald's use of poetic language and parabolic patterns, and it will provide new insight into one of MacDonald's most difficult works of fiction: *Lilith*. It is remarkable how much contemporary discussions on the philosophy of language resonate with George MacDonald's understanding of poetics and the imagination.

---

29. Ronald MacDonald, "George MacDonald," 112–13.

2

Patterns of Subversion and Promise
Jesus' Parables

JESUS WAS A MASTER of using parables to shape the imagination and consequently the lives of his followers and foes alike. While Jesus' parables are in some ways quite different from George MacDonald's Christian fiction, there are significant ways in which MacDonald's works resemble and imitate the way Jesus taught in and through parable. MacDonald's fiction, especially *Phantastes* and *Lilith*, are complex literary creations, and while I shall argue in this book that parabolic patterns reminiscent of the parables of Jesus are an important way by which one can understand these works, it is by no means the only or exclusive way to understand them. Even as we look at the parables of Jesus themselves, we shall find a great variety and complexity among them that defy easy categorization. It is their very particular and often subversive use of language for pastoral reasons that make this comparison a compelling one. We must begin by looking at the parables of Jesus. The aim here is not to provide a tight definition of Jesus' parables, as the wide variety of parabolic speech found in the Old and New Testaments does not lend itself to narrow definitions. Rather, the aim is to explore how Jesus' parables "work," trace patterns and strategic element within them, and then consider in what ways George MacDonald's fiction contains similar elements and how MacDonald consciously continues within the parabolic tradition of Jesus for the formation of his Christian audience. This chapter then explores the nature and function of Jesus' parables.

Towards Understanding the Form and Function of Jesus' Parables

While the usage of parabolic speech increases drastically with Jesus' ministry, it is informative to explore the antecedent of it in the Old Testament. The Hebrew word *mashal* is used in the Old Testament (OT) to denote the English word "parable." It literally means "to imitate, to represent, to be like, to become like."[1] It is used in the OT to describe not only parables but also proverbs and proverbial sayings, prophetic figurative discourse, similitude, poems, wisdom sayings, riddles, comparisons, and example stories. Thus, *mashal* covers a much wider range of sayings and literary compositions in the OT than the English word "parable," and the attempt of form critics to classify them into a clear scheme has turned out to be impossible.[2] The LXX translates *mashal* as *parabolē*, and there are forty-two occurrences of this word in the OT.

An example of a more extended parable used for prophetic proclamation is found in 2 Sam 12:1–19 in which Nathan tells a parable to David, presumably in order to convict him of his sin. Ezekiel also uses an extended parable/riddle in order to confront Israel's sin and rebellion against God. He tells the Parable of the Two Eagles and the Vine (Ezek 17:1–8), the Parable of the Lion (19:1–9), and the Parable of the Vine (19:10–14). Similarly, the prophet Isaiah uses parabolic form prophetically of Israel as God's vineyard and his judgment upon them (Isa 5:1–7). These longer parables in the OT bear some similarities to some parables of the NT, a fact made especially evident when we see the Parable of the Vineyard in Isaiah re-appropriated in the parable of the Wicked Tenants (Mark 12:1–12 par).[3] Parables occur frequently in Rabbinic literature—the earliest written form of which dates back to AD 200.[4]

---

1. BDB 605.

2. Jeremias, *Gleichnisse Jesu*, 13.

3. The Parable of the Two Eagles and the Vine in Ezek 17 reminds one in structure of the Parable of the Sower in Mark 4 par. First, the parable is given (Ezek 17:1–8; Mark 4:1–9), is followed by a remark about the hearers' lack of understanding, and concludes with an allegorical explanation of the parable (Ezek 17:12–21; Mark 4:13–20). The Parable of the Mustard Seed seems to allude to the parable of Ezek 17:22–24. In Ezekiel, God plants a cedar and under it the birds will live. In the Parable of the Mustard Seed, the birds of the air build their nest in the shrub of the mustard seed.

4. The ground breaking work discussing Rabbinic parables in comparison to NT parables was written by D. Flusser. See Flusser, *Rabbinischen Gleichnisse*.

The Greek word *parabolē* is made up of two words. The preposition *para* changes its meaning according to the case of the noun it governs. With a genitive it means "from (the side of)"; with the dative "beside, in the presence of, near"; with the accusative, it means "alongside of." The noun *bolē* means "a throw" or "a stroke."[5] The word *parabolē* etymologically speaking means to throw something alongside of or from the side rather than directly. It is not direct speech. It is indirect; it "strikes" from the side. It is not *prosbolē* but *parabolē*. The etymology of this word gives way to an important dimension of parabolic speech: they confront us indirectly.

The use of *parabolē* in the NT covers some of the same ground as the use of *mashal* in the OT. The Greek *parabolē* covers such forms as proverbs, aphorisms, as well as short and pithy comparisons. Other parables are short stories with a surprising amount of complexity, subtlety, and twist. The latter form is not found in the OT. Examples of longer parables with a realism and complexity not found in OT parables are the parables of the Wicked Tenants (Mark 12:1–12 par), the Good Samaritan (Luke 10), the Prodigal Son (Luke 15), and the Unjust Steward (Luke 16). The most common use of *parabolē* in the Synoptics refers to short stories and what seem to be comparisons such as the Parables of the Leaven, the Mustard Seed, the Treasure, and the Pearl. These are longer than a proverb and can vary from a rather short saying to a short story like the Laborers in the Vineyard.

Altogether, the NT contains fifty occurrences of *parabolē*. Only two of them occur outside the Synoptic Gospels and both are found in Hebrews.[6] The usages of *parabolē* in the Synoptic Gospels are almost exclusively related to Jesus' proclamation of the Kingdom of God. Approximately one third of NT text citing Jesus' teaching comes in the form of parabolic speech, showing that parables are a principal means for his proclamation. NT scholarship has gone through considerable changes in its understanding of what NT parables are and how they should be interpreted. While there has been more consensus over the proverbial sayings and shorter comparative stories, there has been much disagreement over the longer and more complex parables and how they function.

The great variety in NT parables is certainly one aspect that has made it difficult to understand how parables work. In addition, the parables are often much more complex and intricate than one would think at first

---

5. BDAG 144, 611.

6. These two uses of *parabolē* are of a comparative or typological kind.

sight. Klyne R. Snodgrass, in his survey of the history of the interpretation of the parables, puts it succinctly when he asks:

> How do we do justice to the "language event" character of the parables, retain their force, and yet understand the theology they express without reducing them to pious (or not so pious) moralism? The parables have an unquestionable depth. How can we legitimately appreciate their "field of meaning" within the intent of Jesus without turning them into polyvalent modelling clay?[7]

Snodgrass' question is an important one, and the task at hand must be to discern the questions we must ask and address in order to understand the nature of Jesus' parables more fully. Several issues continue to emerge in the history of the interpretation, such as the importance and reliability of the Gospel contexts, the extent to which can we reconstruct the *ipsissima verba*, *ipsissima vox*, and original structure of the parables of Jesus, and equally, identifying criteria which are helpful in such a reconstruction.[8] Closely related to these issues is, of course, the question of genre, i.e., the relationship between parable, metaphor, and allegory. The strong disagreement and wide variety of interpretation shows how complex the parables are and that a careful interpretation of them has to consider a whole range of issues, such as the historical, socio-political, cultural, and aesthetic-literary dimension of the parables. The consideration of historical questions cannot be separated from the aesthetic-literary dimensions. A proper understanding of parables must consider both aspects and see how they inform one another.

The nature of the relationship between the parables, metaphor, and allegory has remained ambivalent in parable studies and needs to be addressed in more detail. Adolf Jülicher sought to correct an overly allegorical interpretation but ended up using Artistotelian categories for understanding the parable genre, thereby setting up a stark contrast between parable on the one hand and allegory and metaphor on the other. C. H. Dodd interpreted parables from an eschatological understanding of the Kingdom of God, seeking to correct an overly futuristic/apocalyptic understanding of the parables and in doing so focused too narrowly on "realized eschatology." Joachim Jeremias also concentrated on the eschatological nature of the parables, seeking a more balanced view

---

7. Snodgrass, "Allegorizing," 27.

8. For a careful discussion of the history of parable interpretation see Kreglinger, "Christian Fiction," 16–42.

of eschatology and arguing that the Kingdom of God is "in the process of being realized." The suspicion of allegory is perpetuated by Jeremias, and his attempted reconstruction of the original form of the parables was informed by the assumption that allegorical elements of the parables are later additions of the Early Church. Jeremias assumed that Jesus' parables and his teaching were much simpler than the ones preserved by the Early Church. Both Dodd and Jeremias neglected the aesthetic dimension of the parables in order to make room for a recovery of the eschatological dimension of the parables of Jesus. The focus was on getting to the *ipsissima vox* of Jesus.

John Dominic Crossan, representative of a wider movement and particularly the New Hermeneutics school, sought to correct the neglect of the aesthetic and literary dimension of the parables. His focus was on the subversive nature of language and the existential dimension of the parables. Kenneth Bailey brought out the complexity of some of the parables by looking at their literary nature and cultural context. William Herzog made the most radical shift as he interprets the parables literally and dismisses the aesthetic-literary dimension as well as the Gospel context of the parables of Jesus. In light of this great ambiguity among NT parable scholars, it is important for understanding the nature of parables to investigate the question of the relation between parable, metaphor, and allegory more closely.[9] By providing clear definition for each, we can differentiate them from one another as well as show how they are related. As the definition of metaphor is the most complex, disputed, and confusing one, we will begin with it.

What Then Is A Metaphor? Clearing the Ground

The earliest accounts we have of metaphor go back to Aristotle and Quintilian. Aristotle's account especially has considerably shaped subsequent discussions of metaphor.[10] Adolf Jülicher bases his definition of parable on categories derived from Aristotle and holds to a substitutionary view

---

9. Even John Dominic Crossan, whose focus was to recover the literary-aesthetic dimension of the parables of Jesus, only provides a very rudimentary discussion of metaphor and allegory and their relationship to and in the parables of Jesus. More recent books on the parables also lack any helpful discussion. See Crossan, *In Parables*; Crossan, *Power*; Bailey, *Jacob*; Schottroff, *Parables*; Stern, *A Rabbi Looks*; Snodgrass, *Stories with Intent*.

10. Soskice, *Metaphor*, 3.

of metaphor.[11] Janet Soskice has challenged such substitutionary or ornamentalist interpretations of Aristotle as too narrow; she argues that Aristotle's understanding of metaphor is, in fact, more complex. In the *Poetics*, we find indications that Aristotle suggested that metaphor may name the unnamed and may, as Soskice puts it, "be active in the extension of our understanding,"[12] a dimension of metaphor to which we will return later on in this chapter.

According to Soskice, it was the empiricists who developed a substitution view of metaphor. The seventeenth-century philosophers such as Hobbes and Locke critiqued the use of rhetoric and figurative speech in philosophical argument because it manipulates the will; it is "verbal trickery."[13] Metaphor was argued to be purely decorative and dispensable, a mere substitute for what can be stated plainly and literally. In this view, metaphor is a figurative substitute for literal expression. Against this view, however, we shall argue along with Soskice that such an understanding of metaphor is reductionistic and unsatisfactory.

Soskice discusses three prevalent theories on how metaphor works. The first is the substitution theory, introduced to the study of the parables by Jülicher. The substitution theory assumes that metaphor is just another way of saying what can be said literally. It gives a fresh spin on worn-out literal language. Metaphor—like décor and ornamentation—is an expendable substitute for literal language.[14] With Soskice, however, we would argue that metaphor does more than just function as a substitute

---

11. Jülicher argues that Aristotle's understanding of metaphor is substitutional. Metaphor, according to Jülicher, is a word that needs to be replaced by another in order for the reader to understand the context in which the metaphor occurs. This is what distinguishes metaphor from comparison. Jülicher, *Gleichnisreden Jesu*, 52.

12. Soskice, *Metaphor*, 9. For similar assessments of Aristotle see Lakoff and Johnson, *Metaphors*, 190; Jüngel, "Metaphorical Truth," 40–44. Jüngel shows that Aristotle's understanding of metaphor goes beyond mere comparison. He argues that for Aristotle, metaphorical language is "bringing together the surprise of linguistic novelty and the familiarity of that which is already known. In this way a gain is always made through metaphor. The horizon of being is expanded in language" ("Metaphorical Truth," 40).

13. Soskice, *Metaphor*, 12. Soskice cites in particular extracts from Locke's "Of the Abuse of Word" in Locke's *Essay Concerning Human Understanding*. Lakoff and Johnson argue along similar lines. See Lakoff and Johnson, *Metaphors*, 190. It was the Romantics who first sought to recover a more balanced view of metaphor, and it is to the Romantics like Novalis and Coleridge that George MacDonald turned in his search for a more balanced view of language.

14. Soskice, *Metaphor*, 24–26.

for literal speech. Metaphor makes, as Soskice puts it, "some addition to significance;"[15] it works actively in the furtherance of the hearer's understanding. Paul Ricoeur's critique of the substitution model is very similar. It is insufficient because it cannot account for the fact that metaphor creates meaning.[16]

Another approach to metaphor that Soskice considers is the emotive theory. The basic emotive theory argues that metaphor does not have a cognitive dimension at all and its impact is affective. As Soskice notes, this idea has much in common with "emotive" accounts of religious and ethical language and shares their problems. Soskice rightly challenges such theories, noting that

> . . . it has been difficult to formulate a convincing theory of "emotive meaning" bereft of cognitive content. There must be some guiding cognitive feature which the emotive response is the response to. We cannot conceive of emotive "import" apart from a cognitive content which elicits it.[17]

The third approach that Soskice considers is incremental theories. The basic idea of this approach is that what is said in a metaphor cannot be said in any other way. The combination of parts created in a metaphor can produce new and unique meaning. In contrast to the substitution theory, where a metaphor simply says something that is already known, an incremental theory proposes that metaphor contributes something new as it increases understanding.[18]

Defining Metaphor: Increment and Interanimation

Of three incremental theories that Soskice discusses, it is the "interanimation" theory that represents her own position.[19] Rejecting both substitutionary and emotivist accounts, this theory seeks to draw attention to the fact that metaphors are not bereft of cognitive import but advance understanding in ways that other modes cannot. Metaphor, Soskice suggests, creates an "intercourse" or "interanimation," not between two

---

15. Ibid., 25.
16. Vanhoozer, *Biblical Narrative*, 63.
17. Soskice, *Metaphor*, 27.
18. Ibid., 25.
19. The other two theories are the "Intuitionist" and "Controversion" theory. See ibid., 31–38.

words but between two thoughts. In order to explain this process, Soskice, employing I. A. Richards's categories, distinguishes between the tenor, which is the underlying subject matter of the metaphor, and the vehicle that presents it.[20] The following example helps clarify the terms and dynamic:

> A stubborn and unconquerable flame
> Creeps in his veins and drinks the streams of life.[21]

Here, the underlying subject matter or "tenor" is the idea of a fever from which someone is suffering. The "vehicle" for it is the description of the flame. The fever is never mentioned in the description, showing that the interaction is not between words but thoughts. The interaction between the two ideas (vehicle and tenor) adds to our understanding of the one subject matter. It is important to notice that the metaphor has only one subject, which is the fever, and the vehicle *is suggestive of* this subject matter. The relationship between them must not be reduced to a mere comparison, even though comparative elements are present.[22] For Soskice a "good metaphor does not merely compare two antecedently similar entities, but enables one to see similarities in what previously had been regarded as dissimilars."[23] It is in this interaction or interanimation of tenor and vehicle that metaphor describes and depicts something in a unique way. The interaction between tenor and vehicle is based on a comparison but goes beyond comparison.

In order for a metaphor to work, there must be a certain amount of similarity and dissimilarity between the vehicle and the tenor. Where there is no similarity, communication breaks down and the metaphor will not work. Eberhard Jüngel, relying on Aristotle, puts it this way: "Metaphors must be successful. If they are to succeed, similarity must be discerned since 'a good metaphor implies an intuitive perception of the similarity in dissimilars.'"[24] Thus, metaphors must also have a certain amount of dissimilarity in order to be able to advance meaning and not

---

20. Ibid., 43.

21. Ibid., 45.

22. A comparison theory of metaphor argues that a metaphor always has two subjects, something that Soskice challenges with her own definition of metaphor. Ibid., 45–47.

23. Ibid., 26.

24. Jüngel, "Metaphorical Truth," 39. For a similar argument see Soskice, *Metaphor*, 26.

collapse into mere comparison. The greater the dissimilarity between the vehicle and the tenor, the more surprising, shocking, and subversive a metaphor becomes. Jüngel also summarizes this dynamic well: "Metaphorical language harmonizes in the most exact way the creative potential of language and strict conceptual necessity, bringing together the surprise of linguistic novelty and the familiarity of that which is already known. In this way a gain is always made through metaphor."[25] Jüngel continues by arguing that the dissimilarity is created by an unusual use of words.[26] A word is taken out of its familiar context/ordinary usage and placed into a new and/or unexpected context.[27] In this way the range of meaning of a word is modified, and this new combination of words creates new meaning as it extends one's understanding of reality.

To describe metaphor as "speaking about one thing and meaning another" is unsatisfactory as it presumes a substitution theory (which is more appropriate when talking about allegory, for example). Metaphor is better described as speaking about one thing in terms that are seen to be *suggestive of* another.[28] The interaction of the two elements of tenor and vehicle contributes new understanding of the one subject matter. Both are needed, each playing its vital part. In this way metaphor purports meaning or, as Soskice puts it, is an "embodiment of new insight."[29] Depending on the level of similarity and dissimilarity between the tenor and vehicle, this often happens in surprising and even shocking ways.

---

25. Jüngel, "Metaphorical Truth," 40.

26. As Soskice points out, this is not only true for words. Metaphors must not be reduced to words only but can occur in larger semantic contexts such as phrases or whole sentences. See Soskice, *Metaphor*, 10. Fletcher's definition seeks to avoid the reduction of metaphor to that of words and defines metaphorical use as follows: "Metaphors . . . convey real transfers of meaning from a standard prose sense to an unusual poetic sense." Fletcher, relying on the work of Aristotle, emphasizes the importance of the element of surprise and therefore liveliness of metaphor: "This extremely important criterion of surprise should, I think, be weighted in the balance whenever we wish to call a figure metaphorical. The more metaphors . . . the greater the amount of liveliness." Fletcher, *Allegory*, 75–76. Fletcher refers to Aristotle's *Rhetoric* 3.12.1412a in this regard.

27. Jüngel, "Metaphorical Truth," 46.

28. Soskice, *Metaphor*, 14.

29. Ibid., 48.

Transcendence, Mystery, and Metaphor

The question of whether metaphorical speech is necessary is, we shall see, closely related to the question of how we can speak of an infinite God in finite language, though it is not limited to the context of theological discourse. For speaking about certain kinds or levels of reality, it seems only metaphor will do. This is the fundamental claim of incremental theories. For Soskice, metaphor is "capable of saying that which may be said in no other way."[30] Any attempt to reduce metaphor to literal equivalent will include a loss of meaning.[31] The elusive nature of reality demands and is reflected in the peculiar structure of metaphorical language, and nowhere more so than in our talk of God. Soskice speaks of

> the radically elusive nature of our subject-matter when we claim to speak about God . . . the fact that when the believer is asked to explain what he means by God's "fatherly kindness" or his "just wrath" he must use expressions equally metaphorical or say nothing at all . . . Put it this way, the sceptic's problem is not a problem with metaphor as such when employed in religious language, but with the possibility of language about God at all. His difficulty is not with the way in which religious metaphors are significant or intelligible, but with the problem of how, even granted the existence of the transcendent God, we can possibly claim to talk about him in finite language.[32]

For Soskice, then, the question of the irreducibility of metaphor is closely linked to the question of how we can speak of a transcendent God within the confines of language at all. Metaphorical language is the inevitable way to speak about God as metaphors are suggestive in nature, not seeking to confine the tenor to the meaning of the vehicle. Strictly speaking, in theological terms the gap between the transcendent and immanent, the uncreated and created, God and the world cannot be bridged by human language as such but only because God took flesh and revealed himself in human terms. We should note, therefore, that the metaphors of Christian discourse are not "discerned" but revealed.

There is a parallel in this regard between the transcendence of God and the mysteriousness of reality more widely (though the case of God

---

30. Ibid., 44.

31. The question of what is the difference between metaphorical and literal language is important and will be addressed at a later stage of this chapter.

32. Soskice, *Metaphor*, 96.

remains *sui generis*). As it is impossible to capture God in human language, so do many areas of reality resist an easy capture in words. The world we live in is far more mysterious and complicated than is often admitted. Soskice refers us to

> the ancient Greeks who made use of metaphor to chart the unexplored reaches of the mind, and . . . the psychologist who speaks of "streams of consciousness" or the political scientist who speaks of the "cold war" or the wine taster trying to differentiate two clarets. There are many areas where, if we do not speak figuratively, we can say very little.[33]

It is easy to forget how thoroughly metaphorical our daily language is not only in matters pertaining to theology but to all spheres of our human existence.

Metaphor, Accountability, and Limitation

If what is said in metaphor cannot be said in any other way, the question must be raised how one might evaluate metaphor. George Lakoff and Mark Johnson, in their excellent study of how widely metaphors permeate everyday language and life, have shown that metaphors are often accompanied by what they call "metaphorical entailments." Metaphors have a field of meaning, and there is an orderliness to them that can be explored systematically. One example Lakoff and Johnson provide is the metaphor "time is money."[34] This metaphor carries with it many entailments such as "I am spending my time," "I am wasting my time," "I lost an hour," "I don't have time," "How much time do you have left," and "This shortcut saved me an hour" just to name a few. By systematically exploring the metaphorical entailment of "time is money," we can come to an understanding of the predominant way in which the Western world has conceptualized time without having been able to express the metaphor "time is money" in literal terms. One way of evaluating metaphors is on the basis of the range and orderliness of their respective sets of entailments.

It is also important to notice that the metaphor "time is money" only provides a very limited understanding of time and in fact hides other aspects of it.[35] Time can be seen as a gift, something to be celebrated

---

33. Ibid.
34. Lakoff and Johnson, *Metaphors*, 8–13.
35. Ibid., 12–13.

like anniversaries, and time can be understood as a place of rest, like the Sabbath. The metaphor "time is money" by no means expresses a full and comprehensive understanding of time. Metaphors do not seek to capture the full meaning of the subject matter but given their suggestive nature, highlight certain aspects while hiding other aspects. The overemphasis on the metaphor "time is money" in the Western world has caused other dimensions of time such as "time is a gift" to fall into the background.[36] Because good metaphors function on the basis of discerning similarities in dissimilars, a given metaphor will emphasize one aspect of a thing while hiding others. A whole range of images may be needed in order to approach the field of meaning of the larger reality.

Metaphors We Live By

Soskice confines her definition of metaphor to that of figures of speech, restricting metaphors to linguistic phenomena only.[37] According to Lakoff and Johnson, though, metaphors shape not only our language but also our pre-linguistic conception and experience of the world. Metaphors play a fundamental and central role in our understanding and ability to conceptualize the world.

Lakoff and Johnson demonstrate this by showing how experiences with physical objects provide the basis for viewing, structuring, and naming non-physical events, emotions, and ideals.[38] One example is what Lakoff and Johnson call orientational metaphors. The experience of human spatial orientation gives rise to such orientational metaphors. "Happy is up" and "sad is down" are two examples. One commonly says "I'm feeling up," "my spirit rose," and "you are in high spirits." Examples of sad are "I am feeling down," "he is really low these days," and "I fell into a depression." These metaphorical usages of spatial orientation are based on the physical experience of a drooping posture while feeling sad and depressed, while an erect position is indicative of a positive emotional state.[39] Lakoff and Johnson make a similar argument for the way we structure our understanding of an argument in terms of the metaphor of war. In argumentation, one attacks, defends, counterattacks, retreats, sur-

---

36. See, for example, Abraham Heschel's book *The Sabbath* where he seeks to emphasize the theological importance of time.

37. See Soskice, *Metaphor*, 74–83, esp. 81.

38. Lakoff and Johnson, *Metaphors*, 59.

39. Ibid., 14–15.

renders, wins, and loses. The metaphor of war and its metaphorical entailments shape the way we view and understand arguments. Of course, war is not the only metaphor we employ to speak about arguments. Another metaphor used to get at the concept of an argument is that of a container. An argument for example can have "little content" or "holes in it." An argument can be said "to be empty" or "full of substance."[40]

Due to the fact that these metaphorical structures have been thoroughly assimilated into our everyday language, we do not notice their metaphorical aspect. As such, they are metaphors "we live by," as Lakoff and Johnson put it. They now appear to be literal speech.[41] What is important to notice here is that metaphors and metaphorical structures are no mere ornament to literal speech but play a central and crucial part in forming a culture's understanding of life and the world. For Lakoff and Johnson, such metaphors shape not just our speaking of the world but the ways in which we experience it.

Metaphors have a particularly important role when one attempts to talk about non-physical things like ideas, feelings, events, and, as already discussed, theological matters. While we will discuss George MacDonald's understanding of metaphor in more detail in chapter 4, it is important to point out the close parallel with MacDonald here. MacDonald, like Lakoff and Johnson, articulates an account of metaphor that is central to the way we engage with reality. The physical world, or, as MacDonald refers to it, the "outer world" or the "macrocosm," provides the language and pattern that is then transferred and used metaphorically to speak about the region of the "inner world" or the "microcosm" such as feelings and thoughts. There exists a deep natural correspondence between the outer world and the inner world, and, according to MacDonald, this correspondence exists because God created it. We quote him at some length:

> "Thinkest thou," said Carlyle in "Past and Present," "there were
> no poets till Dan Chaucer? No heart burning with a thought

40. Ibid., 61–65, 80–81, 92. Another example used by Lakoff and Johnson to demonstrate the extent of metaphorical discourse in everyday language is the concept of love. While one can categorize love in general terms as an emotion, love is primarily spoken of in metaphorical terms, like "love is a journey," "love is patient," "love is madness," and "healthy and sick love." Ideas and thoughts are often talked about in terms of food. There are "half-baked ideas" and "digested thoughts." Lakoff and Johnson, *Metaphors*, 85, 109, 119.

41. Lakoff and Johnson, *Metaphors*, 55, 215. Lakoff and Johnson resist talk about such metaphors as "dead" metaphors as they continue to shape our understanding of the world, thus they are metaphors by which we live.

which it could not hold, and had no word for; and needed to shape and coin a word for-what thou callest a metaphor, trope, or the like? For every word we have there was such a man and poet. The coldest word was once a glowing new metaphor and bold questionable originality. Thy very ATTENTION, does it not mean an *attentio*, a STRETCHING-TO? Fancy that act of the mind, which all were conscious of, which none had yet named, —when this new poet first felt bound and driven to name it. His questionable originality and new glowing metaphor was found adoptable, intelligible, and remains our name for it to this day.". . . For what are the forms by means of which a man may reveal his thoughts? Are they not those of nature? But although he is created in the closest sympathy with these forms, yet even these forms are not born in his mind. What springs there is the perception that this or that form is already an expression of this or that phase of thought or of feeling. For the world around him is an outward figuration of the condition of his mind; an inexhaustible storehouse of forms whence he may choose exponents—the crystal pitchers that shall protect his thought and not need to be broken that the light may break forth. The meanings are in those forms already, else they could be no garment of unveiling. God had made the world that it should thus serve his creature.[42]

Like Lakoff and Johnson, MacDonald shows how deeply our perception of the world is shaped by metaphor, but MacDonald takes Lakoff and Johnson's argument one step further and argues that the reason we can take images from the visible world and use them metaphorically is because there exists a natural correspondence between the physical/outer world and the inner world of a person. This correspondence exists because God put it there and serves to unveil the mysteries that God has hidden since the foundation of the world.[43] It is the poet's task to discover these correspondences and in this way unveil life as God sees it.

We shall discuss two more aspects in regard to metaphor. One of them is the question of how metaphors differ from literal language and analogy, and the other is the importance of the dimension of surprise and shock in metaphors. These two are interrelated, as the former informs our understanding of the latter. It is to these issues that we must now turn.

42. George MacDonald, *Orts*, 5, 8–9.
43. Ibid., 29, 36.

Literal, Analogical, and Metaphorical

Traditionally, in positivistic accounts of language such as those of Hobbes and Locke, it was assumed that there is a great dichotomy between literal and metaphorical language. While literal language was thought to provide direct access to the world, metaphorical language was devalued as it confuses and distorts reality. Metaphors need to be replaced by literal language in order to be capable of expressing truth in a genuine way. Such rationalistic accounts have been challenged, and it is widely accepted now that neither literal nor metaphorical speech provides direct access to the world.[44] In light of this development, it is important to draw attention to the role that metaphor plays in scientific discovery. Both Colin Gunton and Soskice point out that metaphors play a significant heuristic function in science and provide epistemic access to reality in ways that literal language cannot.[45] Gunton concludes from this that the difference between literal and metaphorical language is not as great as it was previously assumed. Rather, the line between metaphor and literal speech is more fluid. For Gunton, the difference lies in the different ways a word is used in discourse. A metaphor always involves transference of words from one context to another. Metaphor is "teaching an old word new tricks."[46] Gunton states: "The common feature that makes a metaphor a metaphor is that words come to be used in a new or unusual way in human speech."[47] It follows from this that no one word can be neatly categorized as literal or metaphorical. Gunton argues that,

> if the relation between words and things is essentially indirect, part of a process of interaction between person and world, that static view had to disappear. There are no words that are "literal" in all times and places, nor can words be neatly divided into two classes in that way. The same word can begin life as a metaphor and become a literal usage, as the example of *muscle* shows. It also shows, however, that there is a difference between the literal and the metaphorical. In process of time, the metaphorical becomes literal. What then is the difference? Not that it now

---

44. See Gunton, *Atonement*, 29–34. Soskice, *Metaphor*, chapter 5. Gunton mentions Wittgenstein as an important philosophical thinker who challenged the notion that language can function as a direct mirror of the world.

45. Gunton, *Metaphor*, 30–33. Soskice, *Metaphor*, chapter 6. Examples of this heuristic function will be given in our discussion of models in the next section.

46. Gunton, *Metaphor*, 28.

47. Ibid., 29.

mirrors its object as once it did not, but that it has come to be accepted as the primary use of the term... Language is dynamic and protean, and words cannot be sorted into mutually exclusive classes. And so metaphors die, but may also be recalled to life, and over a period of time reveal a wide spectrum of movement to and from the metaphorical.[48]

Gunton uses the example of the word *muscle* to demonstrate his point. When first used, the Latin *musculus*, "little mouse," served as a successful metaphor to help physiologists explore and name one part of the anatomy. Over time *muscle* became the primary way of speaking about this part of the anatomy and ceased to function as a metaphor. In this way metaphors die and need to be recalled to life.[49] Literal and metaphorical language does differ, but the difference is not absolute, and language can change over time and usage.

Having discussed the relationship between literal and metaphorical language, we will now turn to the question of the relationship between metaphor and analogy. A comparison of metaphor with analogy will further clarify and draw out the unique nature of metaphor. Soskice defines analogy as follows: "Analogy as a linguistic device deals with language that has been stretched to fit new applications, yet fits the new situation without generating for the native speaker any imaginative strain."[50] In analogy words come to have a wider domain of application rather than a radically new domain. While "riding" was once used only in relation to horses, in analogy it is stretched to bicycles as well.[51] By using the verb "riding" for bicycles, the word "riding" has been stretched to fit a new application. What is important is that the act of riding a bike resembles the act of riding a horse. They are not identical acts, but there is a natural and apparent analogy between them. For Soskice analogy is a category that must be located in between metaphor and literal speech. The way in which Soskice differentiates analogy from metaphor is significant, as it emphasizes an important trait of metaphor:

> Analogical usage can be distinguished from a metaphorical usage by the fact that from its inception it seems appropriate. We feel no jolt or strain saying 'my dog is happy', 'my dog is eager to

48. Ibid., 35, emphasis mine. For a similar definition of literal language see Fishbane, *Garments*, 114.
49. Gunton, *Metaphor*, 34–35.
50. Soskice, *Metaphor*, 64.
51. Ibid., 64–65.

go', or 'the Martians discussed their policy'. We regard such analogy as a legitimate extension of a word's domain of application, and this accounts for our intuitive reluctance to say that 'riding a bicycle' is or ever was metaphorical.[52]

The difference between analogy and metaphor is that an analogy ought to seem like a natural and appropriate extension of a word's domain of application. Metaphor, on the other hand, is not a stretched but figurative usage, where the connection seems strange, surprising, or even shocking. Because metaphor brings into interaction two ideas in a surprising and even a subversive way, the hearer of metaphor is forced to make new connections and is thereby pressed towards new understanding. As Gunton has shown, however, through familiarity metaphor can "die" and lose this capacity for creating new insight. It is always in need of being reinvested with the dimension of surprise and shock that it once had.

Before turning to the nature of allegory, we shall discuss the model as an important relative of metaphor. The model bears some important similarities to both metaphor and allegory, and this discussion will therefore serve as a transition to the next section.

Metaphors and Models

A close relative of metaphor is the model. Max Black, in his book *Models and Metaphors*, distinguishes between various types of models. One of these he identifies is the "theoretical model." Black begins his definition of this type by stressing its similarity with what he calls "a sustained and systematic metaphor," which seems close to what Lakoff and Johnson have designated "metaphorical entailment."[53] Such models are often employed imaginatively in research in order to advance understanding in a scientific field.

By employing theoretical models imaginatively, a scientist is able to explore significant connections and similarities between a theoretical model and scientific phenomena observed and thereby advance understanding of the scientific subject matter. The model can suggest questions that bear the possibility of new discovery, thereby taking the scientist beyond the phenomena that formed the basis for the investigation. It is the suggestive nature of the model, when employed imaginatively rather

---

52. Ibid., 65–66.
53. Black, *Models*, 236.

than rigidly, that can serve so powerfully in scientific discovery.[54] Black stresses the fact that these models have to be employed imaginatively as possible similarities might not fit rigidly with the model employed. There is a continual tension between the similarities and dissimilarities of model and the subject matter under investigation.[55] In this way, theoretical models bear some striking similarities to metaphors.

Ian Barbour provides some helpful examples of where a model has been applied successfully and advanced scientific understanding. One of these examples is the "billiard-ball model" of a gas. By applying a particle model derived from colliding billiard balls to that of the behavior of gas, a theory was developed which suggested patterns in experimental observation.[56] Thus, the "billiard-ball model" was crucial in developing a theory for the behavior of gases. Models thus serve as mental pictures in terms of which to understand complex relations, particularly of invisible realities. Barbour defines a model as follows: "[A] model is a mental construct and not a picture of reality. It is an attempt to represent symbolically, for restricted purposes, aspects of a world whose structure is not accessible to us."[57] Barbour in particular wants to establish the link between scientific and theological models. He argues, "[a]s models of an unobservable gas molecule are later used to interpret other patterns of observation in the laboratory, so models of an unobservable God are used to interpret new patterns of experience in human life."[58]

Soskice defines model similarly to Black and Barbour; she also links the model to metaphor. She defines a model as an object or state of affairs

---

54. Ibid., 239–42.

55. Black does not develop his understanding of an "imaginative" employment of models other than setting it over against a rigid imposition of a model on the subject matter. He argues, "The imagination must not be confused with a strait jacket" (ibid., 242). He further argues that it is this exercise of the imagination in scientific discovery that provides a common ground for science and humanities. For Black, then, while not defining the imagination in any specific way, the human faculty of the imagination plays a significant role in scientific discovery. This is an important link with George MacDonald, as the imagination also plays a central role in his understanding of how human beings engage with God and the world, including science. Barbour also stresses the importance of the imagination for developing theories via models. See Barbour, *Myths*, 36, where he argues, "Theories are the product of creative imagination, often mediated through models, and not the result of simply generalizing from the data."

56. Barbour, *Models*, 31.

57. Ibid., 38.

58. Ibid., 50.

that is viewed in terms of some other object or state of affairs.⁵⁹ Soskice uses the concept of fatherhood as an example of a theological model. When the concept of fatherhood is used to develop one's understanding of God, it functions as a model. A metaphor, while related to a model, must not be equated with the model. Soskice argues:

> ... if we go on to speak of God's loving concern for his children, we are speaking metaphorically on the basis of the fatherhood model. Talk based on models will be metaphorical, so model and metaphor, though different categories and not to be—as frequently they are by theologians—equated, are closely linked; the latter is what we have when we speak on the basis on the former.⁶⁰

Metaphor and model are closely linked, and a metaphor, when linked to a model, is always an aspect of a model.

It is here, we note by way of anticipation, that the model bears important similarities to allegory. Both the model and allegory are extended imaginative devices, though the model not in narrative form. In both cases there is a whole set of elements that corresponds to another set of elements. Thus, both model and allegory are much wider in scope than metaphor, but metaphor is related to each and can occur in conjunction with each. Soskice argues that this is why allegories are sometimes called extended metaphors.⁶¹ It is to allegories, therefore, that we turn next.

Towards an Understanding of Allegory

In order to understand Jesus' parables, it is crucial to understand the nature of allegory and to what extent the parables of Jesus might be allegorical. As indicated before, the question of the relationship between the parables, metaphor, and allegory has remained ambiguous in parable studies. While Jülicher's critique of excessive allegorical interpretation was certainly important, the continual and persistent devaluation of the allegorical mode in Jesus' parables from Jülicher, Dodd, Jeremias, to Crossan in his early work remains problematic because of their influence upon future scholarship.⁶² Interpreters like Bailey sought to be more balanced

---

59. Soskice, *Metaphor*, 55.
60. Ibid.
61. Ibid., 56.

62. Crossan revised this position including his negative stance towards allegory in later works. See Crossan, "Parable."

in regard to the role of allegory in parables, but Bernard Brandon Scott and Herzog dismissed allegorical components of the parables once more as additions of the Early Church. Schottroff, in a recent books on Jesus' parables, continues with Herzog's rejection of allegory in the parables. In her acknowledgement she even announces that she was "enabled . . . to break through the barrier of allegorizing interpretation of the parables."[63] In one of the more recent surveys of the study of parables, Kurt Erlemann concludes that metaphor has received much more attention than allegory. The relationship between the two has remained unclear and is often not discussed at all.[64]

One must be careful in comparing metaphor with allegory since a metaphor, as we have shown, is intrinsically suggestive in nature, refusing to be substituted, while allegory works precisely on a substitution level. The intention of allegory is wholly different from metaphor and allegory is much wider in scope than metaphor. Metaphor, however, is often found in allegories. The point is not to define allegory over against metaphor but to show how they are different from one another and in what way they might work together.

A brief survey of the history of allegory in Western thought will help clarify the nature of allegory and why the parables of Jesus came to be interpreted in a predominantly allegorical fashion.

The History of Allegory: A Brief Survey

Allegory, like metaphor, has a long history. Allegory occurs in the form of two related traditions, i.e., allegorical interpretation and allegorical composition. Allegorical interpretation begins with the interpretation of Homer in the sixth century BC.[65] In order to make Homer speak to the philosophical demands of the time, a method was developed that presumed a dual understanding of the text. Interpretive allegory looks for a

---

63. Schottroff, *Parables*, vii. Schottroff does not even discuss the relation between metaphor and allegory in Jesus' parables and simply concludes: "[O]n the whole the parable imagery is much less rich in metaphors than is supposed by the traditional interpretations. In many essential parts they really are talking about . . . the Roman empire." Thus she strongly encourages a literal reading of the parables. Schottroff, *Parables*, 102.

64. Erlemann, "Gleichnisforschung," 5–7.

65. Whitman, *Allegory*, 3. For a careful discussion of allegorical interpretation in Greco-Roman and Jewish literature see Klauck, *Allegorie*.

deeper hidden truth behind a text and seeks to discover it.[66] Thus, Numenius and Porphyry interpreted Odysseus, once a storm-tossed sailor, as the soul of the philosopher laboriously ascending to the intellectual sphere.[67] Kurt Frör argues that this method should be understood as a result of Platonism with its distinction between the transcendental world of ideas and the earthly reality of shades.[68] Allegorical interpretation can, however, be found in OT books such as Genesis and Ezekiel.[69] It is therefore questionable whether this method was solely an inheritance of Platonism even though the strong influence of Platonism on allegorical interpretation cannot be denied.

The method of allegorical interpretation was taken up by Hellenistic Jews in the first century AD for an allegorical interpretation of the OT. Philo of Alexandria in particular introduced this method into the Jewish world.[70] In the Christian tradition the first allegorical interpretation is found in Gal 4:21–31, where Paul retells the story of Abraham and his two sons and interprets it allegorically to fit his own situation. In all three synoptic Gospels, it is reported that Jesus interprets the Parable of the Sower allegorically, and Matthew's Jesus interprets the Parable of the Weeds allegorically as well. Whether it was Jesus and Paul or the Early Church that began this tradition, these instances contributed in a major way to the popularity of allegorical interpretation in times ahead. Allegorical interpretation was then continued and developed by the early Jewish rabbis and the church fathers, Origen and Augustine in particular.[71] Shaped by both Christian as well as Platonic thought, Origen held to

66. Whitman, *Allegory*, 3; Frör, *Schriftauslegung*, 21.

67. Edwards, "Origen," 239. Edwards provides a very helpful introduction to a Platonic understanding of allegory.

68. Frör, *Schriftauslegung*, 21.

69. See, for example, Joseph's allegorical interpretation of Pharaoh's dreams in Gen 41 or the Parable of the Two Eagles and the Vine and the allegorical interpretation thereof in Ezek 17 as well as Isa 5. We have already mentioned in the previous chapter that the structure of this parable and its allegorical interpretation is very similar to the Parable of Sower and its allegorical interpretation in Mark 4.

70. Frör, *Schriftauslegung*, 21. While his Greek predecessors sought to interpret Homer philosophically, Philo interpreted Genesis allegorically as a description of the attitudes of the soul towards God.

71. Edwards stresses the fact that while Origin incorporated Platonic ideas into his method, it is much more than that. He argues: "Origen steers a middle course between the Platonic method, which sets out to make the text conform to reason, and the fideism of simple-minded Christians—Pauline Christians, as they thought of themselves—who held that reason must give way before the Word . . . In the Church

a twofold understanding of the world. Reality is made up of the material and the spiritual world and they are interrelated.[72] The physical world is charged with spiritual meaning and is thus viewed as a sacramental cosmos through which one ascends to the spiritual realm. For every physical reality there is a spiritual correspondent. Origen transferred this understanding to his interpretation of Scripture. The material and historical realities found in a literal reading of the Bible point to their spiritual counterpart found in an allegorical interpretation of Scripture. The letter of Scripture points to the spirit of Scripture. Origen writes in his *Commentary on the Songs of Songs*:

> But this relationship does not obtain only with creatures; the Divine Scripture itself is written with wisdom of a rather similar sort. Because of certain mystical and hidden things the people is visibly led forth from the terrestrial Egypt and journeys through the desert. All these events, as we have said, have the aspects and likenesses of certain hidden things. And you will find this correspondence not only in the Old Testament Scriptures, but also in the actions of Our Lord and Savior that are related in the Gospels . . . all things that are in the open stand in some sort of relations to others that are hidden.[73]

Allegorical interpretation enabled Origen to discover the spiritual meaning behind a given text. It is based on a metaphysical understanding of the cosmos that is invested with a deep intrinsic correspondence between the outer, physical and the inner, spiritual dimension of reality. Scripture has then more than one level of meaning, and Origen tended to prioritize the spiritual sense of Scripture. Both creation and Scripture serve to unveil the mysteries of God. Origen's metaphysical worldview and method of interpretation were adopted and developed throughout the Patristic period and the Western church of the Middle Ages by such thinkers as Augustine, Jerome, Gregory the Great, Bede, and Hugh of St. Victor, just to name few.[74]

---

tradition, Origen is as much a Latin father as a Greek one" (Edwards, "Origen," 251). For a similar argument see also Dawson, *Figural Reading*, 50–56. Origen not only practiced allegorical interpretation but also contributed through his systematic reflections on the allegorical interpretation in a significant way to its establishment as a prominent method in the patristic and medieval period. Frör, *Schriftauslegung*, 21–22.

72. Dawson, *Figural Reading*, 50–51.

73. Origen, *Commentary on the Songs of Songs* 3.12, quoted in ibid., 51.

74. See Lubac's careful discussion of this development in *Medieval Exegesis*.

Allegorical interpretation finds a prominent place in the Jewish and Christian medieval fourfold interpretation of Scripture, and the popularity of allegorical composition in all its varied forms throughout the medieval period is certainly linked to the prominent place of allegorical interpretation of Scripture. While it is not easy to outline the development of the fourfold method, Henri de Lubac has shown that a clear interpretive tradition had developed by the twelfth and thirteenth century.[75] This tradition sought to discern three to four distinct levels of meaning in the biblical text.[76] These four senses are divided into the literal sense and the spiritual senses, with the spiritual senses being based on and presupposing the literal sense. Underlying these senses is the same worldview Origen had espoused. The literal sense was designated as *sensus historicus* or *sensus litteralis*. The spiritual senses included the allegorical sense as *sensus allegoricus*, the moral application as *sensus tropologicus* or *sensus moralis*, and the eschatological sense as *sensus anagogicus*.[77] The *sensus litteralis* always came first, and its meaning was the most apparent meaning of the text. It took into consideration the presence of metaphor and parable and was not a mere historical or literalizing reading of the text.[78] The *sensus allegoricus* included figurative language as well as allegorical interpretation of historical events and institutions. With the *sensus tropologicus* the interpreters reflected upon the implications of discovered truth for the soul of the believer. It was chiefly structured around virtues and vices at war in the individual soul.[79] The anagogical sense was primarily concerned with the mystical union of the soul with God and its eschatological fulfillment.

A good example of the application of this method upon the biblical text is "Jerusalem." The literal sense identified Jerusalem as a city.

---

75. Ibid., 1:90.

76. Lubac emphasizes that this tradition was much more varied and differentiated than is often admitted. The variations of this method are immense and concern both the number of levels of meaning (usually three or four levels), as well as the order in which these levels were discussed. Some subsumed anagogy into allegory while others allowed tropology to precede allegory for example. See ibid., 90–96.

77. Frör, *Schriftauslegung*, 23; Lubac, *Medieval Exegesis*, 1:87–96. The fourfold method was developed in both the Jewish and Christian traditions. In the Jewish tradition the four meanings of a text were designated as literal (Peshat), allegorical (Remesh), tropological and moral (Derash), and the mystical (Sod). Fishbane, *Garments*, 113.

78. Smalley, *Study of the Bible*, 11.

79. Ibid., 5–6, 201. See also Lubac, *Medieval Exegesis*, 1:96.

The allegorical sense would see Jerusalem as depicting the church, while the tropological sense would see it as depicting the believing soul. The anagogical sense would interpret it as the heavenly city of God. All four senses were not always applied to every biblical text. The spiritual senses were especially helpful in giving meaning to seemingly irrelevant parts of the Bible like passages on legislation, the temple, and long lists of names, as well as morally problematic passages. In applying the spiritual senses to these passages, they sought a more satisfying meaning for such passages. This brief and simplified survey of the four-fold method shows how thoroughly it is built upon a two-fold understanding of the world, viewing the world and Scripture as a sacramental cosmos through which one is able to look into and ascend to the spiritual realm. Allegorical interpretation served to penetrate deeper into the higher mysteries of the spiritual world. Consequently, the spiritual senses continued to be preferred.

A significant change came only with the rise of scholasticism and the study of Aristotle in the later medieval period. Thomas Aquinas in particular sought to integrate Aristotle's ideas into his theology and consequently his method of interpretation. An important shift towards privileging the literal sense of Scripture began.[80] The Reformation developed a radically different understanding of Scripture and the way it should be interpreted. Eventually Luther rejected the allegorical interpretation of Scripture as well as the medieval teaching of the fourfold method. The focus of interpretation became the literal sense of Scripture.[81] The search for the literal sense of Scripture continued throughout the eighteenth and nineteenth centuries with such figures as Bengel, Baumgarten, Reimarus, Lessing, Ernesti, Semler, Gabler, Eichhorn, De Wette, Baur, and such critics as Herder and Schleiermacher of the Romantic period. In parable studies it was Jülicher's radical rejection of all allegorical interpretation of Jesus' parables that marked another halting point for the excesses of allegorical interpretation of the Bible. This radical shift away from any allegorical interpretation of the parables was unsustainable and subsequent scholarship had—and has still—to ask the question to what extent the parables of Jesus contain allegorical elements. Having provided a brief history of allegorical interpretation, we will now turn to the history of allegorical composition or allegory.

80. For a short introduction to this development, see Smalley, *Study of the Bible*, 229–41, 270.

81. Frör, *Schriftauslegung*, 24. See also Preus, *Shadow to Promise*. Preus provides a careful discussion of Luther's hermeneutic.

It is not surprising that the popularity of allegorical composition during the Middle Ages develops out of the prominence of the fourfold method and its emphasis on an allegorical interpretation of the Bible. Allegorical composition during the Middle Ages is complex and often woven into various forms of literature, such as the minnesong, the medieval romance, and hunting stories. According to Jon Whitman, allegorical composition reaches a decisive stage in the twelfth century, when allegorical composition merges with allegorical interpretation. He writes:

> The decisive turning point in this movement is the *Cosmographia* of Bernard Silverstris, written near the midpoint of the century. In this text, the coordinating tendencies of earlier movements in antiquity and the Middle Ages begin to coalesce in a comprehensive, far-reaching design . . . the two allegorical traditions themselves at last converge in a systematic form. Bernard *interprets* the story of creation by *creating* allegorical agents to act out the story; he thus radically integrates the act of interpretation with the act of personification.[82]

Dante's *Divine Comedy* marks another important stage of allegorical composition in the Middle Ages, and this tradition is continued and developed in later works such as Chaucer's allegorical tales, Spenser's *Faerie Queene*, and Milton's *Paradise Lost*. John Bunyan's *The Pilgrim's Progress* signifies an important climax in allegorical composition as its allegory is worked out to such perfection that it became known as the classical example of allegory.

In the nineteenth century Goethe's critique of allegory, setting symbol over against allegory, marked an important turning point in the popularity of allegory in both German as well as English Romanticism. Prominent among the English critics of allegory was Coleridge, who adopted Goethe's criticism.[83] The New Hermeneutics school in parable studies (including John Dominic Crossan) based their understanding of metaphor and allegory on the Romantics' discussion of symbol and allegory, uncritically adopting their negative stance towards allegory.[84] Modern literary criticism has sought to correct this overly negative attitude towards allegory by stressing the great variety in which the allegorical

---

82. Whitman, *Allegory*, 10.

83. See René Wellek's well-known treatment of the discussion of the symbol over against allegory in Goethe and Coleridge. Wellek, *History*, 200–211. Coleridge follows Goethe quite closely in his assessment.

84 See, for example, Crossan, *In Parables*, 14.

mode occurs and that a general devaluation of allegory is an insufficient treatment of a literary mode that occurs in such a wide range of classic literature.[85] Having discussed briefly the history of both allegorical interpretation and allegorical composition/allegory, we shall now turn towards a definition of allegory.

Towards a Definition of Allegory

The history of allegory shows that allegorical writing often occurs within a wide variety of literary forms and traditions. Most often allegory occurs to varying degrees in such literary genres as the medieval romance, myths, fairytales, and fantasy literature. Northrop Frye argues,

> Within the boundaries of literature we find a kind of sliding scale, ranging from the most explicitly allegorical, consistent with being literature at all, at one extreme, to the most elusive, anti-explicit and anti-allegorical at the other. First we meet the continuous allegories, like *The Pilgrim's Progress* and *The Faerie Queene*, and then the free-style allegories just mentioned. Next come the poetic structures with a large and insistent doctrinal interest, in which the internal fictions are exempla, like the epics of Milton. Then we have, in the exact center, works in which the structure of imagery, however suggestive, has an implicit relation only to events and ideas, and which includes the bulk of Shakespeare.[86]

It is no surprise, given the great variety of literature in which allegory occurs, that the term allegory has been employed rather loosely. One of the most popular definitions of allegory since antiquity, introduced to the study of the parables by Jülicher, is allegory as extended metaphor. This definition continues to enjoy some popularity but is rather problematic as it does not distinguish the way metaphor works from the way allegory works. Allegory and allegorical elements operate quite differently from metaphor, and the two must be kept distinct even though metaphors can and often do occur in allegory.[87]

---

85. See for example Lewis, *Allegory*; Honig, *Dark Conceit*; Fletcher, *Allegory*. In the area of theology and exegesis, see Louth, *Discerning the Mystery*, chapter 5; Klauck, *Allegorie*.

86. Frye, *Anatomy*, 91.

87. Romanticism recognized these different ways of operation and expressed it in its discussion of the symbol over against allegory. Whether their distinction is a helpful one is beyond this thesis to discuss.

Before providing a definition of allegory, it is important to ask whether allegory is a genre, a mode, a device, or, as Frye called it, a structural element in literature?[88] We shall call allegory a genre when the predominant modus operandi is that of allegory. The more the allegory is developed, the stricter the allegory becomes. Frye calls such thoroughgoing development of the allegorical mode a "naïve allegory" as it is "so anxious to make its own allegorical points that it has no real literary or hypothetical center."[89] If allegory is not the primary mode of the story and only a part of another genre, we shall call this an allegorical mode or device.

The most basic definition of an allegory is that it says one thing and means another. The OED describes allegory as a "description of a subject under the guise of some other subject."[90] Whitman put it this way: "[a]llegory turns its head in one direction, but turns its eyes in another."[91] Thus, allegories always have a strong thematic interest. A strict allegory is usually a longer unit or story with a set of elements. Each element of the allegory corresponds to or compares with an element of the subject/reality that it seeks to depict. The correspondence between the elements is clear and predictable, and the aim of the allegory is for the reader to see through the guise and detect the resemblance. In allegory the message is encoded and the reader's task is to decode it. The code is usually known and transmitted socially through usage in social contexts. Frye defines allegory similarly but more cautiously: "A writer is being allegorical whenever it is clear that he is saying 'by this I also . . . mean that.' If this seems to be done continuously, we may say, cautiously, that what he is writing 'is' an allegory."[92] C. S. Lewis' definition highlights an aspect of allegory that is crucial and distinguishes allegorical elements from metaphor: "Allegory gives you one thing in terms of another. All depends on respecting the rights of the vehicle, in refusing to allow the least confusion between the vehicle and its freight . . . The light is sharp: it never comes through stained glass."[93]

While allegory distinguishes itself from metaphor in terms of its structure (i.e., allegory, like the model, always consists of a whole set of elements that corresponds to another set of elements and finds its meaning in

---

88. Frye, *Anatomy*, 53–54.
89. Ibid., 91. It is this kind of allegory of which George MacDonald was so critical.
90. OED, s.v. "Allegory," online: http://dictionary.oed.com.
91. Whitman, *Allegory*, 2.
92. Frye, *Anatomy*, 90.
93. Lewis, "John Bunyan," 197.

the accumulative value of the corresponding elements), the other important distinction is that of clarity and simplicity. Allegory avoids confusion and opposition. As discussed before, the relationship between the tenor and the vehicle of a metaphor is opaque and complex. The interanimation between the vehicle and tenor, the tension between their similarities and dissimilarities, presses towards new understanding of the subject matter. Metaphor works on the basis of an unconventional usage of words and cannot be replaced. The vehicle is inextricably involved in creating the meaning of the tenor. Allegory, on the other hand, works on the basis of convention. The relationship between vehicle and tenor of allegorical elements is clear, direct, and without tension. The task of the vehicle is to point to the tenor, the subject matter. The vehicle in allegory is finally transparent and dispensable. At best, the vehicle reminds one of the subject matter because of some inherent similarity. What is also important is that "allegorists flex an inherently rigid control of intention," as Angus Fletcher puts it.[94] There is no doubt about what the vehicle points to and represents. This is also in contrast to metaphor, which allows a "determinate plurality" of meaning due to its suggestive nature.[95]

A prominent tool of allegory is personification. Attitudes, vices, and virtues get simply personified in the story, often without the characters being developed in any way. Bunyan's *Pilgrim's Progress* is a good example of continual personification.[96] Metonymy and synecdoche are also often employed in allegory. In the Joseph story (Gen 40—41), the grapes and the bread stand for the profession of cupbearer and baker. The fat cows and full ears stand for fertile years, while the lean cows and empty ears stand for famine. Sometimes, however, the similarity between the vehicle and tenor of allegorical elements is stretched fairly thin, and the use is solely based on convention. Three rings depict the three world religions in Lessing's parable *Nathan der Weise* adopted from Boccaccio's *Decameron*, not because there is any inherent similarity between the rings and world religions but because of conventional use. The relationship between the vehicle and tenor of allegorical elements can be contrived, and what

---

94. Fletcher, *Allegory*, 20.

95. We have borrowed this term from Edwards, "Origen," 256.

96. It must be said, though, that even *The Pilgrim's Progress* is not an allegory in the strictest sense. Some characters are developed more than others. Many of them function on this allegorical level, but others are more than mere allegorical elements of the story.

matters is not how vehicle and tenor are interrelated but that the reader of the allegory knows the code in order to decode the allegory.

While allegory has been criticized for being artificial, contrived, and mechanical, it must be pointed out here that such a critique usually refers to very thorough and mechanical allegories, i.e., allegories in the strict sense. More often, however, allegory occurs as a mode in other genres of writing and serves a very important purpose. Precisely because allegory is clear, straightforward, and works on convention, it serves to ground the story in a world familiar to the reader and thereby provides a platform from which to explore unknown regions. Timothy Lowell Pagaard argues that allegorical elements of a story serve as a "structural anchor and an imaginative catalyst for the sacramental and sometimes even mythopoeic process."[97]

Degrees of Allegory and the Relationship of Allegory to Other Modes of Writing

As mentioned above, the extent to which each element of an allegory corresponds to elements of the subject that the allegory seeks to depict varies. The *Pilgrim's Progress,* an allegory of the spiritual journey of salvation and sanctification, is an important example of a carefully worked out allegory. The correspondences between the allegorical elements and the elements of the subject it seeks to illustrate are both obvious and highly developed. Christian, the protagonist of the story, represents the believer on his spiritual journey. The people that he meets on the journey are named after the virtue/vice they represent, like the neighbors Pliable and Obstinate, Ignorance, Talkative, and Worldly Wiseman, who dwells in the town of Carnal Policy and who tempts Christian to go the easier path for the village of morality. Other characters are called Giant Despair, Faithful, and Hopeful. Many of the characters are not developed at all and only serve to depict the vices/virtues they are to represent. The allegory is often blatant, with no real need of decoding. The key is given with names in the story. In this way the barrier between the real story and the spiritual meaning is broken down. Even the places in the story have this explicit allegorical function. Christian begins his journey from the city of destruction, which corresponds to the place of the unsaved and those who will perish. Christian and Pliable fall into a slough that is called

---

97. Pagaard, "Parable," 41–42.

despond. There is little ambiguity in these allegorical features. "The light is sharp," as Lewis puts it. When Christian leaps over the wall of salvation and meets Sloth, whom he cannot get to wake up from his slumber, we do not learn anything new about Sloth but are reminded of the danger of sloth on the way of sanctification. Allegory usually helps us remember, while metaphor seeks to advance understanding of the subject matter.[98] One must admit, however, that even in this highly developed allegory of *The Pilgrim's Progress*, the allegorical correspondence is interspersed with description of the countryside that exists for its own sake or character development that goes beyond mere allegorical correspondence.

C. S. Lewis was a strong advocate of allegory, and it is no surprise that we find allegorical features in his works such as *The Lion the Witch and the Wardrobe*. While Lewis' story is not allegorical to the extent that *The Pilgrim's Progress* is and has more merit in its own right, it is obvious that Aslan the Lion works as a Christ figure in the story. Just as Judas betrays Jesus, so does Edmund betray Aslan. Susan and Lucy, like Jesus' disciples in Gethsemane, accompany Aslan into the night as he walks towards his fate. Both Aslan and Jesus are without sin. Just as Jesus dies on the cross vicariously, so does Aslan die on the stone table vicariously.[99] Susan and Lucy, like Mary Magdalene and Mary, watch this event from a distance. Both Aslan and Jesus are resurrected. Aslan breathes on the stone animals just like the breath of God revives the dead in Rev 11. In this way Lewis invites the reader to decode the story, and one almost stops being interested in Lewis' story and is tempted to go straight to the gospel story. It is no surprise that C. S. Lewis' interpretation of MacDonald's *Lilith* is extremely allegorical, thereby reducing the meaning of the story greatly.[100]

Tolkien is on the other opposite side of the spectrum and was extremely critical of allegory. He wrote:

> I cordially dislike allegory in all its manifestations, and always
> have done so since I grew old and wry enough to detect its

---

98. While such a distinction between allegory and metaphor is helpful, it is not an absolute one. Allegory also can help people understand the subject matter better, especially when the reader is unfamiliar with the subject matter of which the allegory speaks.

99. This is despite C. S. Lewis' insistence that Aslan is not an allegorical feature as he does not represent an immaterial Deity in the same way as allegorical features function in *The Pilgrim's Progress*. Lewis admits, however, that Aslan "is an invention giving an imaginary answer to the question, 'What might Christ become like, if there really were a world like Narnia and He chose to be incarnate and die and rise again in *that* world as He actually has done in ours?'" (Lewis, *Letters*, 23).

100. See Hooper, *Letters*, 118–20.

presence. I much prefer history, true or feigned, with its varied applicability to the thought and experience of readers. I think that many confuse 'applicability' with 'allegory'; but the one resides in the freedom of the reader, and the other in the purposed domination of the author.[101]

Tolkien's character Gandalf, for example, suggests at times Christ-like attributes, as when he fights the Balrog and falls with him into the abyss and when he suddenly reappears in white raiment. He is, however, in no way a Christ-figure in the story. *The Lord of the Rings* is not supposed to be a story about something else like *The Pilgrim's Progress* or *The Lion the Witch and the Wardrobe*. It exists for its own sake. When the son of Tolkien's publisher suspected allegory in the struggle between darkness and light in *The Lord of the Rings*, Tolkien insisted that it is not allegory, a mere mimetic expression of reality. Rather, Tolkien argues that the struggle between darkness and light is a particular expression of a wider pattern of reality. For Tolkien then, the presence of such individual correspondence does not make something "allegorical." The story has morals, and its characters reflect universals; otherwise, according to Tolkien, the story would not be worth telling and the characters would not live at all.[102] What is important for Tolkien is how reality is reflected in the story. The more allegorical a story, the less illuminating it becomes: "The nearer the so-called 'nature-myth', or allegory of the large process of nature, is to its supposed archetype, the less interesting it is, and indeed the less is it of a myth capable of throwing any illumination whatever on the world."[103] Tolkien insists that it is those stories that do not seek to be mimetic but are particular expressions of universal truth that are most capable of illuminating reality. This pattern of expressing the universal in the particular is the way reality is accessible to us in general.[104] It is for this reason that one must not confuse myths, legends, poems, and fairy-stories with allegory, and it is here that Tolkien echoes MacDonald's insistence that fairytales are not allegories.[105] The three examples of *The Pilgrim's Progress*,

---

101. J. R. R. Tolkien quoted in Carpenter, *Tolkien*, 190.

102. Tolkien quoted in ibid., 202–3.

103. Tolkien, "On Fairy-Stories," 26.

104. See especially Tolkien's discussion of *Beowulf* in this regard. Tolkien, *Critics*, 7–33. Tolkien argues that the particular in the poem serves a poetical rather than a historical purpose.

105. See George MacDonald, *Orts*, 317. Despite his critical stance towards allegory, Tolkien does not shy away from the use allegory in some of his other writings.

The Lion, the Witch and the Wardrobe, and *Lord of the Rings* are helpful as the first two show varying degrees of allegorical correspondence while the third is not allegorical at all.

Allegory, in sum, says one thing and means another. Allegory in the strict sense is a longer unit or story with a set of elements. The assimilation of correspondence created by the allegorical elements adds up to the overall meaning of the allegory. Allegory avoids confusion and opposition and works on the basis of convention. In allegory "the light is clear," and allegorical elements thus often serve as a structural anchor to explore unknown territory. Having defined the nature of allegory, it is now important to turn to the parables of Jesus and discuss the relation of allegory and metaphor in parables.

What Then Are Parables?

The parables of Jesus clearly are stories that seek to speak of something else. The only exceptions to this are the parables traditionally called "example stories."[106] The question is to what extent the parables are made up of allegorical elements, metaphors, and elements that are merely provided to make the parable work as a story and have therefore neither allegorical nor metaphorical significance.[107]

Tolkien uses the allegory of the tower to talk about the futile attempt to reconstruct the sources of *Beowulf*. Tolkien, *Critics*, 7–8. It has also been suggested that *Leaf by Niggle* is an allegory about Tolkien's struggle to complete *The Lord of the Rings*. Shippey, *Middle-Earth*, 34.

106. These parables do not have metaphorical or allegorical elements. The characters are just themselves used as examples. The way the examples are used in the stories, however, is rather surprising and even shocking. Thus these narratives share an important dynamic with many of the other parables, namely that of surprise and shock. See the Parable of the Good Samaritan (Luke 10) and Pharisee and Tax Collector (Luke 18).

107. The Parable of the Wicked Tenants in Mark's Gospel is a good example of this question. The comment "and he went away on a journey" about the owner of the vineyard has been interpreted to mean that he was an absentee landlord, while others have seen it as a necessary comment to make the story work. Without the owner going away, he would have no need of tenants. See Herzog and Schottroff, who take this phrase as an indication to interpret the whole parable literally. One's decision about the function of this phrase is hugely important for how one interprets the whole parable. For another recent example of this tension see N. T. Wright's strongly allegorical interpretation of the Prodigal Son in *Victory of God*, 125–36. Bailey rightly takes issue with Wright's approach. See Bailey, *Jacob*, 195–201.

We have asserted earlier that parables are not allegories and that the strong reaction against allegorical interpretation from Jülicher came because parables were forced into an allegorical interpretation of an extreme kind. Each element of the parable had to correspond to an element of the spiritual reality they were thought to depict. The parables were interpreted like a cryptogram. A good example of such a cryptic reading is Augustine's interpretation of the Parable of the Good Samaritan in Luke 10, typical of the so-called "spiritual" reading of the text. For Augustine this parable is about the salvation of the world. Each and every element of the story corresponds to a specific element of this reality depicted in the story. The man who gets beaten is Adam, Jerusalem depicts the heavenly city of peace, the thieves are the devil and his angels, the priest and Levite stand for the priesthood of the OT, and the Samaritan is God himself. The binding of the wound is the restraint of sin, the oil is the comfort of hope, and the wine is the exhortation to work with fervent spirit. Lewis rightly argues that such an interpretation is not even appropriate for a proper allegory, let alone parable interpretation. Even such a highly developed allegory as *The Pilgrim's Progress* has elements that are not allegorical elements of the story, and it is futile to find a corresponding element for every iota of the text. Jülicher called Augustine's interpretation a "merciless squeezing out of every drop of blood in the parable."[108] The other extreme of parable interpretation is found in Herzog and more recently Schottroff, who read and interpret the parable of the Wicked Tenants literally. Concluding her literal reading of the parable Schottroff writes: "Thus we have before us a fictional narrative, yet one that is pointed toward reality."[109] How a fictional narrative can be read and interpreted literally is not something that Schottroff seems to think it necessary to discuss.

Parables are stories about something else, and while most parables are not strict or mechanical allegories, they do have allegorical elements. The crucial question is to what extent a parable intends us to trace allegorical correspondence. The degree to which elements in the parable refer to elements of the reality depicted varies greatly and, as the history of parable interpretation shows, has proved to be one of the most difficult questions in the interpretation of the parables. It needs to be assessed on a case-by-case basis. Extreme allegorical decoding and the theory that parables make just one single point, the attempt to read parables literally

---

108. Jülicher, *Gleichnisreden Jesu*, 245.
109. Schottroff, *Parables*, 17.

and the idea that parables are inherently polyvalent have proven to be extremely overstated and therefore unhelpful positions. The truth must lie somewhere in the middle of these extreme positions.

Towards a Definition of Parables

As shown in the last section, the wide variety of parabolic speech in the NT does not allow for a narrow definition of parable. The emphasis in our attempt at definition will thus focus on the function of Jesus' parables. When we use the term "parable," we intend to speak of Jesus' parables in particular and not parables in a more general sense. Our aim here is to draw out central elements of Jesus' parables and then explore in chapter 5 how MacDonald's fiction corresponds to these whilst recognizing that there are also important differences between Jesus' parables and George MacDonald's fiction. In doing so, MacDonald's theological intent in writing Christian fiction will come into focus. The pastoral intent of Jesus' parables and MacDonald's fiction centers on shaping and reshaping the Christian imagination of their respective audiences through the parabolic strategies they use. It will become clear that MacDonald's pastoral intent in writing Christian fiction has much more in common with Jesus' parables than with strict allegory. Jesus' parables must not be confused with strict allegories, though they often contain the allegorical mode as an important parabolic device. Many of the parables contain metaphor and thus have a surprising and even shocking dimension to them. Even example stories, which are not about something else, have a surprising twist to their narrative. Specifically, due to their surprising and sometimes shocking nature, these parables, like metaphor, are more easily prone to lose their revelatory capacity and are in need of being reinvested with the shock-experience that they once had. It is to a discussion of the key elements of Jesus' parables that we must now turn.

Parables as Short Narrative Fiction

Many of the parables of Jesus can be looked at as short narrative fictions. The Parables of the Wicked Tenants, the Unmerciful Servants, the Wise and Foolish Maidens, the Prodigal Son, the Unjust Steward, and the Rich Man and Lazarus are a few examples of parables where a short narrative fiction is used in order to speak about the nature of the Kingdom of God.[110] While it has been established since Jülicher that parables are not strict or mechanical allegories in the sense described above, these short narrative fictions nevertheless share some of the same features as allegory. Both literary forms speak of one thing in terms of another. They point beyond themselves to speak of another subject/reality. Just as John Bunyan's *Pilgrim's Progress* speaks about the salvation and sanctification of a believer, so do the parables speak of specific theological subject matters. The parables cannot be reduced, as Herzog argued, to "earthy stories with heavy meanings,"[111] but serve the theological purpose of Jesus' proclamation of the Kingdom of God. What distinguishes many parables from allegory is that at a certain point in the narrative, the allegorical correspondence breaks down. MacDonald's fictional works, we shall see, are of course much longer than parables but share the basic element of speaking of one thing in terms of another.

God Is Never Explicitly Named

Even though the parables of Jesus are about God and his dealings with humanity or the Kingdom of God, God is never overtly mentioned as the subject matter.[112] While in some parables the allegorical mode makes clear from the beginning that a given parable is in fact about God, in other parables it is not clear that this is the case. In the latter case, this lack of direct reference to God is of course an important device as it creates negative space in which to explore and express new understanding of God and the nature of his kingdom. Avoiding overt "God-talk" is an important strategy that Jesus employs. By luring the reader into thinking the parable is just about everyday life, the defense mechanisms of Jesus' religious audience are down, and they are tricked into an understanding of God that is at least surprising, but often shocking and seemingly unacceptable. The process of creating a familiar world, the realization that the parable needs to be decoded, and the introduction of a shocking element that breaks down the realism or coding is an important strategy in many of Jesus' parables and serves to unveil new understanding about God.

---

110. Examples of parables that we would not slot into this category are the Parables of the Unshrunk Cloth and the New Wine. These parables are too short to be considered even short narrative fictions but are more like extended comparison.

111. Herzog, *Parables*, 3.

112. In some exceptional cases, various characters in the parables do refer to God in order to express their piety or lack thereof. See Luke 15:18 and Luke 18:2, 4.

Ambiguity about God, created by avoiding overt reference of him, is thus an important strategic element in Jesus' parables.

Familiarity as Invitation

Familiarity in the parables happens by creating a familiar world and by using a familiar code. The parables of Jesus are usually taken from every day life, using familiar images, and depicting realistic situations of first-century Palestine, at least initially. It was Jülicher and Jeremias' contribution to reveal the extent to which the parables of Jesus make use of everyday life conditions and experiences of first-century Palestine. In the Parable of the Wicked Tenants, for example, a man plants a vineyard and goes away on a journey, depicting, as Jeremias has shown, a very common situation of first-century Galilee. In the Parable of the Good Samaritan, a man walks from Jerusalem, the Jewish place of worship, back to Jericho and gets beaten up on the way home. Vineyards, fields, sowing seed, fig trees, leaven, oil, sheep, fishnets, servants and landowners, laborers and stewards, priests and Levites, judges and Pharisees, fathers and sons, virgins and widows were all common and familiar to the audience to whom the parables of Jesus were first spoken. Of course, this familiarity is easily lost when the parables are read in different times and contexts, and we will discuss this dynamic towards the end of this section.

Another important feature of Jesus' parables that create familiarity is the use of the allegorical mode. While Jesus' parables are not strict allegories, the allegorical mode plays a vital role in the parables. Above all, the allegorical mode, with its clear and direct correspondences based on convention, creates both familiarity for the reader as well as a structural anchor and imaginative catalyst for the exploration of new territory within the parable and thus Jesus' teaching about the Kingdom of God. It establishes the story amidst that which is known to the reader in order then to explore or introduce that which is unknown. The allegorical mode serves as a bridge to untrodden paths. It is crucial for setting the stage. An example of such convention is the Parable of the Wicked Tenants and its use of Isa 5. Mark 12:1–2 par. presupposes the knowledge of allegorical correspondence between the owner of the vineyard and God as well as the vineyard and God's people. Another example is the Parable of the Prodigal Son. The correspondence between the Father and God as well as the son as Israel was not uncommon and can thus be seen as part of the allegorical mode at work in this parable. The speaker of these parables can expect his audience to make these connections. An important task for the interpreter is to discern where the allegorical mode is at work and where it is not.

Parables, therefore, by the very nature of their literary genre, invite the reader to participate in the story. By placing the parables in the everyday world of first-century Palestine, a familiarity is created between the parable and the hearer that serves as an entry point and invitation into the world of the parable. Familiarity makes it easier for the hearer to identify with and become part of the story.

These familiar elements in the parables can have an allegorical function but are often just elements of the story without deeper meaning. The comment in the Parable of the Wicked Tenants that the owner went away on a journey or the setting of harvest time are elements that do not seem to have a deeper significance. The distant country to which the prodigal son travels and his having to feed pigs also do not seem to have any deeper significance. They are there to make the story work. The worlds that the parables create reflect faithfully the world of which the original audience was part and with which it was familiar.[113] Identification is determined by the carefully crafted story, resonating deeply with the world of the hearer. Even those who might be opposed to the speaker of the parable gain easy entrance as the world created is so extremely familiar and inviting. As many of the more recent interpreters have shown, however, there is usually a twist to the story where the familiarity with the world of the audience is disturbed and purposefully broken down. The hearer is confronted with something unexpected. Many of the parables contain three stages. They begin with creating a familiar world, continue by inviting the reader to decode the story, and end by breaking down the allegorical correspondence in an unexpected and surprising way.

Metaphors and Other Disturbing Factors in Parables

This unexpected dimension of many parables is something that they have in common with metaphor. It is here that the parables are distinct from allegory. In an allegory, the assimilation of correspondences adds up to the overall meaning of the allegory. Each vice in *The Pilgrim's Progress*, for example, adds up to speak about the overall dangers and pitfalls on the spiritual journey of salvation and sanctification. The correspondences between the elements are based on a comparison of similars or

---

113. A notable exception is the Parable of the Unmerciful Servant (Matt 18:23–35).

convention, and therefore the points of reference are straightforward and clear. They accumulate to support the overall theme or subject matter of the allegory.

While parables can begin this way, they often have a twist or a turn in the story that is surprising and breaks in to challenge the norm and say the unexpected. They press towards new understanding of the subject matter. Richard Bauckham and Trevor Hart, in their discussion of Jesus' redefinition of the politically laden term "Kingdom of God," show that Jesus' parables rarely use the figure of a king to represent God. When they do, moreover, it is used in a surprising fashion. They argue: "In the parables Jesus subverts expectations of kings and masters and employers by making the story turn on their surprising actions (e.g., Matt 18:23–27; 20:1–15; Luke 12:37)."[114]

Jesus' parables can be divided into four categories. In the first category there is no or very little surprise in the parable. The Parable of the Lost Sheep (Luke 15), the Parable of the Lost Coin (Luke 15), and the Parable of the Humble Servant (Luke 17) are three examples of this category.[115] As our focus is on those parables with surprise and shock, we shall not discuss these parables but focus on those parables that have surprise in them. The second category consists of the "example stories" mentioned previously. The surprise in these parables is not because of the introduction of a metaphor but because of the surprising and shocking way in which individuals (the Samaritan in Luke 10 or the Publican in Luke 18) are used as examples. What they share with the parables to be discussed in category three and four is the tension they create by subverting that which is normal, conventional, and expected for the audience.

The third and fourth groups are those parables with metaphor in them. As we have shown in our discussion of metaphor, the metaphorical process must not be limited to a word. This is important to keep in mind when one seeks to discern metaphor in parables, as the vehicle of the metaphor might not restrict itself to a word but extend to a sentence or a whole narrative structure. As Ricoeur rightly puts it, the difficulty

---

114. Bauckham and Hart, *Hope*, 165.

115. It should be noted that the association of God with a woman is surprising and without precedent in the OT or the later tradition of the Early Church. Even the comparison of God with a hen in Matt. 23:37 and Luke 13:34 removes the female aspect in degree by comparing God to a female animal. See Crossan, *In Parables*, 38.

and task lies in explaining how the narrative structure and metaphorical process converge in parables.[116]

The third category to be discussed here are parables where the story as such is not surprising but the interaction of the vehicle with the tenor of the metaphor used is surprising. The Parable of the Leaven (Matt 13; Luke 13), despite its shortness, is a good example, as its use of metaphor is sometimes overlooked. The story as such is not surprising. It describes the very natural process of leaven working its way through a dough. The interaction of the idea of leaven (vehicle of the metaphor) with that of the kingdom of God (tenor), however, is rather shocking. The idea of leaven in the cultural and historical context of first-century Palestine was associated primarily, but not exclusively, with a corrupting influence.[117] During Passover week leavened bread was banned from the table. Paul's use of leaven has very strong negative connotations. Thus, to compare the Kingdom of God with leaven creates a sense of shock. It creates a radical disjunction between what is expected and that which is spoken. This parable then not only suggests that the Kingdom comes in hidden ways, it also challenges one's assumptions about what is good and evil. It functions, to use B. B. Scott's words, "to subvert a hearer's ready dependency on the rules of the sacred, the predictability of what is good, and warn that instead the expected evil that corrupts may indeed turn out to be the kingdom."[118] This parable is active in advancing one's understanding of the kingdom. It moves the hearer to reconsider the way God's kingdom comes. By shattering an old rationality, it seeks to open up a new and deeper vision of how God works in this world. Another example of this category is the Parable of the Unjust Judge (Luke 18). Could it be that God's kingdom comes and spreads secretly and silently in the midst of utter human brokenness and sinfulness?

The fourth and last group to be discussed here are parables with a two-fold surprise in them. Here the story as such is surprising, and the interaction of the vehicle with the tenor of the metaphor used is surprising as well. It is here that the vehicle of the metaphor extends beyond a word to that of a whole section of the narrative. Bauckham and Hart stress the fact that the king in the Parable of the Unforgiving Servant does

---

116. Ricoeur, "Biblical Hermeneutics," 30.

117. See for example Exod 12:15, 19; 34:25; Lev 2:11; 6:17; 10:12; Hos 7:4; Matt 16:6; 16:11; Mark 8:15; Luke 12:1; 1 Cor 5:6–8; Gal 5:9. Exceptions are Lev 7:13; 23:17 and Amos 4:5 where the offering includes leavened bread.

118. Scott, *Hear Then*, 328–29.

not act like a king by releasing his servant from his vast debt. His willingness to forgive the huge debt is surprising and unexpected. It breaks the norm of what a king is supposed to do. By bringing into interaction the surprising idea of an "unkingly" king (notice that the vehicle consists of the king acting unlike a king!) with the idea of God (tenor), the parable shifts into metaphorical mode and the surprise is doubled. Jesus employs this metaphor, of course, to disturb our understanding of God and shows that God's rule on earth is quite unlike any earthly ruler. This parable advances new understanding of the nature of God.

The Parable of the Prodigal Son invites the reader to decode the story like an allegory. The story, however, takes a surprising turn. While the depiction of God as a loving and forgiving father in the Parable of the Prodigal Son in Luke 15 seems understandable, commentators have shown that it was nevertheless culturally scandalous because of the father's humiliating action in running towards his son.[119] For the father to run out to the son to welcome him back is a gesture of radical love and forgiveness, but this gesture goes hand in hand with an embarrassing act of humiliation. The father strips himself of all dignity by running out to welcome his son back. The comparison of God with a father was not unheard of in the Jewish tradition (see Isa 63:16: "you, O Lord, are our father; our Redeemer from of old is your name"). The combination of a forgiving father with the humiliating act of running towards the son (notice again that this vehicle consists of both aspects and incorporates them into one idea) not only makes the story as such surprising, it also no longer functions as a mere comparison but as a metaphor. This parable brings together two apparent dissimilars: God on the one hand (tenor) and a father who decides to humiliate himself in order to embrace his son on the other (vehicle). God, it suggests, does not only love and forgive; he loves and forgives to the point of humiliating himself before his creation.

We can find similarly surprising and shocking ideas in other parables, such as the association of the Kingdom of God with a tiny mustard seed that grows into a huge tree (Matt 21–22) rather than a sprig from the mighty cedars of Lebanon (Ezek 17:3, 22, 23), or the upholding of a dishonest steward, who is commended by his master for his dubious action, as a model for the disciples (Luke 16), or the laborers in the vineyard (Matt 20).

---

119. Jeremias, *Gleichnisse Jesu*, 107. Bailey, *Poet and Peasant*, 181–82.

We have sought to show the role of allegory and metaphor in parables. The parable shifts from the allegorical to the metaphorical mode when similars and dissimilars are brought into interaction with one another. In this way the parables of Jesus are active in the extension of one's understanding of the Kingdom of God. Precisely because parables have this revelatory capacity, however, they are more prone to lose this dimension, as the surprising and even shocking dimension of parables is easily lost to a modern reader. It is to this vulnerable dimension of Jesus' parables that we must now turn.

The Loss of Shock and the Need to Continue the Shock Experience of the Parables

It is because of their revelatory nature in extending one's understanding of the subject matter that metaphors and parables are particularly vulnerable to becoming "dead." Gunton argues that it is precisely because of their once successful use that metaphors lose their metaphorical status.[120] The two main reasons why parables can lose their capacity to reveal is over-familiarity with the metaphors used and unfamiliarity with the world and texts to which the parables refer. A dead metaphor might even distort what the parable intended to say in the first place.

Anthony Thiselton, relying on the work of Crossan and Walter Wink, has made a strong argument in this regard with the Parable of the Pharisee and the Tax Collector in Luke 18:9–14. By investigating the position and meaning of the Pharisee, Thiselton shows how the original audience would have identified with the Pharisee and the justification of the tax collector would have come as a shock to them. For the modern reader, however, it is not so. The modern reader, familiar with the biblical text, knows that the Pharisees are the bad ones in the story and would naturally identify with the tax collector, the more positive character of the story. The result, for Thiselton quoting Wink, is a weakening of the message:

> The unreflective tendency of every reader is to identify with the more positive figures in an account. Consequently, modern readers will almost invariably identify with the *publican*. By that inversion of identification, the paradox of the justification of the *ungodly* is lost . . . The story is then deformed into teaching cheap grace for rapacious toll collectors.[121]

---

120. Gunton, *Metaphor*, 39.
121. Wink, *Bible in Transformation*, quoted in Thiselton, *Horizons*, 14.

A similar argument can be made for many of the surprising parables of Jesus. A modern audience is so familiar with the comparison of the Kingdom of God with a mustard seed and the suggestion that God is like a father who runs out to meet his son, for example, that the original surprise and shock of these parables is lost. An important dimension of many parables gets lost because of the audience's over-familiarity with the original story.

Under-familiarity with the parables' first-century context creates similar difficulties. As shown above, the comparison of the Kingdom of God with that of leaven creates a certain amount of jolt and tension for a first-century Jewish audience. A modern audience's unfamiliarity with the negative associations linked to the metaphor of leaven in its original context misses out on an important aspect of this metaphor when used to describe certain aspects of the Kingdom of God. While the metaphor suggests how the Kingdom of God might expand, it also suggests that an easy categorization into "good" and "bad" is not possible anymore, and an important dimension of this parable gets lost. The parables no longer modify understanding of the subject matter in the way they once did. They lose an important part of their revelatory dimension. In order to read them properly, there is a great need to recover and refresh the shock-experience that many of the parables of Jesus once had.

Intertextuality

Jesus' parables are deeply rooted in the Jewish context of the Greco-Roman world, and some of the parables allude to the OT. These references to OT texts are important, and some parables cannot be understood properly without an understanding of this intertextual dynamic. The Parable of the Mustard Seed and the Parable of the Wicked Tenants are a couple of examples that we have briefly touched upon in this regard in the previous section. Kenneth Bailey has devoted a whole book to the possible OT background of the Parable of the Prodigal Son.[122] While it goes beyond the parameters of this book to investigate the intertextual links between Jesus' parables and the OT or ask in what way the OT is appropriated in the parables, it is important to mention that it is a significant aspect of Jesus' parables.[123] These allusions have to be recognized as such, and one

---

122. See Bailey, *Jacob*. A recent paper given by Bernard Jackson suggests the Joseph story as a possible OT background to this parable. Jackson, "Prodigal Son."

123. Recent scholarship has paid more attention to the influence of the OT on the

has to discern how the NT employs OT texts. One has to ask in what way the NT usage is similar and dissimilar to its original setting. In this way OT references in the NT display a similar tension between similarity and dissimilarity to metaphors, as there is a considerable amount of tension generated by the use of a familiar OT reference in a rather unfamiliar and strange setting within the NT. Richard Hays understands Paul's use of the OT in a very similar metaphorical way. He argues: "I contend that Paul's pastoral strategy for reshaping the consciousness of his pagan converts was to narrate them into Israel's story through metaphorical appropriation of Scripture."[124] Some of the parables of Jesus refer to and make use of OT texts, and they often do so in surprising ways. As we have shown in our discussion of metaphor, it is only within this tension of similarity and dissimilarity that new understanding of a given subject matter is achieved. The use of the OT is no exception in serving to press towards new understanding of the subject matter. This intertextual dynamic, finding its beginning in the OT, is continued in the NT and has since shaped the long Western literary tradition such as Dante and Milton, Shakespeare and Bunyan, Novalis and Goethe, just to name a few. It finds a prominent place in MacDonald's parabolic stories, and those stories cannot be understood without recognizing and understanding their intertextual dynamic, especially in regard to the OT and NT.

Imaginative Engagement and a Time for Decision

As we have already suggested, the use of metaphor demands an imaginative engagement on the part of the hearer/listener. While allegorical elements invite the reader into the story and create a world with which the hearer/reader is familiar, metaphor demands a different level of engagement and imaginative participation. Parables, too, and here the etymology of the word *parabolē* is helpful, often "throw" something at the reader "from the side" and demand that the reader make connections that have never been made before. These connections are suggested by the parable but have to be made by those who hear it.[125] Parables then demand

---

parables of Jesus. Bailey, *Cultural Keys*, 194–212; Bailey, *Jacob*. Bailey discusses the intertextual relationship between the parables in Luke 15, Ps 23, and the story of Isaac and his two sons Jacob and Esau in Genesis. Klauck in particular pays careful attention to the intertextual links between Jesus' parables and the OT. Klauck, *Allegorie*.

124. Hays, *Conversion*, xi, 23–24. See also Hays, *Echoes*.

125. Richard Hays argues similarly when he stresses the fact that it is the hearer/

participation and active imaginative engagement on a level that allegory does not. Allegory primarily helps to remember, while parable seeks to advance understanding. The hearer/reader has to use his/her imagination in order to be able to follow the suggestions made and imagine new and radical possibilities. Not only does parable push the hearer towards new discovery by making surprising and even shocking connections, these often go hand in hand with challenging old commitments and thereby pushing the hearer/reader towards making a decision. Parables are not spoken merely to inform, but to confront and push towards decision and embrace of Jesus' proclamation.[126]

Conclusion

Jesus' proclamation of the Kingdom of God is both in continuity and discontinuity with his Jewish heritage and therefore the people's expectation. It is both similar and dissimilar to the tradition, and the hearers are confronted with a reality that they were unable or unwilling to see before. In parables Jesus speaks of the unexpected and the humanly impossible. The message of the Kingdom of God does not meet the general expectations of God's people at the time. The Kingdom of God is by nature surprising and sometimes shocking. It shatters a commonly accepted worldview and moral norms. The radical grace expressed is married with a radical demand on those who are willing to embrace it. Bauckham and Hart put it this way: "The ethics of God's kingdom which Jesus teaches are the radical demand God's rule makes of those who acknowledge it, the corollary of the radical grace with which God's kingdom reaches sinners as freely forgiving love."[127]

It is here that we find a satisfying answer to why Jesus employed parable so prominently. In parables, Jesus' proclamation of the Kingdom of God finds its perfect form. The nature of his proclamation demands parabolic speech. The tension of the new in the old, the discontinuity within the continuity, the already not yet, and the unexpected amidst the expected must find expression in a form that can hold these dimensions in creative

---

reader who needs to make certain connections suggested by a metaphorical use of OT scripture. Hays, *Conversion*, 23–24. See also Klauck, *Allegorie*, 137.

126. We will discuss this aspect of participation and transformation in more detail in regard to George MacDonald's understanding of the parabolic. The transformative power of parable was an important incentive and concern for his own writing.

127. Bauckham and Hart, *Hope*, 163.

tension without reducing them. The parables of Jesus, by juxtaposing dissimilars, are the ideal means by which to proclaim the Kingdom of God. They can hold two sides in tension and in this way press the hearer towards new understanding. They break open the mystery of God's coming kingdom. Form and content are intrinsically related in Jesus' parables. They work together in a powerful way to reveal that which has been hidden since the foundation of the world and is now revealed.

By inviting the audience into a familiar world without using religious language, parables have the capacity to take the audience by surprise. The hearers do not expect religious content and receive news without their defenses in place to protect their preconceived ideas about God and religious life. Parables can literally function, as Franz Kafka has put it so well, like "an ice-axe to break the frozen sea inside us"[128] and radically challenge and transform our understanding of how God acts in the world in and through Jesus Christ.

As we have shown, however, the parables are especially prone to lose their revelatory capacity. In order to continue their surprising and revelatory dimension, new parables need to be created that are similar in intent and effect. This is one important reason why we have chosen to look at George MacDonald within the parabolic tradition. MacDonald understood the significance of language and poetics as a means for revelation. He also understood that language can lose its capacity to reveal and that poetic language is in need of being recovered as poetic language. It was MacDonald's life-long attempt to clothe the message of the Kingdom of God with new form so as to perpetuate its surprising and even shocking aspects.

Another important reason for looking at George MacDonald is the significant correspondence between Jesus' parables and MacDonald's fiction. MacDonald's pastoral intent in writing Christian fiction and many dimensions of his fiction correspond with and are similar to Jesus' parables. While MacDonald's stories are certainly much longer than Jesus' parables, and while he often incorporates a wide of range of different literary genres, it is in these parabolic dimensions just laid out that we discover that MacDonald followed Jesus not just in his life and teaching but also in the way that he taught.

---

128. Kafka here speaks of the impact of books more generally but this depiction of the reading process captures very well the way parables often work. Franz Kafka quoted in Steiner, *Language*, 88.

Before we can look at MacDonald's last and most difficult fiction, *Lilith* (chapter 5), and how it might be invested with the "parabolic" as laid out in this chapter, we must turn to a discussion of the influences that shaped MacDonald's understanding of language, poetics, and the imagination (chapter 3) and explore his decidedly theological understanding of story and the "parabolic" in particular as a means of God's revelation (chapter 4). We shall see that the proclamation of the Kingdom of God in parabolic form is in fact an important reason why George MacDonald's chose *Kunstmärchen* (artistic fairytales) and fiction for his proclamation of the Kingdom of God.

3

Patterns of Subversion and Promise
Romanticism

The Influence of Novalis upon George MacDonald: The Priest as Poet

The influence of Friedrich von Hardenberg, better known as Novalis, is well known in MacDonald scholarship, though few have been able to penetrate the complexity of Novalis' thought, especially in regard to his Christian faith and the extent to which he influenced George MacDonald. C. S. Lewis, however, recognizes the depth of influence and writes:

> As you know, 'Heinrich Von Ofterdingen' wh. I am reading is a very Macdonaldy book—indeed Novalis is perhaps the greatest single influence on Macdonald—full of 'holiness', gloriously German-romantic (i.e. a delicious mingling of earthy homeliness and magic, also of a sort of spiritual voluptuousness with innocence) and to be compelled to spell out such stuff word by word instead of galloping greedily thro' it as I certainly should if I could find a translation really forces me to get the most out of it.[1]

Lewis rightly suggests that Novalis is one of the most important influences on MacDonald, and MacDonald himself acknowledges his indebtedness to Novalis. He writes quite dramatically: "It is, indeed, well with him who has found a friend whose spirit touches his own and illuminates it ... Shall I not one day, 'somewhere, somehow,' clasp the large hand of Novalis, and gazing on his face, compare his features with those of Saint John?"[2]

---

1. C. S. Lewis in a letter to Arthur Greeves in Hooper, *Letters*, 1:922.
2. George MacDonald, *Orts*, 229–30. MacDonald explicitly cites Novalis

In light of such recognition of Novalis' influence, it seems surprising that most discussions have focused merely on the relationship between *Phantastes* and *Heinrich von Ofterdingen* and MacDonald's translation of Novalis' *Spiritual Songs* and are typically of an introductory nature. A more in-depth study of Novalis is necessary both to understand Novalis himself as well as the extent to which he shaped MacDonald's writings.

The influence and importance of *Hymns to the Night* upon MacDonald's thinking has often been neglected. This is surprising considering that MacDonald translated these hymns and included some of them in his poetical works.[3] The extent of the influence that Novalis had on MacDonald, especially in regard to Novalis' Christian faith, has yet to be discussed and can be seen clearly in MacDonald's appropriation of Novalis' *Hymns to the Night*.

Owen Barfield rightly cautions the reader not to read these hymns too superficially. They are complex and deep and deserve careful attention. He writes,

> In a sense one has the feeling that only dead people ought to be allowed to read this *Hymn*. This is where the consciousness soul, like a spiritual policeman, steps in. It never forgets death. It is not going to allow us to forget that, before there can be a resurrection, there must be a death.[4]

We need to heed Barfield's warning, and I shall show that one cannot understand *Hymns to the Night* apart from a broader understanding of Novalis' life and other works. *Heinrich von Ofterdingen* is particularly important for understanding these hymns as they were written about the same time, immediately before Novalis' death in 1801. In *Heinrich von*

---

throughout his writing career, which might give an indication of how extensive the implicit references and influences might be. MacDonald produced a translation of the *Spiritual Songs* by Novalis, which he presented as a Christmas gift to his friends in 1851. It only was published much later and in a revised version. In the introduction to his first translation, he quotes Ludwig Tieck on Novalis' life. He quotes from Novalis several times in *Phantastes* (1859) and *David Elginbrod* (1863), he refers to Novalis in *Adela Cathcart* (1864), "The Golden Key" (1866), quotes from the *Spiritual Songs* in *The Seaboard Parish* (1868), refers to him in *The Marquis of Lossie* (1877), *Dish of Orts* (1882), and *Lilith* (1895), and provides more translations of Novalis in *Rampolli* (1897).

3. George MacDonald, *Poetical Works*, 2:324. The citation is taken from Novalis' fifth hymn.

4. Barfield, *Romanticism Comes of Age*, 139.

Ofterdingen we will focus our investigation on the symbols of dreams to provide an entry point into Novalis' thinking and context.

In the following I will argue that MacDonald was influenced by Novalis' *Hymns to the Night* in his writing of *Lilith*. Novalis' imaginative employment of poetics as a way to probe deeper into the Christian faith was a significant influence on MacDonald. In this chapter we will focus on a discussion of Novalis' *Hymns to the Night* in light of Novalis' understanding of dreams and poetics. In chapter 5 we shall then explore how MacDonald appropriated the imagery and theology of these hymns.

The Poet as Priest: Novalis as a Prime Example for MacDonald

In considering the influence of Novalis upon MacDonald, it is striking that both *Phantastes* and *Lilith* end with the same quotation from Novalis. MacDonald introduces the last chapter of *Phantastes* with this citation, and the very last sentence of *Lilith* reiterates this citation: "Our life is no dream, but it should and will perhaps become one." It is also important to notice that Novalis is one of only two writers to whom MacDonald directly refers in *Lilith*. While most MacDonald scholars at least mention the citation, no one has yet discussed the importance of this quotation for understanding *Lilith*, even though the image of dreams is very prominent in *Lilith*. MacDonald's use of this provocative quote calls for a closer examination of Novalis' influence on MacDonald in this regard. We shall therefore investigate the significance of dreams in Novalis' thinking and how this has shaped MacDonald's understanding of the role of dreams, thereby shedding some light on MacDonald's most difficult novel (chapter 5).

Novalis and his Context Explored through the Symbol of Dreams

Novalis' understanding of dreams is very complex and closely related to his understanding of aesthetics, poetics, fairy stories, the imagination, revelation, and eschatology or, in Novalis' words, his longing for the "Golden Age."[5] In the beginning of *Heinrich von Ofterdingen*, Novalis

---

5. In *Hymns to the Night*, Novalis associates the idea of Golden Future most clearly with his Christian eschatological understanding of the world. The Golden Age, the golden cup, and the golden wine of life all speak of the reality of eternal life that is

provides one of his most comprehensive discussions about dreams. Heinrich has a dream about a blue flower, and he believes that this dream has deeper significance than an ordinary dream.⁶ He shares this dream with his parents, but his father is not keen on Heinrich's new fascination and urges his son to pursue his studies rather than dwelling in the world of dreams. Heinrich's father argues,

> Dreams are spindrift [lit. foam], whatever your learned men may think of them; and you will do well to turn your mind away from such useless and harmful reflections. The times are past when . . . [the divine face] appeared in dreams, and we cannot and will not fathom the state of mind of those chosen men the Bible speaks of. The nature of dreams as well as of the world of men must have been different in those days. In the age we live in there is no longer any direct intercourse with heaven. The old stories and records form our only source of knowledge, in so far as we need it, of the supernatural world; and in place of those express revelations the Holy Ghost now speaks to us indirectly through the minds of wise and well-disposed men and through the way of life and the fortunes of the pious.⁷

Heinrich, on the other hand, has a much more open stance towards dreams:

> But my dear father, what makes you so opposed to dreams? . . . Dreams seem to me to be a defense against the regularity and routine of life, a playground where the hobbled imagination is freed and revived. Without dreams we should certainly grow old sooner; and so we can regard dreams, if not as directly sent from heaven above, at least as divine gifts, as friendly companions on our pilgrimage to the holy sepulchre. Certainly the dream I dreamed last night will not have been an ineffectual accident in my life, for I feel that it reaches into my soul . . . [like a] giant wheel, impelling it onward with a mighty swing.⁸

---

available because of Christ's death and resurrection. Thus he writes about Christ in hymns five: "[T]hy loved ones . . . see thee hasten, full of longing, into thy father's arms . . . and the inexhaustible cup of the golden Future." Novalis in George MacDonald, *Rampolli*, 12. This clear identification of the Golden Age with Christian eschatology is not as present in Novalis' earlier prose, especially his philosophical discussions.

6. Novalis, *Novalis*, 1:243.

7. Novalis, *Henry*, 18. Unfortunately, the English translation available and used here is at times not correct. Thus, I will add my own translation in brackets as needed.

8. Ibid., 19.

The above dialogue shows Novalis' awareness of the current debates of his time towards dreams, and it also sheds some light on his own understanding of dreams. Heinrich's father is very skeptical about the whole idea of dreams and seems to represent an attitude that reinforces Enlightenment skepticism towards the imagination, dreams, and supernatural revelation.[9] Reason is now the sole category by which revelation is evaluated, and since dreams lack order and cannot always be interpreted rationally, they stand in opposition to the pursuit of truth. The way we can know things, according to Heinrich's father, is through "the minds of wise and well-disposed men"; in short, the intellect.

Manfred Engel, in his careful analysis of dreams in the period between the Enlightenment and late Romantic thought, shows that the pre-Enlightenment discourse about dreams was focused on supernatural dreams. Natural dreams were only of marginal interest then, mainly discussed by physicians. With the Enlightenment, however, a significant shift occurred. The emphasis completely changed, and supernatural dreams lost in significance. The idea of a direct revelation from God was challenged, and thus dreams had to be interpreted on merely natural grounds. God does not intervene into the natural order of things and therefore does not send dreams anymore.[10]

Christian Wolff (1679–1754), an important German Enlightenment thinker, is the first to differentiate clearly between dreaming and waking. This is important to notice as MacDonald completely blurs the lines between waking and sleeping in the character of Mr. Vane at the end of *Lilith*. Wolff was able to draw attention to the phenomenology of dreams, but this also included a categorization of dreams into that which is untrue. For Wolff the primary criteria for the evaluation of dreams are the truths and certainties accessible through reason. These truths are marked by a great sense of order, and since dreams often lack order and usually cannot be interpreted rationally, they stand in opposition to truth. Wolff writes, "In the truth everything builds upon one another sensibly, but not

---

9. For a similar argument see Pfefferkorn, *Novalis*, 171–72. Engel shows in more detail how much Novalis was familiar with the dream theories of Enlightenment thinkers. See Engel, "Träumen," 160.

10. Engel, "Träumen," 145–47. Engel relies here on an article on dreams published in the *Grosses Vollständiges Universal-Lexikon aller Wissenschaften und Künste*, published in Germany in 1745.

so in dreams."[11] Thus, according to Wolff, order has now become the sole category by which dreams are evaluated.

The discussion of dreams in Enlightenment thought continued in the context of the battle against supernatural revelation and superstition. While dreams where still important, many thinkers denied that God would still send dreams, as he does not intervene into the natural order of things anymore. As a consequence, in popular Enlightenment thought dreams came to be explained naturally; i.e., either rationally or, at a later stage, empirically and psychologically.[12] For example, the German university preacher Richerz writes in 1785 that his nightmare from the previous night can be explained on the grounds of experiences of the previous day, physical sensations, and his personality.[13]

Novalis, as we have seen in the dialogue above and similarly to George MacDonald, opposes a merely rational and scientific understanding of the world, bemoaning his own time as a period where "divinely, magically and poetically oriented people cannot develop under such conditions."[14] For Novalis divine interventions cannot be encapsulated sufficiently in a mere rational outlook, which deliberately excludes the possibility of divine intervention. Nor can the possibility of God's speech be constrained to a time of old but must be contemplated in the present. In *Heinrich von Ofterdingen*, Novalis writes that "we can regard dreams, if not as directly sent from heaven above, at least as divine gifts, as friendly companions on our pilgrimage to the holy sepulchre."

The development from later Enlightenment thought into German Idealism proved to be a fruitful context for Novalis. A new interest in the role of the imagination and poetics in relation to metaphysics also brought with it a renewed interest in dreams and their metaphysical significance. Johann Gottfried von Herder and Jean Paul, for example, closely associate dreams and poetics. Jean Paul calls dreams the mother country of the imagination, and for Herder dreams are the ideal of the

---

11. Christian Wolff, *Gesammelte Werke*. I. Abt. Bd. 2, 76, quoted in Engel, "Träumen," 145, translation mine.

12. Ibid., 147–51. With the rise of empiricism, the study of dreams became a main focus with anthropological studies as it sought to understand the experiences of the soul ("Erfahrungsseelenkunde") on empirical grounds.

13. Ludwig Anton Muratori, "Über die Einbildungskraft des Menschen," quoted in ibid., 147.

14. Novalis, "Vorarbeiten 1798," 322, translation mine.

fairytale genre as well as all novels.[15] It is here that one has to locate the early Romantic voice of Novalis. For Novalis the imagination—or to render the German more literally, the power and ability to imagine (German: *Vorstellungskraft, Einbildungsvermögen*)—becomes the foundational force for all knowing and the role of dreams crucial.[16] In dreams "the hobbled imagination is freed and revived," as Heinrich argues with his father. Thus, in response to a merely ordered and rational understanding of the world that privileges the use of prose, Novalis puts forth the poet-dreamer as a person that enables his readers to a renewed and more comprehensive vision of the world, especially a renewed vision for the supernatural and divine.[17] It is the task of the poet, according to Novalis, to point to the Golden Age.[18]

In light of this, Novalis believed that the poet should employ stylistic devices such as an arbitrary use of the world of the senses, non-coherence in the plot, and non-closure in the narrative.[19] Deirdre Christine Hayward calls this technique a "strain[ing] against the barriers of conven-

---

15. Engel, "Träumen," 151.

16. Ibid., 152. While MacDonald also emphasizes the role of the imagination, he emphasizes that the imagination must work in relation to all the other human faculties. See George MacDonald, *Orts*, 11.

17. Novalis' understanding of the role of the poet has at times strong idealist tendencies and thus becomes problematic, especially because he seeks to recover a theological understanding of the poet. At times the poet becomes deified and seems to be the sole mediator between the transcendent and the immanent and at other times, especially in Novalis' later works such as *Heinrich von Ofterdingen* and *Hymnen an die Nacht*, Novalis places poetics and dreams into the context of God's revelation. A certain ambivalence remains, especially in his earlier philosophical works. Novalis writes for example, "Through poetics the highest sympathy and coactivity is achieved, the most intimate communion between the finite and the eternal" (Novalis, *Novalis*, 2:322, translation mine). At another place Novalis argues that the artist makes himself into all that he sees and wants to become; see ibid., 2:324.

18. The Golden Age is an important idea in Novalis' thinking and is closely connected to his eschatological understanding of the world. In *Christenheit oder Europa* Novalis bemoans the loss of faith in the modern world and envisions an undivided Christian Europe. The pre-Reformation period is seen as the ideal world where people still had a childlike faith. Through the Reformation and the scientific discoveries, the Europeans lost their respect for the earth and their heavenly home. Novalis, *Christenheit*, 69. It is no accident that Novalis places *Heinrich von Ofterdingen* into the medieval period where Heinrich can discover his poetic gifts quite freely. While both of these works seem to idealize the medieval world in a sense it is clear that this is only a stylistic device. Novalis reflects quite critically on the crusades in *Heinrich von Ofterdingen*, for example.

19. Kasperowski, *Mittelalterrezeption*, 176.

tional narrative."[20] The subversive use of images and symbols is another important device. In this way the rational world has to submit to and serve this fresh poetic expression.

The use of symbols is also very important in Novalis' work. Symbols serve to suggest things, to create associations that are meant to open up one's vision in contrast to the use of prose, which, for Novalis, has a tendency to narrow down meaning. He argues that "[o]ur language is either mechanical, atomistic or dynamic. The true poetic language ought to be organic and alive. How often do we feel the poverty of words, which seeks to express several ideas with one swoop."[21] MacDonald's view of symbols, as we shall see, is quite similar, and it is no surprise, then, that MacDonald would refer to and lean on Novalis for the creation of his two most "Romantic" and symbolic fantasy novels, *Phantastes* and *Lilith*.[22]

It is in this context that one has to understand Novalis'—and I would also suggest MacDonald's—use of the symbol of dreams. True to his Romantic spirit, Novalis' employment of the symbol of dreams is complex and fluid rather than systematic, and we will focus on just one aspect here, where the symbol of dreams serves as a poetic device to open up one's vision to the divine. Novalis distinguishes between various qualities of dreams. There are of course ordinary dreams, which have no deep significance. The highest form of dreams happens in a synthesis of dreaming and waking. In this synthesis the experience of the individual is brought into the spiritual world created by the imagination. For Novalis this synthesis of waking and dreaming is best mediated in poetic dreams of the fairytale genre.[23] I shall argue that it is in this sense that one has to understand Mr. Vane's state at the end of *Lilith*, where he is not sure anymore whether he is dreaming or awake. Mr. Vane is awaiting the fulfillment of the "other" world that he has begun to discover in the world of the seven dimensions. "I wait; asleep or awake, I wait" are his last words, and the novel closes with the Novalis citation "Our life is no dream, but it should and will perhaps become one."[24]

---

20. Hayward, "Three German Thinkers," 209. Hayward focuses her discussion especially on the role of incoherence and non-closure in fairytales.

21. Novalis, *Novalis*, 2:255.

22. MacDonald begins *Phantastes* with an extended citation from Novalis on the nature of the fairytale (Märchen).

23. Novalis, *Novalis*, 2:448. See also Engel, "Träumen," 164.

24. George MacDonald, *First and Final*, 398.

For Novalis then, dreams and fairytales became poetic "strategies" for drawing the reader into the world created by the poet. Novalis does not differentiate between dreams and fairytales anymore. It is in this context that one has to understand the Novalis quotation in *Phantastes*:

> One can imagine stories without rational cohesion and yet filled with associations, like dreams; and poems that are merely lovely sounding, full of beautiful words, but also without rational sense and connections—with, at the most, individual verses which are intelligible, like fragments of the most varied things. This true Poesie can at most have a general allegorical meaning and an indirect effect, as music does . . .[25]

Stories without rational cohesion, images that seek to suggest and cause one to make associations are thus literary tools by which Novalis, and MacDonald in his own way, sought to de-familiarize the reader in an aesthetic way. The genre of fairytales becomes the place where a certain rationality is destroyed only to establish a fresh and more profound vision of the world.[26] In this way the Romantic fairytale works similarly to the more subversive parables of Jesus. Engel describes Novalis' use of dreams as follows:

> dreams are for Novalis, like other insertions as poems and fairy stories, a model for a specifically romantic, anti-realistic style of writing, in which 'dream-like' streaks break out the enclave of a clearly defined dream sequences and enter into the main body of the narrative.[27]

The line between dreaming and waking is purposefully blurred, and a literary style is created that seeks to transcend the orderly, rational, and systematic world in order to awaken the reader to the supernatural, spiritual, and poetic world in which Novalis so strongly believed. In this way dreams can become for Novalis prophetic dreams.

It is important to emphasize that neither Novalis nor MacDonald understood such literary creation as irrational. Reason was still a very important dimension of these newly created worlds. They sought to

---

25. Novalis, quoted in George MacDonald, *Phantastes*, 3.

26. For similar argument see Hayward, "Three German Thinkers," 213, where Hayward defends both Novalis and MacDonald against accusations of irrationality and meaningless and argues that "the way to new kind of rationality (the project of MacDonald and Novalis) goes via a deconstruction of ordinary logic."

27. Engel, "Träumen," 167.

re-establish a "rationality" that would see the spiritual not in opposition to the rational and empirical world.[28] It was important for Novalis to seek an integration of the physical with the spiritual rather than merely transcending from the physical to the spiritual. Novalis' elevation of the state between waking and dreaming as the superior state emphasizes this very important concern of integration.

Dreams to what End?
Dreams, Revelation, and the Face of God

As mentioned above, Novalis sought to recover a more comprehensive view of the world for his own time, especially in regard to the integration of the spiritual world and poetics into a time and culture that focused on the physical and rational. His poetic expression, however, was not so much for the discovery of something new but for the recovery of something old. Novalis writes: "All truth is ancient. The alluringness of the new lies in the variety of expression. The greater the contrast in appearance, the greater the joy of recognition."[29] Dreams have a revelatory dimension to them; they reveal something that is there but not so easily grasped. In the conversation between Heinrich and his father in *Heinrich von Ofterdingen*, Novalis offers us some important insights into what this revelation might be. While Heinrich's father argues that the times are past when "the divine face appears in dreams," Novalis, in the voice of Heinrich, holds to a more medieval understanding of revelation.[30] While he does not equate dreams with a direct revelation from God, he does understand them as "divine gifts, as friendly companions on our pilgrimage to the holy sepulchre." Novalis certainly does not attribute a deeper meaning to every dream. He does, however, consider the possibility that God can reveal himself in dreams and that they therefore have a revelatory dimension with eschatological significance to them. Heinrich, in response to his father's skepticism, says about his dream: "Certainly the dream I dreamed last night will not have been an ineffectual accident

---

28. Ibid., 164. George MacDonald's novel *At the Back of the North Wind* is a great example of such an integration of dream sequences into the realistic framework of the story.

29. Novalis, *Novalis*, 2:290.

30. In the medieval period dreams and dream visions were often thought to be divinely inspired. See Kruger, *Dreaming*. He provides a careful discussion of the role of dreams in the medieval period.

in my life, for I feel that it reaches into my soul . . . [like] a giant wheel, impelling it onward with a mighty swing." Dreams have thus the potential of revealing truth but only because they are sent by God as "a divine gift." The source of such revelations is not dreams in themselves, but God who reveals in and through them.[31] George MacDonald, as we shall see in chapter 5, holds to a very similar view of dreams and revelation. In *Lilith*, he firmly situates Mr. Vane's dreams in the reality of God's presence in the world. The source of Mr. Vane's dreams is not his own subconscious but God who gives dreams.[32]

It is in the context of this understanding of revelation in dreams that one needs to understand the Novalis quotation of which MacDonald was so fond. "Our life is no dream, but it should and will perhaps become one" becomes now a metaphor for an understanding of life where the spiritual dimension of reality becomes an integral part of life and that finds its ultimate fulfillment only in the future. In dreams one can be freed from a fixation on a mere material world and open up one's eyes to the spiritual world.[33] The open-ended nature of this statement has eschatological and, as Engel calls it, prophetical overtones. Dreams have the ability to "impel one onward" towards the ultimate destination of humanity, one's homecoming. For Novalis, this homecoming is closely linked with his belief in Christ, as both *Hymns to the Night* and his *Spiritual Songs* suggests.[34]

Hymns to the Night as an Example of Novalis' Symbolic World

In *Hymns to the Night*, we see Novalis' poetic genius at work in creating a cycle of hymns that seek to "reach into one's soul like a giant wheel," impelling the reader onward "with a mighty swing."[35] Novalis' theory of poetics and dreams, as well as his belief in God, now takes on concrete form. These hymns literally function, I will argue here, like "a divine gift, a friendly companion on our pilgrimage to the holy sepulchre," and I will argue that it is because of their subversive nature as well as their

---

31. Novalis is not always as clear about the source of revelation as he is in this part of *Henrich von Ofterdingen*. See Hayward, "Three German Thinkers," 219–20, who discusses Novalis' more idealist understanding of poetry.

32. George MacDonald, *First and Final*, 396. MacDonald makes a similar argument in his first essay on the imagination. See idem, *Orts*, 25.

33. Engel, "Träumen," 163.

34. See also Sepasgosarin, *Tod*, 220–24, 255.

35. Novalis, *Henry*, 19.

emphasis on Jesus as the fulfillment of Novalis' longing that they had such a strong hold on MacDonald and served as an inspiration of his last fantasy novel *Lilith*.

As the title of this cycle of six hymns suggests, the main subject is the night. It is surprising, then, that these hymns begin with an appraisal of the light. Novalis writes, "Before all the wondrous shows of the widespread space around him, what living, sentient thing loves not the all-joyous light, with its colors, its rays and undulations, its gentle omnipresence in the form of the wakening Day?"[36] After such an introduction one would expect a continuation of the praise of the day and the light, but already in the second paragraph an important turn occurs, which Novalis continues throughout these hymns. Rather than turning towards the light, Novalis turns himself downwards to the "holy, mysterious, inexpressible night."[37] Thus, in the very beginning, he sets up a stark contrast between night and light. It is also important to notice that he uses these symbols in a subversive way. The century of enlightenment associated the light and the day with reason, darkness with sin and guilt, and the night stood in contrast to the light of God's revelation. Such a subversive use of imagery seems at first confusing and disturbing.

In light of the conversation between Heinrich and his father discussed above, however, Novalis' intention becomes clearer. In true Romantic spirit he challenges the contemporary over-emphasis on reason by subverting the use of light and night as he reconstructs a reality in which the symbol of the night becomes central. In this way he emphasizes both the limitations of enlightenment thinking and the fact that some of the most important aspects of the Christian faith cannot be apprehended on a merely rational basis. He believes that they have to be experienced by a turn towards the night, an important idea in Christian mysticism.[38] Novalis' final aim, however, is not to set up a false dichotomy

---

36. Unless otherwise indicated, the translation of these hymns is taken from George MacDonald in *Exotics*. There are two different German versions of *Hymns to the Night*. MacDonald's translation relies on the later published version. It is noteworthy that the hand-written version does not have "waking day" but merely "day." Novalis, *Novalis*, 1:148–49.

37. Ibid. 149. In the last verse the move downwards is stressed once more. Novalis, *Novalis*, 1:177.

38. Gerhard Schulz argues along similar lines when he states that these hymns seek to explore a dimension of the Christian faith that the Enlightenment world with its focus on the day and the light is unable to grasp. Schulz, "Novalis," 46. See also Biser, *Abstieg*, 34–36.

between reason and a Romantic mystical outlook. As the hymns develop, he works towards an integration of the light and the night. The final goal is their union, a concern very close to MacDonald's own heart.[39] Novalis reflects in hymn four: "Now I know when will come the last morning: when the light no more scares away the Night and Love, when sleep shall be without waking, and but one continuous dream."[40]

Hayward describes Novalis' subversive use of traditional imagery well when she calls it a "re-orientation of classical Christian Doctrine."[41] Novalis describes his own use of poetics as a way "to de-familiarize in a pleasant way, to make an object strange, and yet familiar and enticing, that is Romantic poetry."[42] But what is this reorientation, and what is it exactly that Novalis' wants to entice his readers into? Hayward suggests that death and absorption have become the prime impulses of an erotic mystical love affair, and she concludes that these hymns "offer anarchic ideas. Love is seen in terms of erotic desire, spiritual union in terms of overt sexual activity; death is seductive and alluring."[43] It is significant that Hayward, in her discussion of these *Hymns*, leaves out a very important part of *Hymns to the Night*, where Novalis reflects on Christ's death and resurrection. For Novalis, it is only in Christ's suffering, death, and resurrection that redemption is found. Death in itself does not offer life or redemption as Hayward suggests when she writes, "For Novalis, as for MacDonald, death was the great link between the two worlds, the absolute necessary step towards finding the way home."[44] I shall challenge Hayward's view, and I will show that the erotic and sexual language that Novalis employs in these hymns has to be understood in his return

---

39. See especially the fairytale "The History of Photogen and Nycteris: A Day and Night Mährchen." George MacDonald's plea for the reintegration of the academic disciplines in this fairytale, I would suggest, might quite possibly rely on Novalis' metaphors of day and night in *Hymns to the Night*.

40. Novalis, quoted in George MacDonald, *Rampolli*, 6.

41. Hayward, "Three German Thinkers," 206.

42. Novalis, *Novalis*, 2:839, translation mine.

43. Hayward, "Three German Thinkers," 206, 204.

44. Ibid., 240. Hayward's discussion of death in Novalis is problematic for various reasons. While she begins her discussion of Novalis with an analysis of *Hymns to the Night*, she then establishes her understanding of death in Novalis on various quotes taken from Novalis' philosophical reflections called "Fragments." Methodologically speaking, this is very difficult to do, as these fragments were written over a long period of time and Novalis' understanding of death was rather complex. For a more careful discussion of Novalis' understanding of death, see Sepasgosarin, *Tod*.

to medieval imagery and mystical ideas in order to express a profound Christian mystery.[45] A couple of examples shall suffice here to support my argument. Novalis, before moving into erotic language, praises the victorious cross of Christ in hymn four:

> Inconsumable stands the cross,
> —Victory-flag of our race.

He then continues in the voice of a passive lover:

> Oh, powerfully suck me, beloved,
> Draw till I'm gone;
> That, fallen asleep, I
> Still may love on.[46]

In the fifth hymn, after reflecting on Christ's resurrection, it is Christ's death that calls the believer to the wedding feast, and it is to Mary that thousands will lift their hearts.[47] Novalis ends this cycle of hymns by calling the reader once more down into the night:

> Blest be the everlasting Night,
> And blest the endless Slumber! . . .
> To our home we have to go
> That blessed time again to know . . .
> Down to the sweet bride, and away
> To the beloved Jesus![48]

The bridal imagery used interchangeably for Christ, his beloved Sophie, and Mary was quite common in medieval Germany, and some of the erotic language is reminiscent of the Song of Songs in the OT.

Already in *Heinrich von Ofterdingen* we can see this return to medieval imagery in Novalis. The novel is set in medieval Germany, and references to medieval imagery abound. Novalis weaves into one of the fairy stories the red carbuncle, a medieval symbol for Christ. At another place, Heinrich compares his beloved Mathilde with a sapphire,

---

45. Roder provides a careful analysis of a variety of medieval symbols that Novalis employs in his writing. He also discusses Novalis' use of mystical ideas. Roder, *Novalis*, 427, 636–784.

46. Novalis, quoted in George MacDonald, *Rampolli*, 8, translation in part mine.

47. It is noteworthy that MacDonald does not directly name Mary, as Novalis does, but refers to her as "mother maiden," which might indicate that MacDonald was quite uncomfortable with Novalis' adoration of Mary.

48. George MacDonald, *Rampolli*, 15–16, translation partly my own, partly MacDonald's.

a medieval symbol for Mary as well as wisdom.[49] The experience of the death of Mathilde now becomes like a higher revelation of life.[50] Thus the lost Mathilde, like the lost bride in the above hymn, referring to Novalis' real loss of his fiancée Sophie, has taken on the role of a mediator.[51] Novalis clothes this conviction in yet another medieval image when he has the miner explain to Heinrich at another point in *Heinrich von Ofterdingen* that the gems of life are only found in depths of the mountain.

But what has this melding of Romantic love with imagery of Mary, the beloved Mathilde/Sophie, and Christ to do with the night? Eugen Biser argues convincingly that the key to understanding *Hymns to the Night* is found in an experience that Novalis had after the tragic loss of his fiancée Sophie.[52] Novalis struggled with depression and suicidal thoughts, wanting to follow his beloved into death. One day at her grave, however, he had a profound spiritual experience through which his grief and depression were transformed into a new hope:

> The hillock became a cloud of dust, and through the cloud I saw the glorified face of my beloved. In her eyes eternity reposed. I laid hold of her hands, and the tears became a sparkling bond that could not be broken. Into the distance swept by, like a tempest, thousands of years. On her neck I welcomed the new life with ecstatic tears. Never was such another dream; then first

---

49. "There is engraved an enigmatic token, full deep into the jewels' glowing blood. The stone is comparable to a heart, in which the image of the unknown woman rests" (Novalis, *Henry*, 41). The last two lines are my own translation. Roder, in his careful biography on Novalis, provides a collection of medieval images that depict the relationship between Christ and Mary/Sophia in mystical fashion. See especially the German medieval depiction of the Trinity with Sophia/Mary in the middle as well as the image of Mary and Jesus with the blue flower linking the two. Roder also provides a discussion of the meaning of these symbols, both lining out their historical significance and how Novalis appropriates these symbols for his own purpose. His emphasis lies with their aesthetic and metaphysical significance. Unfortunately, he does not stress their theological import enough. Roder, *Novalis*, 261, 433, 689–92, 733.

50. Novalis, *Novalis*, 1:370–71. This is also based on a medieval image, where a young man has to break a sapphire in order to get to the carbuncle that is enclosed in the sapphire. See the image in Roder, *Novalis*, 733.

51. Hans Urs von Balthasar also recognizes and emphasizes the importance of Sophie's mediating role in Novalis' philosophy. See Balthasar, *Prometheus*, 273.

52. Biser, *Abstieg*, 12–13. Roder argues along similar lines. Roder, *Novalis*, 639. Hymn three bears such striking similarities to an entry into Novalis' diary on May 13, 1797 regarding a profound spiritual experience by Sophie's grave that the connection between the two is commonly acknowledged.

and ever since I hold fast an eternal, unchangeable faith in the heaven of the Night, and its Light, the Beloved.[53]

Novalis' own experience of loss and the subsequent mystical encounter beside Sophie's grave made him understand a central and yet seemingly paradoxical mystery of the Christian faith: the very place one would naturally consider as "dark"—one's losses, one's suffering, and the harsh reality of death—becomes now the very place where God reveals himself. This is why Novalis can write *Hymns to the Night*, not because he intends to celebrate death, loss, and suffering as such but because of what is revealed in the night.

In the first hymn Novalis asks of the night: "What holdest thou under thy mantle, that with hidden power affects my soul?" In hymns four and five Novalis answers this rhetorical question: "the Night became the mighty womb of revelation." This revelation is centered for Novalis around the birth, life, death, and resurrection of Christ, which he reflects upon in the last four hymns. Novalis writes, "Inconsumable stands the cross, victory-flag of our race," and "In death eternal life was made known, you are death and thou first makest us whole."[54] Novalis' fascination with the night and death is not with death as such, as Wolff and Giorgio Spina have argued for example.[55] Rather, it is because of Christ's death and resurrection that one's own experience of suffering and loss can become the very place we encounter God. In Christ, one's own experience of loss and suffering can be redeemed. This is why Novalis urges his reader again and again to go down into the "holy and blessed night," a clear reference to the *latin exsultet* and its the praise of the Easter night: *o vere beata nox*. This journey downward into the night and his longing after death is really a longing after home, which is for Novalis closely connected with his faith in the beloved Jesus. He writes at the very end of these *Hymns*, "Down to the sweet bride, and away to the beloved Jesus! Courage! The evening shades grow grey, of all our griefs to ease us! A dream will dash our chains apart, and lay us on the Father's heart."[56] Death in itself cannot save or redeem nor give birth to hope and new life. The experience of loss and death can, however, become the very place where Christ meets us and where we can come to know Christ and be unified with him in

---

53. George MacDonald, *Rampolli*, 6.
54. Hymn five, translation mine.
55. Wolff, *Key*, 22–23; Spina, "Contrapositions," 30.
56. Novalis, *Hymns to the Night*, quoted in George MacDonald, *Rampolli*, 16.

his suffering and somehow, also in his resurrection. Significantly, for Novalis this great mystery is best expressed in poetical dreams, which in turn help the reader both to imagine and learn to participate in this great mystery, and somehow be laid into "the Father's heart."

Conclusion

The uniqueness of *Hymns to the Night* lies in its employment of Romantic poetics as a way to enter into one of the most difficult and profound Christian mysteries.[57] These hymns do not offer anarchic ideas as Hayward suggests. On the contrary, they seek to provide guidance in the midst of a frantic existence where the experience of loss and suffering does not necessarily have to lead into despair and hopelessness. The movement down into the night becomes a way through the abyss to a solid place that Novalis calls "the beloved Jesus." For Novalis, poetics serves the greater purpose of expressing the great mystery that "is revealed to all and yet remains for ever unfathomable," as he puts it in *Heinrich von Ofterdingen*.[58] For Novalis the task of the poet and priest are intimately connected, and he sees it as the challenge of his time to recover their unity. He writes: "Poet and priest were one in the beginning and only in later times were they separated. The true poet is always priest, just as the true priest remains always a poet—and should the future not seek to re-establish the old order of things?"[59]

This unified vision of the role of the priest as poet as well as Novalis' profound grasp of the mystery of Christ's death and resurrection

---

57. Christianity is for Novalis superior to Ancient Greek mythology, for example, precisely because it is able to make sense of death in light of Christ's death and resurrection. In hymn five, Novalis incorporates the Ancient Greek myths and gods into his hymn, a popular undertaking in the Romantic period, and laments the inability of the Greek gods to make sense of death.

58. Novalis, *Novalis*, 1:361. The relationship of poetics and religion in Novalis' works is very complex; the question of whether art is subservient to religion or the other way around is a difficult question to answer and beyond the scope of this thesis. In *Hymns to the Night* one can clearly argue for poetics as a handmaiden to religion, but at other places in Novalis' works it might seem the other way around. See Pfefferkorn, *Novalis*, 187–90. She discusses this issue and concludes that "his stronger inclination is toward the service of art to the truth, to the divine, and that for this reason his truly religious poems, the *Geistliche Lieder*, are his most successful poetic work" (Pfefferkorn, *Novalis*, 189). The same can be said for *Hymns to the Night*.

59. Novalis, *Novalis*, 2:255, translation mine. The quote is taken from the collection called "Blüthenstaub."

in light of his own suffering had a strong appeal to MacDonald as he sought to bring these two callings together in his own life; he also faced tremendous suffering and the loss of many of his loved ones. While MacDonald's *Lilith* is of a very different genre, we shall show in chapter 5 that both in theme and his usage of subversive imagery, these hymns had a significant impact on MacDonald. In the next part of this chapter, we shall explore MacDonald's theological understanding of the imagination in light of Samuel Taylor Coleridge. MacDonald's view of the imagination is foundational for understanding his theological rationale for story and the "parabolic" that we shall discuss in chapter 4.

MacDonald's Understanding of the Imagination in Light of Coleridge

In the first part of this chapter, we explored the influence of Novalis upon MacDonald and especially Novalis' understanding of the relationship between priestly and poetic activity. Closely connected to this theme is George MacDonald's understanding of the imagination. The imagination, as we shall see, became a central concept in MacDonald's understanding of human experience and activity and therefore also his view of how God reveals himself to humanity, especially in and through poetics.

The Christian imagination has received much attention of late. The rise of interest in the role of aesthetics for theology and spiritual formation is remarkable and extremely important for moving the arts back to the center of theological inquiry and the life of the church. But what actually is the imagination and how is it at work? MacDonald wrestled with these very questions and sought to answer them for his own Victorian audience. It is not a simple subject matter, and in order to grasp MacDonald's understanding of the imagination, we have to place him within the Romantic tradition that strongly shaped his thinking in this regard. Coleridge in particular was an important influence on MacDonald. Coleridge in turn drew heavily upon Immanuel Kant and German Idealism in his articulation of the wide-ranging scope of the imagination. Therefore, we must at least consider briefly the development of this tradition, the issues that arose, and how both Coleridge and MacDonald responded to them. The distinction we shall draw between degrees of Idealism and creative/constructive perception are fine but crucial for understanding both Coleridge and MacDonald's response to him. Coleridge sought to blend Idealism with theology. MacDonald went in a rather different direction. Only by locating MacDonald within this tradition will we be able to recognize his thoughtful appraisal and critical reception of it and in what way he contributed to a theological understanding of the imagination from a decidedly Christian perspective.

Kant and Schelling as the Backdrop for Coleridge's Thinking

The imagination became a major subject within German Idealism and Romanticism, both of which were heavily indebted to Immanuel Kant's established categories in his books *Critique of Pure Reason* (1781) and more particularly in *Critique of Judgment* (1790). Kant together with Friedrich Wilhelm Joseph Schelling had a profound impact on Coleridge's understanding of the imagination, and it should prove fruitful to look at each of these influences.

Kant argued that the imagination plays a major role not only in artistic expression but also at a much more fundamental level in human perception of the world. In his writing Kant distinguishes between the empirical and transcendental imagination. The empirical imagination works on a pre-cognitive level and presents objects of the world to the mind by identifying objects as being of a certain kind and by making an image of the object.[60] The transcendental imagination has a more constructive function and is called the "productive" imagination by Kant, as it is an active power. Mary Warnock describes these categories as follows:

> It seems that in Kant's system the imagination, whether empirical or transcendental, lies half-way between the purely intellectual part of our knowledge of the world, the part, that is, which consists of our having abstract concepts or thoughts about things [a priori], and the purely sensory part, which, as we have seen, he regards as totally chaotic and unorganized, if considered on its own. Without imagination, we could never apply concepts to sense experience. Whereas a wholly sensory life would be without any regularity or organization, a purely intellectual life would be without any real content. And this amounts to saying that with either the senses or the intellect we could not experience the world as we do. The two elements are not automatically joined to each other in their functions. They need a further element to join them. The joining element is the imagination; and its mediating power consists in its power to

---

60. Warnock, *Imagination*, 27–28.

bring the chaos of sense experience to order according to certain rules, or in certain unchanging forms.[61]

Kant, then, ascribes to the imagination a crucial and active role in human knowledge, as he sees the imagination synthesizing a priori concepts and sense experience, thereby producing a structured and meaningful perception of the world.

While it is beyond the scope of this chapter to discuss Kant's understanding of the aesthetic imagination, it is important to point out that there are some significant connections between Kant's cognitive and aesthetic functions of the imagination, as Warnock detailed previously.[62] In both cases, Kant claims, the imagination functions to bring order to the chaos of sense experience, no matter whether the order is imposed upon sense experience (as in cognition) or whether the order is intrinsic to the object (as in aesthetic judgment).[63] This close relationship further suggests that he understands the imagination to be far more fundamental to human experience and action than previously acknowledged. In light of this it seems surprising that Kant never contemplates the constructive role that the imagination might have for religion.

Johann Gottlieb Fichte and Friedrich Wilhelm Joseph Schelling in particular molded the latter's categories into a decidedly Idealist framework, doing away with Kant's important category *"Das Ding an sich"* (the thing in itself). Kant had established an important distinction in his metaphysical system where he clearly differentiates between human perception of the world and the world that exists independent of the mind, *"Das Ding an sich."* As a consequence, he kept in place the theologically important distinction between humanity, the created world, and God. Hart explains:

> [B]y continuing to speak of a *Ding an Sich*, and thus to differentiate *something* from the phenomenal (which . . . is how we know or experience the world *humanly*), his refusal to concede the absolute *givenness* of "creation" relative to the mind and its productivity nonetheless preserves some account of the world's *otherness* from us and our human way of experiencing it, and thereby, in theological terms, the otherness of its Creator (God) in the same regard. In other words, while emphatically denying a certain sort of givenness, Kant holds back from denying

61. Ibid., 30.
62. See ibid., 41–42, esp. 50–62.
63. Ibid., 50.

givenness altogether and as such, leaving room for the genuine existence of that which is other than us.[64]

For the Idealist hoping to overcome the Kantian "dualism" between man and nature, this distinction had to be done away with. For Schelling there no longer existed a reality independent of the mind. He created a system in which the infinite mind (*Geist*) had to be understood, as Isaiah Berlin puts it, as "a kind of self-developing principle of consciousness."[65] Schelling believed that the world's intelligibility is dependent upon this infinite intelligence (*Geist*) and its unfolding of consciousness.

He saw the human and finite mind in turn to be part of this absolute and infinite mind.[66] In the finite mind's interaction with the world it comes to increasing consciousness of itself as part of the infinite mind. According to Schelling, nature itself is alive as its patterns, laws, and its very essence are identical with infinite *Geist* not come into consciousness yet.[67] Frederick Copleston describes Schelling's view of nature as "a teleological system, as the necessary self-unfolding of the eternal Idea."[68] As such a "teleological system" nature strives but is not aware of it.

It is only when the mind begins to strive that it brings the universe to a higher level of self-consciousness.[69] Through the mind's engagement with nature, the eternal idea intrinsic to nature becomes apparent, and in this way nature (in its ideal sense) becomes the product of the mind. According to Schelling nature only comes fully into its own when it is brought into consciousness through the mind, and thus it exists in its most complete sense only in the mind. Warnock explains this as follows: "What we order by means of the categories of our understanding is not mere appearances, it *is* the things themselves. For the things are also our own ideas. And therefore it can be said that the categories or rules of the mind do more than order; they create."[70] The finite mind as part of the infinite mind is thus capable not only of bringing order to the world but

---

64. Hart, *Creation*, 5. See also Warnock, *Imagination*, 66.

65. Berlin, *Roots*, 98.

66. Hart, *Creation*, 5; Copleston, *History*, 7:18–19.

67. Störig, *Kleine Weltgeschichte*, 455.

68. Copleston, *History*, 7:110–11.

69. Berlin, *Roots*, 97–98.

70. Warnock, *Imagination*, 66. See also Hart, *Creation*, 5; Copleston, *History*, 7:109–10.

also creating the world (in its ideal sense), thereby moving to increasing self-consciousness.[71]

For Schelling then, there is no clear distinction anymore between the finite (human) mind and the world or between finite (human) and infinite (divine) mind.[72] In Christian terms, the distinction between Creator, creature, and the created world is collapsed into the category of "*Geist*" as the underlying unifying principle of existence, progressively moving towards consciousness of itself.[73] The otherness of God is swallowed up, and the artist emerges as the central player in unfolding consciousness. Richard Kearney puts it this way: "By so collapsing the onto-theological dichotomy between divine and human creation, Schelling put an end to the traditional understanding of imagination as a second-hand imitation of God's original being."[74]

For Schelling the imagination plays a major role in this process both on an unconscious and conscious level. It is the role of the artist to press deeper into the mysteries of the infinite, thereby moving towards a higher level of union between the finite and infinite mind.[75] While an absolute union can never be achieved, it is the responsibility of the finite mind, infused by infinite power, to strive towards the infinite "*Geist*."[76] This process of coming into consciousness and into union includes the resolution of conflicts. It is the aim of the artist to show that beneath the apparent conflicts there is an underlying unity and harmony of the universe towards which we should strive.[77]

Schelling differentiates between two kinds of art in this regard. Only those works of art that break open the infinite world of consciousness are

---

71. That such a system could easily lead to a glorification of the individual, who can create reality arbitrarily, is pointed out by Berlin in his discussion of the excesses of "unbridled romanticism" (Berlin, *Roots*, 89, 93).

72. Kearney, *Wake*, 180; Hart, *Creation*, 8. Copleston notes that this is a general principle in Idealist and Romantic thought. Copleston, *History*, 7:18–19.

73. Störig, in his discussion of Schelling's understanding of nature, quotes a poem in which Schelling explains this process of coming into consciousness. It is only through mankind's active engagement with nature that the "Riesengeist" (giant spirit) hidden in nature is released. Störig, *Kleine Weltgeschichichte*, 455–56.

74. Kearney, *Wake*, 180.

75. Hart, *Creation*, 7.

76. See Hart's insightful discussion here on the fusion of human and divine activity in Schelling's thought explicating as a general metaphysical principle the incarnation where human and divine unite to reveal God. Ibid., 8.

77. Warnock, *Imagination*, 93.

valuable and to be considered true works of art. Artistic works that are conventional and mimetic, reiterating what has already come into consciousness, are "dead," as they do not contribute to this vital and mystical coming into consciousness. Berlin explains Schelling's distinction as follows:

> Life in a work of art is analogous with—is some kind of quality the work has in common with—what we admire in nature, namely some kind of power, force, energy, life, vitality bursting forth . . . When this is lacking, when the whole thing is wholly conventional, done according to rules, done in the full self-conscious blaze of complete awareness of what one is doing, the product is of necessity elegant, symmetrical and dead.[78]

According to Berlin, it was this view of art that would shape Romantic thought in general and Coleridge's thought in particular.[79]

Coleridge: Between Faith and German Idealism

While MacDonald scholars have pointed out the particular influence of Coleridge on MacDonald's understanding of the imagination, this influence deserves more investigation and analysis, as the philosophical underpinnings of Coleridge's comments on the imagination in *Biographia Literaria* are often not taken into consideration. This is in part due to the fact that Coleridge's thinking has remained obscure to many as his philosophical musings are not part of one coherent philosophical system, nor are they recorded in any coherent way. Understanding Coleridge's philosophical understanding of the imagination will elicit MacDonald's unique contribution.

The degree to which Coleridge integrated Idealist thinking into his own work is somewhat disputed. Jonathan Wordsworth, for example, argues that Coleridge's understanding of the imagination did not change in a significant way over his lifetime. Wordsworth compares Coleridge's earlier comments on the imagination, especially the comments in *Lecture on the Slave Trade* (1795), with his definition in *Biographia Literaria* (1817) and sees no significant difference. He concludes: "[I]magination is for

---

78. Berlin, *Roots*, 98–99.

79. Ibid., 98–102. See, for example, Wordsworth's definition of imagination, which carries traces of Schelling's definition of "true art." Wordsworth, "Preface," xxi–xlii.

Coleridge an act of faith . . . the primary [imagination] in its full potential showed man at his closest to God . . . [I]t is a statement of faith."[80]

Wordsworth's comparison of Coleridge's two statements is, however, not differentiated enough. In 1795 Coleridge writes regarding the imagination: "To develop the powers of the Creator is our proper employment—and to imitate Creativeness by combination our most exalted and self-satisfying Delight . . . Our Almighty Parent hath . . . given to us Imagination."[81] In *Biographia Literaria* (1817) his wording is quite different: "The primary Imagination I hold to be living power and prime agent of all human perception, and as a repetition in the finite mind of the eternal act of creation in the infinite I AM."[82] While Coleridge speaks of the imagination in 1795 in quite a traditional (and Christian) way, namely that the human imagination is a mere imitation of the Creator God, our parent who gives us the imagination in the first place, his wording in 1817 has a decidedly different ring to it. The human imagination is now a "repetition . . . of the eternal act of creation in the infinite I AM." Coleridge's later definition creates some theological problems. If the human and primary imagination is a "repetition" of the "infinite I AM," then the distinction drawn between the divine and human becomes blurred and the human imagination is elevated to a manifestation of the divine. A decidedly Christian understanding of the imagination must come to terms with God's transcendence and the ways in which he is "other" than his creation. One can detect the influence of German Idealism on Coleridge here, which tended to conflate the finite and the infinite.[83]

It is also unclear what exactly Coleridge means by "the eternal act of creation in the infinite I AM." Is the "infinite I AM," as Kearney suggests, a veiled allusion to the "transcendental I" of Schelling?[84] He does not elaborate on this, but the words themselves suggest that Coleridge believes in an actual deity rather than a mere infinite consciousness. Warnock puts it this way:

> How far did Coleridge go with Schelling and Kant? It may be said that he is not completely committed, at least in this passage,

80. Wordworth, "Infinite I Am."
81. Coleridge, *Lecture on the Slave Trade*, cited in ibid., 28.
82. Coleridge, *Biographia Literaria*, 159.
83. Coleridge in later life grew closer towards an orthodox Christian perspective. While one can see this clearly in his *Confessions of an Inquiring Spirit*, his reflections in *Biographia Literaria* are more ambiguous.
84. Kearney, *Wake*, 183.

to idealism; for the work of actual creation is ascribed to the deity, while the human imagination is a repetition in human terms of this divine activity.[85]

Coleridge's comments therefore reflect a certain tension here. His choice of words echo one of the OT names for God (Exod 3:14), but how personal and biblical is his "infinite I AM"? In placing the divine in such close proximity with the human, he seems subtly to remove any transcendence from his presentation of the divine. It seems that Coleridge wants to hold on to some kind of faith in a deity, but he also tends towards the Idealist notion of conflating the finite and infinite.

MacDonald's Response

In light of this tension and ambiguity within Coleridge's account of the imagination in *Biographia Literaria*, it is noteworthy that MacDonald, while following Coleridge in placing the human imagination in a theological context, leaves the reader in no doubt about his understanding of the relation between divine and human imagination. He goes out of his way to differentiate clearly between the creative activity of God and human creativity. MacDonald establishes God as the one who created the world out of nothing and mankind as part of God's creation. God's transcendence can never be swallowed up into the category of finite and infinite mind. He writes:

> We must not forget . . . that between creator and poet lies the one unpassable gulf which distinguishes—far be it from us to say *divides*—all that is God's from all that is man's; a gulf teeming with infinite revelations, but a gulf over which no man can pass to find out God, although God needs not to pass over it to find man; the gulf between that which calls, and that which is thus called into being; between that which makes in its own image and that which is made in that image. It is better to keep the word *creation* for that calling out nothing which is the imagination of God. Everything of man must have been of God first; and it will help much towards our understanding of the imagination and its function in man if we first succeed in regarding aright the imagination of God, in which the imagination of man lives and moves and has its being.[86]

---

85. Warnock, *Imagination*, 91. Prickett and Copleston also notice the tension in Coleridge here. See Prickett, *Romanticism*, 20–25; Copleston, *History*, 8:155.

86. George MacDonald, *Orts*, 2–3. MacDonald emphasizes this distinction

For MacDonald, then, humanity always works within the givenness of the created order, and consequently, he reserves the term *creation* for the primary creative act of God. The human imagination is subordinate to God's, and its primary function is that "of following and finding out the divine imagination in whose image it was made."[87]

MacDonald further reinforces this distinction by making the theologically important observation that the human imagination, unlike God's, is capable of bringing forth evil.[88] While the aim of MacDonald's essay, like Coleridge's, is certainly to emphasize the importance and wide-ranging scope of the imagination in human life and action, he does stress, unlike Coleridge, that the imagination can go astray, can be "ill-bred" and "uncultivated," and is in need of redemption.[89]

According to MacDonald, a denial and suppression of the imagination will not do, though, to avoid the potential towards evil; rather, it will make it worse.[90] He insists that the imagination is central to human cognition and must be cultivated, as it is by the imagination that God takes hold of us and calls us to a true and creative life.[91] With this in mind, it will be helpful now to consider why both Coleridge and MacDonald understand the imagination to be of such central importance to human life and action.

---

throughout this essay and this might very well be in response to its absence in Coleridge's work.

87. George MacDonald, *Orts*, 12. See also ibid., 10. This is in contrast to Robb, who argues that MacDonald, like Coleridge, conflates the two. Robb, *God's Fiction*, 53.

88. George MacDonald, *Orts*, 26.

89. Ibid., 12. See also MacDonald's critique of the painter in the short story "The Cruel Painter" in idem, *Adela*, 379–416. Ironically, the misled artist of the story is called "*Teufelsbürst*," German for "devil's brush." For another depiction of the imagination gone astray see MacDonald's gothic character Herr von Funkelstein and Euphra, who is under his occult influence in *David Elginbrod*. MacDonald cites Novalis in this novel and affirms with him that "*Wo keine Götter sind, walten Gespenster*" (Where no gods are, ghosts reign—translation mine). Idem, *David Elginbrod*, ch. 10.

90. George MacDonald, *Orts*, 29–30. It is the imagination, according to MacDonald, which elevates the intellect and passions "to their true and noble service" (ibid., 30).

91. Ibid., 2–5, 36–38. MacDonald argues, for example, that it is via the imagination that Lady Macbeth is not allowed to rest in her evil scheming, but is driven to a noble unrest. Ibid., 32.

Coleridge: *The Primary and Secondary Imagination and Fancy*

In order to understand the continuities and discontinuities between Coleridge's and MacDonald's concepts of the imagination, we must first come to terms with Coleridge's dense and suggestive comments on the imagination in *Biographia Literaria*, chapter 13.[92] The famous passage, to which we have already referred, is worth quoting in full:

> The Imagination then I consider either as primary, or secondary. The primary Imagination I hold to be the living power and prime agent of all human perception, and as a repetition in the finite mind of the eternal act of creation in the infinite I AM. The secondary Imagination I consider as an echo of the former, co-existing with the conscious will, yet still as identical with the primary in the *kind* of its agency, and differing only in *degree*, and in the *mode* of its operation. It dissolves, diffuses, dissipates, in order to recreate: or where this process is rendered impossible, yet still at all events it struggles to idealize and to unify. It is essentially *vital*, even as all objects (*as* objects) are essentially fixed and dead.[93]

The distinction drawn between the primary and secondary imagination is an important one. The primary imagination as the "prime agent in human perception" is reminiscent of Kant's cognitive, pre-conscious function of the imagination working in all human perception and knowledge of the world.

Here, however, Coleridge follows more closely Schelling's version of the "productive imagination," as Coleridge adopted the Idealist notion that humanity and nature have to be seen as part of one single dynamic unity.[94] He believes that the primary imagination, as a living and actively

---

92. *Biographia Literaria* is a somewhat unstructured collection of reflections of personal, metaphysical, and literary nature. While some reflections are clear and systematic, other passages seem convoluted and difficult to penetrate. Holmes calls it a "genuine literary self-portrait" of Coleridge. Holmes, *Darker Reflections*, 379.

93. Coleridge, *Biographia Literaria*, 159–60.

94. Hart, *Artistry*, 10–11, 13–14. Warnock, *Imagination*, 91–92. See also Richards, *Coleridge*, 65; Copleston, *History*, 8:154. It is commonly acknowledged that Coleridge borrowed many of his ideas from German Idealism, Schelling, and Fichte in particular and German Romanticism. While he has often been accused of plagiarism, it is clear that Coleridge did not merely copy the Germans but brought his own originality to the subject matter. See Wellek, *Modern Criticism*, 151–87; Holmes, *Early Visions*, 42–43, 232, 344–45; idem, *Darker Reflections*, 253–55, 275–80, 400–403, 406; Helmholtz, *Indebtedness*.

shaping power, in some sense creates reality as Coleridge locates reality not in something outside of the self but in the self's perception of the object.[95] While Coleridge does not elaborate on how this might work, he insists that nothing that exists in the mind is *given* to the mind, but the imagination works upon the material provided by sense experience; in this way perceiving and creating are the same thing for him.[96] For example, in his poem "Dejection: An Ode" (1802) he writes: "O Lady! We receive but what we give, / And in our life alone does Nature live."[97]

And yet, as we have shown above, Coleridge does not espouse a completely Idealist framework here, admitting to a divine presence which is other from the self, the "infinite I am." The result of this balancing act, according to Hart, is

> an epistemology that, although it places a huge emphasis upon the mind's creative and constructive activity—and thereby renders the status of the "reality" of which we are conscious ambiguous relative to the reality of the self—nonetheless does so in the interests of a profoundly felt sense of responsibility in the face of something or someone Other to which "response" of an appropriate sort is indeed properly due.[98]

How profound this responsibility towards the "Other" might be is difficult to say, as Coleridge does not elaborate on the relation between human and divine action. What is important for our discussion, however, is that Coleridge, like Kant and Schelling before him, emphasizes that the imagination is fundamental to human life as it plays an active role in human cognition.

According to Coleridge, the secondary imagination then works upon the material received by the primary imagination.[99] In contrast to the primary imagination, it is not pre-conscious, but works within the reign of the "conscious will." It is an activity in which we choose to make something out of the material that we have received through human cognition.

---

95. Richards, *Coleridge*, 49, 51, 53, 57. Hart, *Artistry*, 13.
96. Richards, *Coleridge*, 56–57.
97. Coleridge, *Works*, 365.
98. Hart, *Artistry*, 9.
99. Engell, *Imagination*, 344. Engell rightly points out that one should not infer that the adjective "secondary" indicates in any way a lesser power. Rather, it is secondary because it has to rely on the primary imagination for the material with which to work. Coleridge, in this distinction follows closely Schelling's distinction between productive intuition and the poetic faculty. See Warnock, *Imagination*, 92.

It re-creates the material as it "dissolves, diffuses, dissipates" it.[100] While the secondary imagination works in a wide spectrum of human creative activity, it is to poetry and the symbol that Coleridge turns to demonstrate its function.[101] He explains in the next chapter of *Biographia Literaria*:

> The poet, described in ideal perfection, brings the whole soul of man into activity . . . He diffuses a tone and spirit of unity, that blends, and (as it were) *fuses*, each into each, by that synthetic and magical power, to which I would exclusively appropriate the name of Imagination.[102] This power, first put in action by the will and understanding, . . . reveals itself in the balance or reconcilement of opposite or discordant qualities: of sameness, with difference; of the general with the concrete; the idea with the image; the individual with the representative; the sense of novelty and freshness with old and familiar objects.[103]

Coleridge continues his explication by alluding to a poem by Sir John Davies to demonstrate this profound duty of the imagination:

> Thus does she, when from individual states
> She doth abstract the universal kinds;
> Which then re-clothed in divers names and fates
> Steal access through the senses to our minds.[104]

Coleridge's reflections on the function of the secondary imagination are highly suggestive and raise several questions. First, what does he mean by such verbs as "dissolve," "diffuse," "dissipate," and "reconcilement of opposite or discordant qualities"? How does the imagination "blend . . . and fuse . . . each into each"? And what is "magical power"?

Owen Barfield's discussion of Coleridge offers us a way into his thinking. Barfield suggests that Coleridge's unifying theory of the imagination needs to be understood in terms of polarity.[105] This polarity cannot

---

100. Coleridge, *Biographia Literaria*, 159.

101. Engell suggests that Coleridge primarily means poetry, criticism, and fine arts when he talks about the secondary imagination. Engell, *Imagination*, 345.

102. The term "imagination" here does not refer to the philosophical concept of primary and secondary imagination as whole but rather to the secondary imagination and its function in poetry. Coleridge employs the term "imagination" in a free manner, sometimes to refer to the imagination as a whole, sometimes to the unique function of the secondary imagination. Ibid.

103. Coleridge, *Biographia Literaria*, 166.

104. Ibid., ch. 14, 166.

105. Barfield, "Either: Or," 28. The concept of polarity is integral to all of Coleridge's

be understood as logical opposites that are contradictory in nature. Rather, according to Barfield, it needs to be understood in terms of "polar opposites [that] are generative of each other—and together generative of new product. They are thus agents of genuine transformation."[106] For Barfield, then, Coleridge's poetic imagination, by comparing similarities in things that look unlike, and by bringing together ideas that seem different, is able to look into the underlying unity of the universe and in this way gain new understanding of the world.[107] Coleridge invents the term "esemplastic" power for this reconciling and unifying dimension of the imagination, which "shapes into one."[108]

While Barfield's exposition seems to be a possible explanation of the secondary imagination, some of Coleridge's terminology suggests more than a mere "looking into." The verbs "dissolve" and "recreate" raise the question of whether the secondary imagination can change reality into something new. To dissolve something certainly suggests a complete destruction of a form in order to recreate the material into another shape. Has Coleridge taken on board the paradoxical stance of Idealism that "discovering" and "creating" are in some sense the same thing? Coleridge's poem "Dejection: An Ode" supports this Idealist view. He writes:

> O Lady! We receive but what we give,
> And in our life alone does Nature live:
> Ours is her wedding garment, ours her shroud!
> And would we aught behold, of higher worth,
> Than that inanimate cold world allowed
> To the poor loveless ever-anxious crowd,
> Ah! From the soul itself must issue forth
> A light, a glory, a fair luminous cloud
> Enveloping the Earth—
> And from the soul itself must there be sent

---

thinking. See here also Prickett, "'Living Educts,'" 19–20; Perkins, "Religious Thinker," 187, 193.

106. Barfield, "Either: Or," 28. Warnock, on the other hand, suggests that Coleridge here relies on Schelling's idea of the poetic imagination being able to resolve conflicts. Warnock, *Imagination*, 93.

107. Barfield, like Dearborn, interprets this process in light of Coleridge's later Trinitarian perspective, drawing on Coleridge' later work *Aids to Reflection*. In *Biographia Literaria*, however, Coleridge does not explicate the imagination in Trinitarian terms. Barfield, "Either: Or," 30–33.

108. Coleridge, *Biographia Literaria*, 82. Kearney, *Wake*, 182. Coleridge apparently coined this word to express what he thought the German word "Einbildungskraft" indicated. See Warnock, *Imagination*, 92.

> A sweet and potent voice, of its own birth,
> Of all sweet sounds the life and element! . . .
> This light, this glory, this fair luminous mist,
> This beautiful and beauty-making power . . .
> Which wedding Nature to us gives in dower
> A new Earth and new Heaven . . .
> My shaping spirit of Imagination.[109]

There are several issues to notice here. This section of the poem evokes very similar ideas to Schelling's poem "*Epikureisches Glaubensbekenntis Heinz Widerporstens.*" Nature only comes alive in mankind's imaginative engagement with it.[110] This interaction with Nature is a recreation—or as Schelling puts it, a second creation (*zweite Schöpfung*).[111] It is the imagination that "makes beauty," and Coleridge even argues that the imagination gives us "a new heaven and new earth." He also implies in these lines that the light/voice is "of its own birth," somehow born within the poet rather than given by a creator. The poet, in his conscious interaction with the world, changes and recreates reality. Consequently, the secondary imagination is then also not a mere imitation but "a repetition in the finite mind of the eternal act of creation in the infinite I AM."[112]

From a Christian perspective, such a position is highly problematic as it collapses once more the distinction between divine and human action. MacDonald, we should note, quotes "Dejection: An Ode" in *Phantastes*, but he does not espouse the Idealist notions embedded within these lines. Rather, MacDonald, in chapter 9, shows what the world would look like without an imaginative perspective: cold and degraded to

---

109. Coleridge, *Works*, 365–66, stanzas 4, 5, 6. It is noteworthy that MacDonald reserves such terms as "dissolve" and "dissipate" for God's action in the world. Sadler, *Expression of Character*, 274.

110. Schelling writes: "*Die Natur muß sich unter Gesetze schmiegen, / ruhig zu meinen Füßen liegen. / Steckt zwar ein Riesengeist darinne, ist aber versteinert mit seinen Sinnen / . . . tut nach Bewußtsein mächtig ringen. / . . . In einen Zwergen eingeschlossen / von schöner Gestalt und graden Sprossen, heißt in der Sprache Menschenkind, / der Riesengeist sich selber find't*" (Störig, *Kleine Weltgeschichte*, 455–56).

111. "*[Z]um ersten Strahl von neugebornem Licht, / das durch die Nacht wie zweite Schöpfung bricht / und aus den tausend Augen der Welt, den Himmel so Tag und Nacht erhellt,' hinauf zu des Gedankens Jugendkraft, / wodurch Nature verjüngert sich wieder schafft*" (ibid., 456).

112. This is further supported by Coleridge's quotation of Sir John Davies. He writes: "As fire converts to fire the things it burns,/ As we our food into our nature change" (Coleridge, *Biographia Literaria*, 166).

mere matter. It is a shadow that seeks to lure the protagonist Anodos into such a perspective, and Anodos slowly gives into his view of the world:

> I now began to feel something like satisfaction in the presence of my shadow . . . I need his aid to disenchant the things around me. He does away with all appearances, and shows me things in their true colour and form. And I am not one to be fooled with the vanities of the common crowd. I will not see beauty where there is none.[113]

The more Anodos listens to his shadow, the less can he see nature imaginatively. What MacDonald seems to argue here is that only through the imagination do we see nature in some degree as it really is.

There is another important function of the secondary imagination to be addressed here. For Coleridge the poet must seek to understand the underlying general principles in nature and provide novel and fresh ways for expressing "old and familiar objects." Why is this important? In doing so, he suggests, the poet "steal[s] access through the senses to our minds."[114] Coleridge does not explain what he means by this, but "to steal access" suggests communication of an indirect and subtle sort, which does not allow a conscious closing off of one's faculties to that which confronts us. This function of the secondary imagination might be what we sought to point out about Jesus' parables: they also "steal access" by surprising the reader with a familiar object used in an unfamiliar context. For Coleridge this process happens "through the senses," and this suggests a way of knowing that is not "pure reason" and logic but comes of the senses.[115] More recent discussions on the imagination take Coleridge's suggestions further, arguing for the importance of the imagination in scientific inquiry.[116]

Like Schelling, Coleridge distinguishes between two levels of creative activity here. If this synthesizing and reconciling power provides

---

113. George MacDonald, *Phantastes*, 61.

114. Coleridge, *Biographia Literaria*, 166.

115. Coleridge might be alluding to a way of knowing that Wordsworth in his poem "Expostulation and Reply" calls "wise passiveness."

116. Bohm, *On Creativity*, ch. 3. Bohm argues that the imagination serves to pursue new ways of looking at reality that are not based on familiar patterns of experience and thought. Imaginative engagement with the world enables thought-patterns that provide original insight to reality, the essence of which cannot be captured. He insists that the nature of the whole is irreducible, and both art and science will never be able to capture it fully.

new understanding and recreates reality, if it is fundamentally "vital," then Coleridge considers it a work of the imagination. If it merely reiterates what we already know, if it is a mere mimetic representation of reality, he considers it to be a work of fancy.[117] Aside from its Idealist stance, Coleridge's distinction reminds one of our discussion of allegorical correspondence and metaphor in chapter 2. What sets apart metaphor is its heuristic function as it is able to break open the nature of reality previously unknown. Allegorical correspondence, by contrast, establishes and reiterates that which is already known.

What becomes clear from Coleridge's discussion in *Biographia Literaria* is that he developed a more nuanced and complex understanding of the imagination that draws insights from both Kant and Schelling. He now admits the imagination to have a primary place not only in human creative activity but also more fundamentally in human perception, and the two are intimately related as the secondary imagination is an "echo" of the primary imagination, "identical in kind," and only "differing in degree."[118]

Coleridge's reflections also raise some important questions in regard to our knowledge of reality. In what way and to what extent does the poet change the world? For him the poet's interaction with the world is an intense and dynamic process whereby something is given to the world. But does the poet really create "a new earth and a new heaven"? Coleridge provides no answers to this difficult question. He also remains highly ambivalent about the relationship between God and humanity, an issue of utmost importance for Christian theology. He leans heavily towards an Idealist interpretation of reality, a perspective he changed towards the latter part of his career but which he did not incorporate into his discussions on the imagination.

George MacDonald's Understanding of the Imagination

MacDonald discusses the imagination primarily but not exclusively in his essays called "The Imagination: Its Function and Its Culture" (1867) and "The Fantastic Imagination" (1893), and he acknowledges a variety of influences. In our discussion we shall focus on these two essays and the particular influence of Coleridge.

To varying degrees, MacDonald takes up the questions raised by Coleridge. MacDonald considers them carefully and provides some

---

117. Coleridge, *Biographia Literaria*, 160, 167.
118. Ibid., 159–60.

thoughtful answers, particularly to the complex question of the relation between human and divine action. As discussed above, MacDonald, like Coleridge, looks at the human imagination within a theological context. While MacDonald clearly distinguishes between divine and human, infinite and finite, he affirms that the imagination is that which we have in common with our Creator: "The imagination of man is made in the image of the imagination of God . . . in which the imagination of man lives and moves and has its being."[119] Just as God created the world, so mankind is called to use the imagination not to "create," as MacDonald reserves this term for God's creative activity in forming the world out of nothing, but to follow and discover God's imaginative work.[120]

MacDonald, like Coleridge, offers an account of the imagination that is much more fundamental to human life than just conscious creative activity. He attributes to the imagination a central place in human cognition. He writes: "The imagination is that faculty which gives form to thought."[121] It works upon sensory experience and shapes into form the "thoughts" and "feelings" that arise from our engagement with nature.[122] Nature provides us with physical forms by which we are able to speak about "immaterial conditions" such as the emotional, mental, moral, and spiritual aspects of reality.[123] We should note, however, that according to MacDonald the resemblance that exists between physical forms and "immaterial conditions" and the thoughts themselves that express this resemblance are never born in the human mind but are "given" as God created the material world in such a way that it should serve us to speak of the immaterial.[124] For MacDonald, then, the imagination is a

---

119. George MacDonald, *Orts*, 3.

120. This is something that MacDonald stresses throughout the essay. See ibid., 4–6.

121. Ibid., 2.

122. Ibid., 5. MacDonald explains this process in some detail at a later stage of the essay: "It is the farseeing imagination which beholds what might be a form of things, and says to the intellect: 'Try whether that may not be the form of these things;' which beholds or invents *a* harmonious relation of parts and operations, and sends the intellect to find out whether that be not *the* harmonious relation of them—that is, the law of the phenomenon it contemplates. Nay, the poetic relations themselves in the phenomenon may suggest to the imagination the law that rules its scientific life" (George MacDonald, *Orts*, 12). It is clear that MacDonald does not see the imagination in contrast to the intellect but sees them co-operating in the closest proximity with and dependency upon one another.

123. Ibid., 8.

124. Ibid., 5.

crucial link between the visible and invisible dimension of existence that together make up reality.

In light of this, we can see that MacDonald's account of the imagination is significantly intertwined with his understanding of metaphor. He argues that by using forms from nature metaphorically, we are given the imaginative capacity to explore and name those dimensions of our lives that are not easily accessible and remain intangible. He provides a variety of examples to demonstrate this phenomenon. We have already referred to his discussion of the word "attention" in our chapter on parable/metaphor. The word designates a mental activity, but originally it was derived from the bodily function of *attentio*—a stretching to.[125] It is by an activity of the imagination that someone first noticed the correspondence between the physical form of "stretching to" and a certain activity in our mind that we now call "attention." In this way, according to MacDonald, the imagination is at work in every sphere of human activity.[126] It is by the use of the imagination that we are able to perform the most basic human act of developing language or gain new scientific knowledge of the world. Just as the artist is in need of a creative imagination, he suggests, so is the scientist, the metaphysician, historian, and the psychologist.[127] Consequently, our imaginative engagements with the world happen on a much more basic level than previously acknowledged. It is here that we find another important link to our discussion of metaphor, where we sought to show how thoroughly our linguistic and pre-linguistic conception and experience of the world is shaped by metaphor.

The Relation between Humanity and Nature

MacDonald's exploration of the faculty of the imagination includes important reflections on the relation between humanity and nature. Even though he saw a high level of correspondence between the human mind and nature, he did not go as far as Schelling and Coleridge, who saw them as part of one single, dynamic unity, with the human mind in some sense

---

125. Ibid., 8.

126. Ibid., 7. Coleridge makes a similar argument about the correspondence between the idea of liberty and the physical movements of the wind and the sea in his poem "France: an Ode."

127. Ibid., 7–9, 12, 13, 15. MacDonald explicitly refers to Coleridge here. He writes: "Coleridge says that no one but a poet will make any further *great* discoveries in mathematics" (ibid., 15). For a more recent and very similar appeal to the significance of the imagination in scientific discovery, see Polanyi, "Imagination."

creating the world. Some of his comments might tend this direction, such as when he states that "the world around . . . [man] is an outward figuration of the condition of his mind."[128] Or that "the world is . . . the human being turned inside out."[129] Such comments, however, must always be understood within MacDonald's larger theological argument. He understands the world to be created by God, and any correspondence between the physical and spiritual dimension exists because God placed it in his creation. MacDonald argues: "The meanings are in those forms already, else they could be no garment of unveiling. God has made the world that it should thus serve his creature . . . The man has but to light the lamp within the form: his imagination is the light, it is not the form."[130] The role of the human imagination is always and only that humble task of "following and finding out the divine imagination in whose image it was made."[131] For MacDonald, then, tracing patterns is never a human projection upon the world, and he refuses any Idealist understanding of the imagination when he writes: "Indeed, a man is rather *being thought* than *thinking*, when a new thought arises in his mind."[132] While such a comment might beg the question of whether there is any active contribution on the poet's side, it firmly situates human creativity within the context of God and the givenness of the created world. This humble view of the imagination is an important contribution to the recovery of a decidedly Christian understanding of the imagination.

The Poetic Imagination in MacDonald

While MacDonald does not differentiate between the epistemic (primary) and poetic (secondary) functions of the imagination as Coleridge does and certainly would not want to polarize the imagination into two distinct functions, he still singles out a "higher" function of the imagination that is at work in poetry.[133] Like Coleridge, MacDonald believes that these two functions are intricately related.[134] Unlike Coleridge, he suggests that the better designation for the poet is the French *Trouvère*, the

128. George MacDonald, *Orts*, 5.
129. Ibid., 9, 18.
130. Ibid., 5.
131. Ibid., 10, 20.
132. Ibid., 4.
133. Ibid., 14, 18.
134. Ibid., 15.

finder rather than the maker.[135] Insisting that even the poet never creates in any primary sense of the word, MacDonald advances his argument by admitting that the poet does have a creative power.

> [The poet] . . . can present us with new thought-forms—new, that is, as revelations of thought. It has created none of the material that goes to make these forms. Nor does it work upon raw material. But it takes forms already existing, and gathers them about a thought so much higher than they, that it can group and subordinate and harmonize them into a whole which shall represent, unveil that thought.[136]

He further describes this operation of the imagination as "choosing, gathering, and vitally combining the material of a new revelation."[137] It is important to notice that for MacDonald the imagination is creative only in so far as it combines in a life-giving way ("vitally combining") already existing forms. In contrast to Coleridge, he restrains himself from using verbs like "dissolve" as such a verb would then demand some kind of recreation and elevate the poet to a maker rather than a finder.

For MacDonald figures are arranged in a completely new way, and in this way "the meaning contained is presented as it never was before" and as a consequence it "makes us feel the truth of it afresh."[138] This re-echoing or re-embodying of truth is the primary idea by which MacDonald seeks to explicate the function of the poetic imagination. Similar to Coleridge, then, MacDonald understands the task of the poet to be a conscious activity by which the poet finds new ways of expressing old and even familiar things. In doing so, the poet is able to explore their meaning more fully. MacDonald writes: "And every new embodiment of a known truth must be a new and wider revelation. No man is capable of seeing for himself the whole of any truth: he needs it echoed back to him . . . and still its centre is hid in the Father of Lights."[139]

---

135. Ibid., 20; see also ibid., 24. See also Martin Buber who argues that *"Erfinden ist finden. Gestaltung ist Entdeckung"* (Creating is finding. Forming is discovering). Buber, *Ich Und Du*, 17.

136. George MacDonald, *Orts*, 20. In *Phantastes* he explains the poetic process similarly: "[H]e combines into new forms of loveliness those images of beauty which his own choice has gathered from all regions wherein he has travelled. Ibid., *Phantastes*, 59.

137. George MacDonald, *Orts*, 22.

138. Ibid., 21, 22.

139. Ibid., 22.

In later life he singles out the fairytale genre as an important way for allowing the poetic imagination to be at work.[140] It is by creating one's own "little world" that the poet comes closest to that primary act of creation that he ascribes singularly to God.[141] In his discussion of the nature of the fairytale, following once more Coleridge's lead, MacDonald also distinguishes between imagination and fancy.[142] When such literary creations "are new embodiments of old truths," they are considered works of the imagination. If they merely reiterate, rearrange without a deeper purpose and meaning, if they serve to illustrate a point already made, or, as MacDonald puts it, if they are a "hunting after resemblances that carry with them no interpretation," they are works of fancy.[143] This distinction between the two differs from Coleridge in a significant way. For Coleridge works of the imagination somehow recreate reality. For MacDonald works of the imagination are new embodiments of old truths by which we are able to grasp its truth more fully. Shakespeare, Tennyson, and Fouqué are three important examples for MacDonald as they were able to rescue old and "drearily told" tales and re-embody them into their new creations.[144] MacDonald's fairytales, he hopes, follow this tradition by clothing old truths into new forms.

His definition of fancy, on the other hand, seems to be quite similar to that of Coleridge, even though MacDonald does not set up such a stark contrast between imagination and fancy. Fancy is mimetic and has no newness of expression by which we may feel the truth afresh. It is of an ornamental nature and somehow aids the imagination in the arrangement of the newly created thought forms. MacDonald explains: "[B]eauty is the only stuff in which Truth can be clothed; and you may, if you will, call Imagination the tailor that cuts her garments to fit her, and Fancy his journey man that puts the pieces of them together, or perhaps at most

---

140. He discusses this in his essay called "The Fantastic Imagination." MacDonald, after having spent a significant part of his career writing fairytales, feels he can now provide a more mature judgment of the fairytale. Ibid., 314.

141. Ibid.

142. "Fancy," it must be noted here, is not to be confused with "fantasy." While fancy is a mode of thought in Coleridge's writing, fantasy is a literary genre.

143. George MacDonald, *Orts*, 314; ibid., 41. It must be noted here that MacDonald does not employ the term "fancy" in a systematic fashion. Elsewhere he uses "fancy" to mean a (false) opinion without foundation or an illusion. See idem, *England's Antiphon*, 150, 190, 233.

144. George MacDonald, *Orts*, 22–23, 313.

embroiders their button-holes."[145] For MacDonald, then, the imagination and fancy work together in the creation of new thought forms.

He concludes his reflections on the unique task of the poetic imagination by insisting once more that even these new thought forms and revelations are given and never created by the poet. While Coleridge believes that we have a light/voice within that is somehow "of its own birth," MacDonald argues that ultimately any light that exists within us comes from God. New thought forms might arise from the depth of the poet's subconscious but even there God is at work. He writes:

> But God sits in that chamber of our being in which the candle of our consciousness goes out in darkness, and sends forth from hence wonderful gifts into the light of that understanding which is His candle. Our hope lies in no most perfect mechanism even of the spirit, but in the wisdom wherein we live and move and have our being. Thence we hope for endless forms of beauty informed by truth . . . If the dark portion of our own being were the origin of our imaginations, we might well fear the apparition of such monsters as would be generated in the sickness of a decay which could never feel only—declare—a slow return towards primeval chaos. But the Maker is our Light.[146]

Two important aspects in this passage deserve attention. First, MacDonald seeks to refute objections that ultimately our ideas and beliefs about reality are the man-made products of one's sub-conscious.[147] This addresses the larger question, hotly debated since the mid-Victorian period, of the nature of reality and whether dreams and the phenomena of the subconscious are to be explained on natural grounds alone.[148] MacDonald, against an increasing secularizing trend in Victorian England, wants to affirm that even in our sub-conscious God can be and is at work.

---

145. Ibid., 315.

146. Ibid., 25.

147. MacDonald argues along similar lines in *Lilith*, where the protagonist Mr. Vane wonders whether his dreams are the product of his own sub-consciousness or given by God. Feuerbach, as part of the left-wing reception of Hegel, propagated the idea that religion is the product of our self-consciousness in *Essence of Christianity*. This book was instrumental in "converting" the evangelical Marian Evans into the non-Christian George Eliot. It also contributed significantly to the secularization of Victorian England. Davis, *Victorians*, 147–48.

148. This question ties in with our discussion of the nature of dreams in the previous section. For a helpful introduction to some of the issues, see Brown, "Dreams."

Second, MacDonald understands the imagination to be the overarching faculty that unites all other faculties including the sub-conscious under its umbrella. For both Coleridge and MacDonald, the intellect is not the primary mode of seeing and experiencing the world. Both insist that the intellect does not stand in opposition to the imagination, but it is the imagination that is able to bring the intellect into interaction with feelings, for example, and thus produce a more harmonious and comprehensive understanding of the world.[149] It is also the imagination and not the intellect that stretches beyond the conscious awareness to regions of the sub-conscious.

Both Coleridge and MacDonald seek to put into place and context the enlightenment emphasis upon the intellect. Those who think that the intellect is the supreme human faculty Coleridge describes as dwarfs.[150] It is noteworthy that MacDonald picks up the same imagery of the dwarf to criticize the destructive forces of the intellect, when not married with a more balanced view of other human faculties.[151] He argues:

> We spoil countless precious things by intellectual greed. He who will be a man, and will not be a child, must—he cannot help himself—become a little man, that is, a dwarf. He will, however, need no consolation, for he is sure to think himself a very large creature indeed.[152]

It is also of importance that for MacDonald, it is primarily by the imagination that God takes holds of us as it is "likest to the prime operation of the power of God" and allows us to become finders and "playfellows" in this divinely inspired human act of knowing reality, ever moving towards a more comprehensive grasp of its facets, breaking open the surface of things, plumbing its depths, discovering layers of meaning. In doing so, he argues, we are striving towards harmony and unity with the patterned world and God who created it.

---

149. We have already quoted MacDonald's description of thought-process where it is the imagination that "sends out" the intellect to see whether certain connections can be made. George MacDonald, *Orts*, 157. See also ibid., 30, 33, 35–36.

150. Coleridge, *Biographia Literaria*, 157.

151. While MacDonald does not clearly define what he means by "intellect," he seems to think of it in terms of logic and analysis. See also Jadwiga Swiatecka, *Symbol*, 156; George MacDonald, *Orts*, 322. C. S. Lewis later picks up the image of the dwarf in his book *The Great Divorce*, in which George MacDonald is depicted as C. S. Lewis' guide just as Virgil is in Dante's *Divine Comedy*.

152. George MacDonald, *Orts*, 322.

This is not only true for human cognition of the world. MacDonald emphasizes that it is by the imagination that God draws us into his redeeming presence, a point that Coleridge does not address at all. Dearborn rightly points out that for MacDonald "God's imagination is operative not only in creation, but also in God's penetration into human life with grace and guidance."[153] While MacDonald hesitates to explore how God's imagination relates to his redemptive work in any detail—he focuses primarily on God's imaginative work in creation—he does argue that the human imagination resembles God's in all its aspects, and therefore it is primarily by the imagination that God draws us closer to himself, bringing about redemption.[154]

For MacDonald the world is fallen and alienated from God, and its ultimate destiny is to be brought back into communion and harmony with God and his divine order.[155] Shakespeare's character Lady Macbeth serves MacDonald to demonstrate his point. Only by suppressing her imagination is Lady Macbeth able to take refuge in "materialism" and "idealism," convincing herself and her husband to believe only in the reality that she creates in her own mind.[156] MacDonald argues that it is by her will that she chooses evil and not good. The imagination is also at work, however, but on a different level and in a rather different capacity. MacDonald writes:

> Her will was the one thing in her that was bad, without root or support in the universe, while her imagination was the voice of God himself out of her own unknown being . . . Lady Macbeth's imagination would not be repressed beyond its appointed period . . . It arose, at length as from the dead, overshadowing her with all the blackness of her crime.[157]

For MacDonald, then, the imagination is the primary faculty by which God's reconciling work breaks into our lives and calls us forth to renounce evil and embrace truth. It is here that MacDonald elevates the role of the imagination far beyond that of Kant and Coleridge whilst also

---

153. Dearborn, *Baptized Imagination*, 69.

154. George MacDonald, *Orts*, 3. MacDonald rightly contends that we cannot know God's consciousness.

155. Ibid., 30–36.

156. Ibid., 31.

157. Ibid., 31–32.

delineating its limitations when compared to divine creativity in a way that Coleridge, for example, does not.

Conclusion

With Coleridge, MacDonald affirms that the imagination is much more fundamental to human life and action than previously acknowledged. According to both men, it is at work in all spheres of life both on a conscious and subconscious level. MacDonald sees the imagination at work in human cognition; in creative, artistic expression of which the poet is his prime example; and in humanity's reception of God's redemptive work. In contrast to Coleridge, though, he establishes the imagination within a carefully developed Christian framework and counters Coleridge's strong tendency towards Idealism. The poet does not create the world in any way, and therefore his work must not be seen as repetition of God's primary act of creation. Rather, he seeks to discover new forms by which to express and recover old truths. MacDonald favors the fairytale as an important vehicle for allowing the poetic imagination to be at play. As a consequence, story more widely plays a significant role within his understanding of how God reveals himself to humanity. The next chapter explores MacDonald's theological rationale for story and more specifically the "parabolic." It is in the discussion of *Lilith* in the last chapter of this book that we shall see MacDonald's own imagination at work and how he found new and rather shocking forms to present to his readers old and familiar truth.

4

George MacDonald's Theological Rationale for Story and the "Parabolic"

GEORGE MACDONALD'S THEOLOGICAL RATIONALE for story and the "parabolic" is closely connected to his understanding of Scripture, language, creation, and how God reveals himself in and through it. In order to understand MacDonald's view of Scripture, especially as related to the "parabolic" and the role Scripture plays in his understanding of revelation and spiritual transformation, it is important to locate him in his historical context. Only by outlining the general attitude towards Scripture and closely related questions such as the role of science in Victorian Britain can we properly understand MacDonald's response to the challenges of his time and the views he developed on Scripture, revelation, and how believers might be formed through the parabolic. The discussion of this chapter then falls into four parts. First, we shall discuss the current Victorian attitude towards Scripture and MacDonald's response to it. Second, we shall examine his understanding of revelation. Third, we will discuss his view of the symbol, allegory, and Scripture, and closely related to this we shall then be able to look at MacDonald's understanding of the "parabolic" as a literary space for revelation and spiritual formation in the fourth part.

Reading Scripture in Crisis and George MacDonald's Response

MacDonald's time was a season of great turmoil in regard to reading Scripture. Scientific discoveries had shaken traditional understandings of Scripture and questioned many long-held beliefs about it. By the time

MacDonald began his writing career, the Victorian crisis of faith concentrated on the seemingly irresolvable dichotomy between theology and science. In our discussion of MacDonald's response to this crisis of faith, we will therefore focus on this issue, as one of MacDonald's key concerns was to reintegrate the academic disciplines, especially the sciences with theology. MacDonald's fairytale "The Light Princess," first published in 1863, will serve to show both MacDonald's critique of his time as well as reveal his fundamental beliefs about the nature of reality. We will conclude with some reflections on the relationship between theology and science in George MacDonald's thought.

The Rise of Fundamentalism in Victorian Britain

At the threshold of the Victorian era, the Bible was firmly established in society as the Holy Bible, inspired by God and therefore regarded as authoritative to rule matters of faith and life. While more skeptical and critical views regarding the Bible had been articulated since the age of Enlightenment, the general public was unaffected by such voices.[1]

In reaction to the more critical and liberal approaches to the Bible that were becoming popular in Germany and Switzerland, certain Evangelical thinkers, such as the Scottish churchman Robert Haldane of Airtherey, moved to set forth a more precise theology of verbal inspiration than had been common in Scottish Evangelicalism.[2] Haldane, according to Andrew Drummond and James Bulloch, became the founding father of Scottish fundamentalism.[3] These Evangelicals sought to make the highest possible claims on Scripture and its divine inspiration, using such terminology as "infallible," "inerrant," and "perfect."[4]

The acceptance of the theory of verbal inspiration with its consequent belief in the infallible nature of Scripture would prove to be a major stumbling block as Victorian Britain was confronted with geological discoveries. These archaeological discoveries challenged belief in the verbal inspiration of Scripture by questioning and undermining the timeline of Creation as described (and interpreted literally) in the book of Genesis. Significantly, this challenge would eventually lead to the popular opinion

---

1. Cheyne, "Bible," 192.
2. His book *The Books of the Old and New Testaments proved to be Canonical and their Verbal Inspiration maintained and established* was first published in 1828.
3. Drummond and Bulloch, *Church*, 251.
4. Cheyne, "Bible," 194.

in late Victorian society that religion and science stand in opposition to one another, viewing science as irreconcilable with religion.⁵

Samuel Taylor Coleridge (1772–1834), an important Victorian thinker and writer, describes in his *Confessions of an Inquiring Spirit* the popular opinion of the Bible in Victorian Britain as follows:

> [T]he Bible was not to be regarded or reasoned about in the way that other good books are or may be—that the Bible was different in kind, and stood by itself... What is more, their principal arguments were grounded on the position, that the Bible throughout was dictated by Omniscience, and therefore in all its parts infallibly true and obligatory, and that the men, whose names are prefixed to the several books or chapters, were in fact but as different pens in the hand of one and the same Writer, and the words of God himself;—and that on this account all notes and comments were superfluous, nay, presumptuous,—a profane mixing of human with divine, the notions of fallible creatures, with the oracles of Infallibility,—as if God's meaning could be so clearly or fitly expressed in man's as in God's own words!⁶

The general attitude towards biblical inspiration in the first half of the nineteenth century was marked by a belief in the verbal inspiration of the text by God and an absolute affirmation of the infallibility of Scripture. Coleridge did not share this position, and as we shall see later, it was an attitude towards the Bible that MacDonald found intolerable.

Coleridge's Confessions of an Inquiring Spirit

Coleridge, already familiar with the results of biblical criticism coming from Germany, was an early voice in England that challenged fundamentalist approaches to the Bible. Anthony Harding suggests that Coleridge argued primarily against literalism, the doctrine that the Scriptures do not err, and certain attempts to use miracle stories as scientific proof texts for the truth of Christianity.⁷ For example, in his *Confessions of*

---

5. See Chadwick, *Secularization*, esp. ch. 7 on science and religion.

6. Coleridge, *Confessions*, 62–63. See also the dialogue on the issue of inspiration, a literal reading of the Bible, and the threat of German neology in MacDonald, *David Elginbrod*, 15–16. It is remarkable that Ruskin, 27 years after Coleridge's assessment, describes a much broader approach to the Bible in Victorian England. It shows how rapidly the attitude towards the Bible changed during this period. See Ruskin, *Time and Tide*, 27–29.

7. Harding, *Coleridge*, 74–75. It is noteworthy that MacDonald also insisted that

an Inquiring Spirit, a collection of letters, he sets forth an understanding of the Bible strongly influenced by German criticism.[8] In what follows we will explore Coleridge's understanding of the Bible as set out in this collection of letters.

Coleridge is important here because he was a significant influence on such writers as F. D. Maurice, Thomas Carlyle, Charles Kingsley, and George MacDonald. MacDonald called him a sage who "more than any man in our times . . . has opened the eyes of the English people to see wonderful things."[9] His character Margret Elginbrod reads Coleridge as part of her spiritual and intellectual growth.[10] MacDonald's father-in-law, James Powell, knew Coleridge well and writes to George MacDonald on the subject of Scripture in 1850:

> If in my earlier life I had been asked what I thought of your reading the Scriptures, I should have given an answer of approval, because you avoided monotony by giving the emphasis natural to the various speakers in the narrative parts. But the remarks of my illustrious friend, S. T. Coleridge, modified my opinion . . . I wish I could give you a tithe of his eloquent words, but his meaning was that in reading the Scriptures, while monotony is avoided, the divine source should never be forgotten, and they should be delivered more as the Oracles of God than the opinions of man.[11]

This letter shows that MacDonald was confronted with Coleridge's thought from the very beginning of his writing career, and it is therefore appropriate to discuss Coleridge's work in some detail and compare it to MacDonald's view at a later stage.[12] As we consider Coleridge's thought,

---

the miracles of Jesus should not be understood as proof of his divine mission. See George MacDonald, *Hope*, 74.

8. In his first letter of the collection, Coleridge explains that his reading of *Bekenntnisse einer schönen Seele* by Goethe caused him to reflect on the subject. See Coleridge, *Confessions*, 39.

9. George MacDonald, *England's Antiphon*, 307. For a discussion of Maurice's response to the rise of historical criticism see Prickett, "F. D. Maurice."

10. George MacDonald, *David Elginbrod*, 12, 30. As we saw in our discussion of MacDonald's view of the imagination, however, he did not appropriate Coleridge's thinking uncritically.

11. Greville MacDonald, *MacDonald and Wife*, 137.

12. His first reference to Coleridge appears in a letter written to his father in 1847. Hein, *George MacDonald*, 63. His first reference to Coleridge in his novels can be found in *Phantastes*, published in 1858.

we should keep in mind that his understanding of the Bible and biblical inspiration is formulated in reaction to a certain strand of Victorian culture that clung to verbal dictation, the idea that the Bible is infallible and literalism. Every word of Scripture was thought to be inspired and had some spiritual significance. Coleridge's response, while seeking to provide a more balanced perspective, leaves many subsequent questions unanswered.

In his first letter of *Confessions of an Inquiring Spirit*, Coleridge firmly establishes that the beginning point for a reflection on revelation is Christ as "the light of man." Alluding to the prologue of the Gospel of John (1:1–4), Coleridge writes: "There is a Light higher than all, even *the Word that was in the beginning*;—the Light, of which light itself is but the *shechinah* and cloudy tabernacle; the Word that is light for every man, and life for as many as give heed to it."[13] From this foundation, Coleridge then reflects on the relationship between the Word that is Christ, the written letter, the Bible, and the reader of Scripture. He emphasizes throughout his letters that one must not equate the written word, or one's interpretation of it, with the truth:

> I, who hold that the Bible contains the religion of Christians, but who dare not say that whatever is contained in the Bible is the Christian religion, and who shrink from all question respecting the comparative worth and efficacy of the written Word as weighed against the preaching of the Gospel, the discipline of the Churches, the continued succession of the Ministry, and the communion of Saints, lest by comparing I should seem to detach them . . . Every sentence found in a canonical Book, rightly interpreted, contains the *dictum* of an infallible Mind;—but what the right interpretation is,—must be determined by the industry and understanding of fallible, and alas! more or less prejudiced theologians.[14]

While Coleridge affirms the importance of the Bible as containing "the religion of Christians," he rightly contends that truth in its fullness can only be found in "The Light," which is Christ. It is the sun (Christ) that gives the light and the moon (the Bible) merely reflects its light.[15] He holds on to some yet undefined sense of inspiration, but he does not address

---

13. Coleridge, *Confessions*, 42.

14. Ibid., 61.

15. Ibid., 42. It is noteworthy that MacDonald picks up the same imagery of the sun and the moon to speak about the relationship between Christ and Scripture.

the tension that exists between divine inspiration and human authorship. Instead, Coleridge focuses on the tension between divine inspiration and human, thus fallible, interpretation.

In light of his insistence that the Bible does not contain the fullness of truth, Coleridge insists that the Bible needs to be read and interpreted within the context of Christian practices while having to be aware that every interpretation of Scripture is always a partial one, as every reader comes to the text with presuppositions. This position, however, raises critical questions such as the extent of an interpreter's "prejudice" and whether any meaning can be gained from the text given such a subjective stance. In contrast to MacDonald, he does not anticipate this question.[16]

Coleridge also refuses to locate the proof of Christ's and the Bible's divine authority in Scripture or in historical evidences. Its authority lies in itself and gives witness to itself as the reader engages with Scripture and is transformed by it. Coleridge, drawing on the wisdom of Solomon, puts it this way:

> In short whatever finds me, bears witness for itself that it has proceeded from the Holy Spirit, even from the same Spirit, which remaining in itself, yet regenerateth all other powers, and in all ages entering into holy souls maketh them friends of God, and prophets (Wisd Vii).[17]

And in a later letter he continues by asserting: "Friend! The truth revealed through Christ has its evidence in itself, and the proof of its divine authority in its fitness to our nature and needs;—the clearness and cogency of this proof being proportionate to the degree of self-knowledge in each individual hearer."[18]

There are two important points that Coleridge makes in these passages. First, he argues that the truth revealed in Christ has its evidence and authority in itself. It does not receive its authority from being written down in the Bible or from historical and archaeological evidence.[19] Its

---

16. MacDonald addresses this question in his essay on the nature of the fairytale. George MacDonald, *Orts*, 316.

17. Coleridge, *Confessions*, 42. Coleridge quotes here from the OT Apocrypha Wisdom of Solomon 7:27. Solomon praises the workings of wisdom in this passage and Coleridge replaces "wisdom" with the "Holy Spirit."

18. Ibid., 64.

19. Coleridge sees the search for the evidence of Christianity as part of an "inward withdrawing from the Life and Personal Being of God" and a turning to mere abstract and intellectual reflections about impersonal attributes of God. Coleridge, *Aids to Reflection*, 309.

authority is of an internal character. What he means by this is unclear, but we can see the influence of Lessing who argues "The Christian religion is not true because the Evangelists and Apostles taught it, but they taught it because it is true. Written traditions must be interpreted by their internal truth, and all the written traditions can give Religion no internal truth, if it have none."[20] While it is commendable that Coleridge seeks to critique naïve beliefs about finding proof of the Christian faith in "natural theology," which contributed in a significant way to the Victorian crisis of faith in the years to come, his decision to locate this proof in the very vague realm of "internal evidence" creates other critical problems as he does not define this "internal evidence" in any way. It also begs the question of whether one can so easily separate this truth and its "internal evidence" (meaning) from its manifestation in words (signification).

Second, he argues that the proof of Scripture's divine authority is anchored in its applicability to the human condition. This second point is also problematic, as he seems to make the authority of divine truth dependent upon its fitness to human nature and needs. What does Coleridge mean by phrases like "whatever finds me," "its fitness to our nature and needs," and "what you find therein coincident with your pre-established convictions"?[21] Does he, as Owen Chadwick suggests, rest inspiration upon the Bible's effect in religious experience?[22] And does the Bible merely confirm faith, or does it also engender faith?

What we would like to draw attention to here is that Coleridge's latter statement might somehow relate to his earlier reference to the Jewish wisdom tradition, where the Spirit works within the souls of men, making them into friends of God and thereby being a proof of divine authority. What seems evident from the former quotation is that he believes that whatever truth comes from the Holy Spirit shows itself as true by making people into "friends of God." Coleridge is not concerned with establishing an abstract and intellectual concept of truth. Rather, he seeks to focus on the relational dimension of truth and how God reveals himself to his creatures by transforming them into friends of God.[23] Here also MacDonald will follow Coleridge quite closely in understanding truth

20. Lessing's *Schriften*, quoted in Green, "Introduction," 20.
21. Coleridge, *Confessions*, 64–65.
22. Chadwick, *Victorian Church*, 1:529.
23. This becomes clear in *Aids to Reflection*, where Coleridge expresses his concern that theological discussion and language move away from personal knowledge to abstract concepts and ideas. Coleridge, *Aids to Reflection*, 309–11.

primarily in relational terms with a strong transformative emphasis. Unlike Coleridge, though, he has very clear conceptions of what it means to be transformed into followers of Jesus. Coleridge never defines what he means by "friends of God." This is problematic as the phrase is vague and invites speculation of all kinds about what it means to be a friend of God. While Coleridge raises important issues regarding the nature of Scripture and its relationship to Christ, his choice to manifest the proof of Scripture's divine authority in human experience is clearly problematic. Coleridge does not adequately address the implications of such an emphasis on subjective experience. He sought to stress the importance of personal knowledge of God rather than abstract speculations about him. Such an emphasis, however, does not do justice to the urgent mid-Victorian question of Scripture's divine authority. If one cannot trust in the historical accuracy of the Bible's accounts, where does one find assurance that what it says is true? It is no surprise that Coleridge's new theory of inspiration was not received with much enthusiasm. The Free Church Professor James Bannermann reflects in 1865 upon the unfortunate impact Coleridge's "subjective theory of inspiration" had on his own country.[24] It is on this point, as we shall see, that George MacDonald parts with Coleridge as he resists the temptation to provide proof of Scripture's divine authority. For him truth is found in Christ, and this truth cannot be proven but has to be received in faith.

Not only did Coleridge challenge verbal inspiration and a literal reading of the Bible, he was also the first one in England to assert that the Bible should be read like any other book.[25] Coleridge still held to the belief that the Bible was inspired, but he wanted to emphasize that the Word of God comes to us through human channels and needs to be read as such.[26] Coleridge's plea to read the Bible like any other book was not because he thought the Bible to be like any other book but because God gave us the Bible through human channels. It was this human dimension that had been completely suppressed with the theory of verbal inspiration and which Coleridge sought to recover. He writes:

> . . . the more tranquilly an inquirer takes up the Bible as he would any other body of ancient writings, the livelier and steadier will be his impressions of its superiority to all other books, till at

---

24. Bannermann, *Inspiration*, 144, quoted in Drummond and Bulloch, *Church*, 250.
25. Tulloch, *Movements*, 25.
26. Coleridge, *Confessions*, 44.

> length all other books and all other knowledge will be valuable in his eyes in proportion as they help him to a better understanding of his Bible. Difficulty after difficulty has been overcome from the time that I began to study the Scriptures with free and unboding spirit, under the conviction that my faith in the Incarnate Word and his Gospel was secure, whatever the result might be . . .[27]

His plea was not to place all other great books on equal footing with the Bible but for a certain freedom in reading and interpreting Scripture. Coleridge realized that the Bible was composed over a long period of time, written in different genres and from various perspectives and historical circumstances by different composers, and yet these composers were all prompted by one "pure and holy Spirit."[28] All these factors, according to Coleridge, need to be taken into consideration as one seeks to understand the Bible.

While Coleridge encouraged a critical reading of the Bible, he also emphasized that the Bible needs to be read with a posture of faith in order to be understood properly. Coleridge makes this point by comparing the Bible with the eating of manna in the wilderness:

> The fairest flower that ever clomb up a cottage window is not so fair a sight to my eyes, as the Bible gleaming through the lower panes. Let it but be read as by such men it used to be read; when they came to it as to a ground covered with manna, even the bread which the Lord had given for his people to eat . . .[29]

For Coleridge, then, the Bible cannot be reduced to a historical or moral document. It has to be read as a book given by God and received with faith.[30] What Coleridge fails to deal with adequately, however, is the unique nature of the Bible as the word of God as distinct from the writings of Shakespeare, for example.[31]

In summary, we can say that Coleridge sets forth his understanding of Scripture in conjunction with a discussion of its impact upon the

---

27. Ibid., 75.

28. Ibid., 51–52, 58–59. Coleridge especially refers to all the figurative speech in the Bible that must not be read literally. He also bemoans that a doctrine of verbal inspiration completely ignores the rich and shaping tradition of the church.

29. Ibid., 76. It is noteworthy that MacDonald picks up the imagery of manna in relation to reading Scripture when he discusses the use and abuse of the Bible.

30. See Tulloch for a similar evaluation of Coleridge. Tulloch, *Movements*, 30.

31. See on this issue Swiatecka, *Symbol*, 48–67, esp. 65.

reader. Coleridge emphasizes the relational dimension of revelation. The fact that God has spoken in Christ, that his words come through human channels, as well as the believer's reception of this written word are important dimensions in Coleridge's discussion of the Bible. Christ reveals himself in and through Scripture to the believer, and the transformation of human beings into friends of God is, as he puts it, a sure sign of the Bible's divine authority.

Coleridge's contribution lies in the fact that he raised important questions about the Bible in light of the rise of historical criticism from a perspective of faith rather than skepticism. He rightly challenges important assumptions such as verbal inspiration and the infallibility of the Bible as the basis for its divine authority or naïve attempts to find proof for the Christian faith in nature. Coleridge also raises important questions such as the relationship between divine inspiration and human authorship, the relationship between Christ and Scripture, and the relational dimension of revelation. His insistence that we must hold things in tension is important. And yet, he provides no clear answers and, in consequence, raises a different set of critical questions that he does not even acknowledge. In comparing Coleridge to MacDonald, we shall see that MacDonald recognizes the importance of Coleridge's concerns in regard to the Bible but considers more carefully subsequent questions. While many rejected Coleridge's theory because of its emphasis on a subjective assessment of God's truth, in MacDonald, Coleridge's ideas found fertile yet not uncritical ground.

Coleridge's "loose" view of biblical inspiration seems mild in comparison to some of the works that would soon disturb the slumber of Victorian Britain in regards to German Higher Criticism. In the following, we will look at four important factors that radically challenged traditionally held beliefs about the Bible.

Four Cultural Landmarks and the Crisis of Victorian Faith

There are a number of cultural landmarks that sparked an age of questioning and skepticism, to which we are referring as the Victorian crisis of faith. In this section, we will deal with four significant landmarks in particular: the translation of F. D. Strauss's *Life of Jesus* by George Eliot in 1846, geological discoveries, Charles Darwin's publication of *On the Origin of Species* in 1859, and the publication of *Essays and Reviews* in

1861. These books and events were all important landmarks that changed the attitude towards the Bible in Victorian Britain considerably.

George Eliot's translation of Strauss's *Life of Jesus*, followed by a translation of Feuerbach's *Essence of Christianity* in 1854, was an important contribution to the advance of historical criticism in England. Strauss radically questioned the historical reliability of the Gospel accounts. Matters of faith were completely discarded in the consideration of the origin of Christianity. The miracles of Jesus should not be understood as instances of immediate divine interventions but can be explained as "mythi." Hegel, in his search for the Absolute Spirit (*Geist*), had relegated images, stories, and myths to be primitive representations of God and Strauss followed him in this assessment. Strauss specifically for his project develops an understanding of myth that he then applied to the Gospel writers, setting the category of historical (fact-reporting) writing over against mythical writing.[32] He then demythologizes the Gospel narratives in order to reconstruct the life of Jesus. Thus Strauss argues that "the resurrections in the New Testament are nothing more than mythi, which had their origin in the tendency of the early Church, to make her Messiah agree with the type of the prophets, and with the messianic ideal."[33] The feeding of the multitudes is the product of a common legend in Jewish tradition, and the miracle of the withered fig tree has to be understood as a parable transformed into history.[34] Miracles cannot be historically true as they would be a violation of the laws of nature, and, according to Strauss, such a worldview was no longer tenable.

Strauss became a major-stumbling block to orthodoxy in Victorian England, and according to Chadwick, the country was ill equipped to deal with the challenges that a work like Strauss's brought with it as English conservatism had kept the critical study of the NT out of the curriculum of its universities. According to Chadwick, "The name of Strauss became a ghostly whip, a bogey, a talisman. The blasphemy laws prevented daring publishers from risking their reputation."[35]

In a similar manner to Strauss's German Higher Criticism, a rising interest in geological studies brought unique challenges to Victorian Christian thought. Geology became the most popular science of the first half of the nineteenth century. Chadwick writes: "Between 1820

---

32. Frei, *Biblical Narrative*, 241–42.
33. Strauss, *Life of Jesus*, 495.
34. Ibid., 519, 534.
35. Chadwick, *Victorian Church*, 1:532.

and 1840 geology became the science of the day. It captured popular imagination ... A skilfully produced survey of geology sold more copies than a novel by Sir Walter Scott."[36] While many attempts were made to harmonize geological discoveries with the creation account of Genesis, geological discoveries eventually challenged a literal reading of the creation account and forced a reconsideration of the origin and age of the world.[37] Slowly but surely, science and theology came to be seen in opposition to one another, and according to Chadwick, "Genesis and Geology went to war."[38] Tennyson's Romantic poem *In Memoriam* (1850), a favorite of Queen Victoria, expresses this crisis of faith and anxiety in light of the tension between science and religion in the most moving and powerful way:

> Be near me when my light is low ...
> Be near me when my faith is dry ...
> Be near me when I fade away ...
> Are God and Nature then at strife,
> That Nature lends such evil dreams? ...
> I stretch lame hands of faith, and grope,
> And gather dust and chaff, and call
> To what I feel is Lord of all,
> And faintly trust the larger hope.
> 'So careful of the type?' but no.
> From scarped cliff and quarried tone
> She cries, 'A thousand types are gone:
> I care for nothing, all shall go ...
> Man, her last work, who seem'd so fair,
> Such splendid purpose in his eyes,
> Who roll'd the psalm to wintry skies,
> Who built him fanes of fruitless prayer,
> Who trusted God was love indeed
> And love Creation's final law—
> Tho' Nature, red in tooth and claw
> With ravine, shriek'd against his creed—
> Who loved, who suffer'd countless ills,
> Who battled for the True, the Just,

---

36. Ibid., 558–59.

37. See for example Goodwin, "Mosaic Cosmogony."

38. Chadwick, *Victorian Church*, 1:559; Turner, *Science and Religion*, 1–2. One should note that such a "war" was between a very specific and narrow understanding of both science and a natural theology that had developed during the earlier part of the nineteenth century in England.

> Be blown about the desert dust,
> Or seal'd within the iron hills?
> No more? A monster then, a dream,
> A discord. Dragons of the prime,
> That tare each other in their slime,
> Were mellow music match'd with him.[39]

This poem makes clear that Darwin's *On the Origin of Species* (1859) was published in an atmosphere where faith in the Bible had already been unsettled by discoveries in geology as well as the historical study of ancient texts. The debate between faith and science came to a climax in the 1860s, and Darwin's evolution theory began to take root in the general consciousness of the Victorian mind. Philip Davis writes: "Analogous to the physical shift in population from rural to urban areas . . . was an equivalent shift in the mental map from religious to secular ways of seeing the natural world."[40] George MacDonald read geological works from as early as 1845, and he mentions Darwin, in particular, in several of his novels, although mostly in the 1870s when Darwin's ideas gained in popularity.[41] For example, he applies Darwin's evolution theory in a metaphorical manner to speak about the moral and spiritual development of his characters. More specifically, we observe that Curdie, the protagonist of *The Princess and Curdie*, has to learn to discern whether people are growing from beastly form into truly human form or are degenerating into beastly form. In all of this, we notice that MacDonald is not overtly concerned with the problems that Darwin's theory may introduce to Christian thinking. What is central for MacDonald's theology is mankind's moral and spiritual growth and lack thereof rather than humanity's physical developmental history.[42]

Our final landmark that contributed to the Victorian crisis of faith is the publication of *Essays and Reviews* in 1861. With these essays, a group of English theologians, mostly Oxford men with liberal inclinations,

---

39. Tennyson, *In Memoriam*, stanzas 5, 15, 16.

40. Davis, *Victorians*, 55.

41. MacDonald read Dr. Page Smith's work on geology and Darwin's account of a voyage around the world. Hein, *Victorian Mythmaker*, 63. MacDonald mentions Darwin in *The Vicar's Daughter*, published in 1872; *Malcolm*, published in 1875; *Thomas Wingfold*, 1876; and *Mary Marston*, 1881. The character Mr. Vane in *Lilith* might suggest MacDonald's stance towards Darwin's theory: Mr. Vane reads Darwin and Maxwell, but he is much more interested in Ptolemy, Dante, Bacon, and Boyle.

42. George MacDonald, *Curdie*, 90–97. Darwin before him had applied the metaphysical concept of evolution to his own theory.

encouraged a free engagement with controversial issues in theology.[43] Historical criticism in the first part of the nineteenth century was not developed in England or Scotland, and according to Chadwick, the English had to choose between what was offered from Germany, mostly the Tübingen school with F. D. Baur as a major exponent, and English scholarship with J. B. Lightfoot, which was relatively conservative.[44] *Essays and Reviews* played an important part in opening up the discussion in England and Scotland. Even though the essays varied greatly in quality and content, they had a strong impact at the time.[45] A fundamental issue that was addressed in numerous essays was the question of on what basis revelation was to rest. Benjamin Jowett's essay "On the interpretation of Scripture" deals specifically with this issue. Jowett writes:

> The sciences of geology and comparative philology are steadily gaining ground; many of the guesses of twenty years ago have become certainties, and the guesses of to-day may hereafter become so. Shall we peril religion on the possibility of their untruth? On such a cast to stake the life of man implies not only a recklessness of facts, but a misunderstanding of the nature of the Gospel . . . the idea of inspiration must expand and take them in. Their importance in a religious point of view is not that they impugn or confirm the Jewish history, but that they show more clearly the purposes of God towards the whole human race. The recent chronological discoveries from Egyptian monuments do not tend to overthrow revelation, nor the Ninevite inscriptions to support it.[46]

Jowett argued for a redefinition of the nature of revelation. In particular, he wanted to overcome what he thought a superficial separation between "natural" and "revealed" religion. For Jowett no clear separation between the two was possible. Like Coleridge, he argued that the Bible needs to be studied like any other book, adhering to the spirit of the Bible rather than rigid adherence to the letter.[47] *Essays and Reviews* was bitterly attacked and lawsuits were brought against two of its contributors. In 1864

---

43. Reardon, *Religious Thoughts*, 309.

44. Chadwick, *Victorian Church*, 2:69. See also Drummond and Bulloch, *Church*, 242, 247.

45. See Chadwick's evaluation of the collection of essays in *Victorian Church*, 2:76.

46. Jowett, "Interpretation of Scripture," 349–50.

47. Reardon, *Religious Thoughts*, 310.

Convocation of Canterbury condemned the book, and the controversy continued to grow throughout the decade.[48]

We must keep this context and the general attitude towards Scripture in mind as we turn to MacDonald and his approach to Scripture and revelation. As we have seen, the theological climate was complex in its development. The rise of a more rigid belief in the inerrancy of Scripture and verbal inspiration went hand in hand with an increasing awareness and reception of German Higher Criticism, which sought to put aside the question of revelation and focused on historical criticism as the deciding factor for "accurate truth." George Eliot's translation of *Life of Jesus* as well as discoveries in geology intensified the questions at hand, shaking the old foundations of faith and religion. With the publication of *Essays and Reviews*, the development was brought to a crisis. Even though the book was strongly attacked, it helped to bring into the open questions that had been discussed freely in Germany for a considerable time. Increasingly, the Victorian understanding of science and theology was held to be irreconcilable.[49] In this context MacDonald started his writing career and formulated an understanding of revelation and Scripture that bears some significant similarities to Coleridge but also has some important differences.

George MacDonald's Response: Inversion of Priorities

While George MacDonald was well aware of German Higher Criticism, there is little evidence that he engaged with it to any serious degree. He often mentions the issues and questions involved but does not think that one can validate the claims made by Christianity on historical-critical or scientific grounds. Unlike Coleridge, he does not seek to locate proof of Scripture's divine authority in human experience. Rather, he acknowledges the doubts and anxieties a believer might feel in the face of these challenges. In an essay written in 1880, MacDonald describes the dilemma of a man in doubt:

---

48. Ibid., 311.

49. Cosslett points out that the reason the two came to be seen in such opposition is that Victorian Protestantism had invested heavily in natural theology and therefore scientific investigation in the aid of theology. He concludes: "the new science merely showed up the inadequacies of natural theology, and forced those theologians who had not done so already to rethink their faith in a more profound, spiritual, and sometimes traditional way" (*Science and Religion*, 23–24).

What if the whole idea of his mission was a deception born of the very goodness of the man? What if the whole matter was the invention of men pretending themselves the followers of such a man? What if it was a little truth greatly exaggerated? Only, be it what it may, less than its full idea would not be enough for the wants and sorrows that weaken and weigh him down! He passes through many a thorny thicket of inquiry; gathers evidence upon evidence; reasons upon the goodness of the men who wrote: they might be deceived, but they dared not invent; holds with himself a thousand arguments, historical, psychical, metaphysical—which for their setting-forth would require volumes . . . But at least he is haunting the possible border of discovery.[50]

For MacDonald the limitations or "borders" of scientific discovery cannot be overcome by human searching, but ultimately any truly searching person has to turn in faith and obedience to Christ as the revelation of the Father and ultimate truth.[51] He was not opposed to historical-critical inquiry as such, but he questioned an uncritical embrace of a scientific approach without considering its limitations in leading to knowledge of the transcendent. Thus, he chose not to engage in the debate.[52]

MacDonald shows a stronger engagement with the natural sciences versus theology debate. He insists that theology and science should not be seen in opposition to one another. While he was very interested in science himself, having studied physics and chemistry at Aberdeen University, he did not believe that one would arrive at theological truth via the sciences. His concern was that the emphasis on science and especially geology would reduce reality to its material manifestations. In true MacDonald fashion, it is in his fairytale "The Light Princess," first published in 1863, that his critique of Victorian culture and its movement away from a theological understanding towards a merely scientific account of reality becomes apparent. A closer look at this story will help unveil MacDonald's critique of his time and culture as well as reveal his own beliefs.

50. George MacDonald, *Orts*, 70–71.

51. Ibid., 71–74.

52. Ibid., 2. This does not mean, however, that MacDonald does not deal with the biblical text in a critical way. He uses the latest critical edition of the Greek text by Westcott and Hort, published in 1881 in the third volume of *Unspoken Sermons*, published in 1889, for example. See Gerold's various discussions on MacDonald's critical engagement with Scripture. Gerold, *Gotteskindschaft*, 86–87, 166, 174. MacDonald also has Donal, the main character of *Donal Grant*, read the *Wisdom of Solomon*, a book of the *Apocrypha*. George MacDonald, *Donal Grant*, ch. 17. The inclusion of the *Apocrypha* into the Bible was a highly disputed issue at the time.

MacDonald makes clear that this story has a deeper meaning when he gives the story the motto "more is meant than meets the ear" in a later publication.[53] While this fairytale at first sight seems to be just for amusement, a closer look at its structure betrays a careful assessment of his time. The story goes as follows. A king and queen, after a long period of impatient waiting, have a baby daughter and forget to invite the king's sister, Princess Makemnoit, to the christening.[54] In true fairytale fashion, the princess, in her anger, decides to curse the child, but rather than causing the princess to fall into a deep sleep, the curse takes its effect in the loss of the child's gravity. It is here that MacDonald deviates from the traditional fairytale to address his own time by playing with the physical laws, making gravity a variable. The parents seek help by consulting the college of Metaphysicians. With wit, irony, and hyperbole, MacDonald presents the cures offered by the spiritualist Kopy Keck and the materialist Hum Drum. Kopy Keck asserts:

> There is not fault in the princess; body or soul; only they are wrong put together . . . At that decisive moment, when souls seek their appointed habitations, two eager souls met, struck, rebounded, lost their way, and arrived each at the wrong place. The soul of the princess was one of those, and she went far astray. She does not belong by rights to this world at all, but to some other planet, probably Mercury. Her proclivity to her true sphere destroys all the natural influence which this orb would otherwise possess over her corporeal frame. She cares for nothing here. There is no relation between her and this world.

Kopy Keck's other-worldly diagnosis is followed by a this-worldly oriented cure:

> She must therefore be taught, by the sternest compulsion, to take an interest in the earth as the earth. She must study every department of its history—its animal history; its vegetable history; its moral history; its political history; its scientific history; its literary history; its musical history; its artistical history; above all, its metaphysical history. She must begin with the Chinese dynasty and end with Japan. But first of all she must study geology, and especially the history of the extinct races

---

53. George MacDonald, *Adela Cathcart*, 57. The motto is taken from John Milton's *Il Penseroso*.

54. MacDonald here alludes to Perrault's fairytale *Sleeping Beauty*.

of animals—their natures, their habits, their loves, their hates, their revenges.⁵⁵

This diagnosis and prescription is followed by Hum-Drum's no less absurd analysis:

> 'Hold, h-o-o-ld!' roared Hum-Drum. 'It is certainly my turn now. My rooted and insubvertible conviction is, that the causes of the anomalies evident in the princess's condition are strictly and solely physical. But that is only tantamount to acknowledging that they exist. Hear my opinion.—From some cause or other, of no importance to our inquiry, the motion of her heart has been reversed. That remarkable combination of the suction and the force-pump works the wrong way—I mean in the case of the unfortunate princess: it draws in where it should force out, and forces out where it should draw in. The offices of the auricles and the ventricles are subverted. The blood is sent forth by the veins, and returns by the arteries. Consequently it is running the wrong way through all her corporeal organism-lungs and all. Is it then at all mysterious, seeing that such is the case, that on the other particular of gravitation as well, she should differ from normal humanity?'⁵⁶

The materialist's prescription is as ridiculous as the spiritualist's, and it comes as no surprise that neither of them gets to try their cure on the princess. These over-exaggerated and comical caricatures are important as MacDonald seeks to speak to a time where society moved rapidly away from a theological worldview. U. C. Knoepflmacher even suggests that these characters, given the association of Hum-Drum with the materialist and Kopy Keck with the spiritualist, might be MacDonald's critique of "the absurd misapplication of the philosophical positions held, respectively, by Hume and Kant."⁵⁷

In "The Light Princess" MacDonald seeks to subvert this trend by emphasizing that the deepest reality a Christian can know is found in self-sacrificing love. The contemporary Victorian tendency to move from theology to metaphysics to empiricism, and thus a solely material and

---

55. George MacDonald, *Fairytales*, 27.

56. Ibid., 27–28.

57. Knoepflmacher, "Introduction," 344. The Victorian Idealist philosopher J. F. Ferrier complains in 1854 about the undisciplined engagement with philosophy in Britain. He writes in this regard, using the metaphor of the sailor: "All the captains are sailing on different tacks, under different orders, and under different winds" (Ferrier, quoted in Davis, *Victorians*, 161).

scientific understanding of reality, is inverted in this story.[58] This inversion comes to its climax in the princess's eventual cure at the very end of the story. A prince, appropriate for the fairytale genre, breaks all class boundaries and abases himself to become a shoe black in order to be near the princess. He eventually gives his life for the cure of the princess: "His head fell back; the water closed over it, and the bubbles of his last breath bubbled up through the water . . . he was past breathing."[59] He embraces death for her sake. Before he drowns, the princess feeds him wine and biscuit, and in this symbolic last supper MacDonald ties the prince's sacrificial death to the Eucharist and therefore to Christ's sacrificial death. Of course the prince's death is not final, and he awakes only to be united with his beloved princess. It is striking that the princess is being healed as the prince drowns. Realizing that the prince is drowning, she throws herself into the water to rescue him. The associations with baptism in this episode are striking: "Love and water brought back all her strength."[60] The princess is healed from her superficial and uncaring personality, and she is finally able to care.[61] When the prince comes back to life, the princess bursts into tears and finds her gravity as she falls on the floor. Thus, the light princess becomes weighty in a dual sense of the word. She is first healed of her flighty character and then finds her gravity restored, after she is able to cry.

The ending of the story expresses MacDonald's deepest conviction about the nature of reality. Ultimate reality is neither found in metaphysics nor materialism and empiricism but in self-giving love of which Christ's death is the prime example. Truth, as MacDonald reiterated in his *Unspoken Sermons* over and over again, is only found in the person of Christ. A comprehensive understanding of reality and the world—physical, metaphysical, moral, and spiritual—finds its ultimate answer only in Christ, and particularly in his sacrificial death. MacDonald cleverly inverts the predominant development of his time by moving

---

58. The turn to philosophy in the mid-Victorian period was marked by what Davis calls "a series of incongruous contests without the possibility of common resolution" (Davis, *Victorians*, 161).

59. George MacDonald, *Fairytales*, 50.

60. Ibid.

61. The young princess' questionable moral behavior is of course another important critique of Victorian society. Her ability to feel compassion at the end of the story is an important part of the cure as MacDonald himself stresses in his comments on the story in *Adela Cathcart*.

in this fairytale from gravity as an icon for empiricism to metaphysics to theology as the ultimate key to human existence and its cure from illness. In true MacDonald fashion, more is meant than meets the ear in "The Light Princess." It is of importance that he articulates his argument in a fairytale. We should note by way of anticipation that for MacDonald, as it is for Jesus' parables, form and content are closely related in his fairytales.

As MacDonald continued his writing career, it was an urgent concern for him to show that science and theology are not in conflict. Science occupies an important place in MacDonald's thought. It remains important, however, for him to emphasize that science is limited and consequently unable to give a complete account of reality. Thus he argues: "Those who put their faith in Science are trying to live in the scaffold of the house invisible."[62]

MacDonald reiterates this argument in many different ways throughout his writing career. The incident of the globe in *Phantastes* (1858), which has puzzled many a reader, may be helpfully interpreted in this connection. Anodos' shadow disenchants reality for him and he begins to see the world differently, more scientifically: "I will not see beauty where there is none. I will dare to behold things as they are."[63] He continues his journey and meets a girl with a mysterious globe. In his greedy desire to know about the globe—the way things really are—he breaks the globe. Anodos' desire for accurate knowledge has disastrous results, foreshadowing, unknowingly on MacDonald's side, the ecological crisis of today. The globe shatters into pieces.[64] He addresses similar issues in the fairytale "The Day Boy and the Night Girl" first published in 1882. The story begins with the description of a witch who wants to know everything: "There was once a witch who desired to know everything. But the wiser a witch is, the harder she knocks her head against the wall when she comes to it. She cared for nothing in itself—only for knowing

---

62. George MacDonald, *Orts*, 58. See also his essay "Wordsworth's poetry" in the same volume for similar arguments. MacDonald has a high regard for science as these essays show, but he refuses to accept that science can provide an accurate and complete description of reality as it cannot capture the moral, aesthetic, or spiritual dimension of life. Thus, the mark of a mature person is the ability to integrate the scientific with the poetic.

63. George MacDonald, *Phantastes*, 61.

64. Ibid., 61–62. For a similar incident see Mr. Vane's attempt in *Lilith* to catch a bird-butterfly rather than contemplating its beauty. Vane admits that he is contemplating a metaphysical argument. Idem, *First and Final*, 74–75.

it. She was not naturally cruel, but the wolf had made her cruel."[65] The whole story is a plea for a re-integration of the intellectual disciplines. The separation of the disciplines is portrayed as being demonic both in *Phantastes* and "The Day Boy and the Night Girl." The theme of night and day as metaphors for scientific and mystical knowledge are most likely borrowed from Novalis.[66] The scientific has to be held in tension with a theological and mystical view of the world. They must not be separated.[67] As MacDonald argues elsewhere, "It is not that Madam Science shows any antagonism to Lady Poetry; but the atmosphere and plane on which alone they can meet as friends who understand each other, is the mind and heart of a sage, not of the boy."[68] A merely scientific view of the world will have devastating results for the earth.

In summary, we can say that for MacDonald science aids our understanding of reality but has severe limitations. It is unable to reveal and express reality in all its complexities, especially its emotional, moral, and spiritual dimensions. Importantly, this insight ties in with our discussion of metaphor in chapter 2, where it was argued that language, like science, is limited in its ability to express the complexities of reality. For MacDonald, while not denying the role of science in our search for knowledge and understanding, truth can only be found in Jesus Christ. Science, language, and, as a consequence, the Bible are all limited in their ability to express reality comprehensively. To quote MacDonald once more:

> Use all the symbols that we have in nature, in human relations, in the family—all our symbols of grace and tenderness, and loving-kindness between man and man, and between man and woman, and between woman and woman, but you can never come up to the thought of what God's ministration is. When our Lord came he just let us see how his Father was doing this always. He "came to give his life a ransom for many." It was in giving his life a ransom for us that he died; that was the consummation and crown of it all, but it was his life that he gave for us—his whole being, his whole strength, his whole energy—not alone his days of trouble

---

65. George MacDonald, *Unspoken Sermons*, 304.

66. Novalis writes in hymn four of *Hymns to the Night*: "Now I know when will come the last morning: when the light no more scares away the Night and Love" (George MacDonald, *Rampolli*, 6).

67. George MacDonald, *Unspoken Sermons*, 304. See MacDonald's sermon on truth, published much later in his writing career in 1889, for a very similar argument. Ibid., 465.

68. George MacDonald, *Orts*, 51.

and of toil, but deeper than that, he gave his whole being for us; yea, he even went down to death for us.[69]

For MacDonald, then, the crux of revelation is anchored in Jesus Christ, who came to fulfill the created glory, employing the images and material of this world to reveal the heart of the Father. He does this most profoundly in his sacrificial death. It is no surprise therefore that MacDonald did not embrace the historical criticism of his time with its naïve belief that historical investigation will provide direct access to reality and especially the realities about which the Bible speaks. We must now consider more carefully MacDonald's Christological understanding of revelation before exploring MacDonald's understanding of Scripture, language, and the parabolic.

George MacDonald's Christological Understanding of Revelation

In the previous section we sought to place MacDonald into his mid-Victorian context. In particular, we provided a rough outline of the Victorian mindset towards the Bible and MacDonald's response towards its philosophical underpinnings. In the following we shall argue that MacDonald developed a decidedly theological understanding of story and more particularly the parabolic mode, as story has the capacity to provide a literary space in which God reveals himself in unforeseen ways.

In order to understand MacDonald's view of the Bible and the parabolic particular, it is important to place it into his larger theological framework, especially his Christology, and his understanding of creation and revelation as these are inextricably connected. Language, for MacDonald, emerges out of Christ's created order and plays an important role in his understanding of revelation in Christ. His strong and continual emphasis on the relational dimension of the Godhead, especially the relationship between the Father and the Son, as well as his relational understanding of revelation are crucial for understanding MacDonald's view of the role of the language, the parabolic, and the Bible more generally. In what follows, our aim is to discuss MacDonald's Christological understanding of revelation.

---

69. Ibid., 302.

Christ the Son and Child of God is One with the Father

As we suggested in the previous section, MacDonald reacted against a merely scientific view of the world and espoused a thoroughly Christocentric worldview. He also rejected certain aspects of scholastic Calvinism, especially its emphasis on a highly mechanical, impersonal, and legal understanding of the atonement, focusing on humanity's utter depravity, God's wrath, and the absolution thereof. Kerry Dearborn in particular has gone to great lengths to show the kind of theory of atonement that MacDonald sought to critique and move away from.[70] In reaction and as a corrective, his theological emphasis is on the person of Christ, his relationship with God the Father, the importance of creation, and Christ as the one who reveals the Father not in opposition to creation but as the one who comes into his own, fulfilling his created glory. It was an important concern for MacDonald to move the atoning work of Christ from the center of his theology and focus on the person of Christ instead. For him the overemphasis on a certain understanding of atonement rather than on Christ himself leads to a distorted understanding of Christ and therefore of God. MacDonald writes: "Even if your plan, your theories, were absolutely true, the holding of them with sincerity, the trusting in this or that about Christ, or in anything he did or could do, the trusting in anything but himself, his own living self, is a delusion."[71] MacDonald's plea was for a renewed trust in the atoner himself rather than a certain system of thought about the atonement. It is no surprise, then, that one finds very little reflection on Christ's atoning work. Rather, MacDonald focuses on Christ as the one who reveals the Father.[72]

In addition, MacDonald, as we shall see, argues against a literal reading of the Bible and the notion that the whole truth about God can be found in the Bible. Language can never encompass truth, even if it is the words of the Bible. From the very beginning of his writing career,

---

70. Dearborn, "Prophetic or Heretic," 100–129.

71. MacDonald, *Unspoken Sermons*, 391–92.

72. This is in contrast to Dearborn who argues that "The Atonement was pivotal in George MacDonald's thinking" ("Prophet or Heretic," 149). While Dearborn is correct in arguing that MacDonald's emphasis is on the Son as the true revelation of the Father, the atoning work of Christ receives little emphasis in MacDonald's work. Even if one seeks to understand his statements on the atonement in light of a more relational understanding of God, there is little reflection in MacDonald on what actually happened on the cross, and Dearborn admits her ambiguity at this point. Dearborn, "Prophet or Heretic," 150.

MacDonald upholds Christ as the one who alone is and encompasses the truth.[73] While the Bible plays a central role by which we come to know Christ, it is in the person of Christ himself that truth is found. Therefore, truth has to be understood above all in relational terms rather than a mere theoretical system of thought, something into which MacDonald felt Federal Calvinism had slipped by using primarily legal metaphors rather than relational metaphors in regard to God.[74]

For MacDonald the center of the universe lies in Christ who is the son of the Father and who is one with the Father. He argues: "He is the Son of God because the Father and he are one, have one thought, one mind, one heart. Upon this truth—I do not mean the dogma, but the truth itself of Jesus to his father-hangs the universe . . . 'I and the Father are one,' is the centre-truth of the Universe."[75] MacDonald reiterates this Christo-centric view of the world throughout his writing career.[76] C. S. Lewis goes so far as to argue that

> The Divine Sonship is the key-conception which unites all the different elements of his thought. I dare not say that he is never in error; but to speak plainly I know hardly any other writer who seems to be closer, or more continually close, to the Spirit of Christ Himself. Hence his Christ-like union of tenderness and severity. Nowhere else outside the New Testament have I found terror and comfort so intertwined.[77]

Lewis' words capture well MacDonald's balanced perspective, where an emphasis on the love of the Father is closely tied into the demand to follow Christ in obedience.

Above all MacDonald stresses that the relationship between the Father and the Son is marked by love.[78] God is love, and love is the deepest

---

73. This is contrast to Reed-Nancarrow, who argues that for the early MacDonald revelation is mostly a matter of inner experience. Reed-Nancarrow, "Remythologizing," 33.

74. See Dearborn, "Prophet or Heretic," 117–25.

75. MacDonald, *Unspoken Sermons*, 490–91.

76. He repeats this throughout his *Unspoken Sermons* published between 1867 and 1889, his *Diary of an Old Soul* first published in 1880, his sermons in *The Hope of the Gospel*, published in 1892, and many other places. See Ibid., 37, 79–80, 283, 286, 288, 326, 417–18, 534; idem, *Hope/Miracles*, 38, 53, 55, 124, 152–54, 256; idem, "Diary," March 23, 24, 26, 29; April 22, 23; May 10, 19, 30.

77. Lewis, *MacDonald*, 19.

78. George MacDonald, *Unspoken Sermons*, 417–18; idem, *Hope/Miracles*, 260. See also Gerold, *Gotteskindschaft*, 66; Raeper, *George MacDonald*, 243.

and most important reality of his being: "I know nothing deeper in him than love, nor believe there is in him anything deeper than love—nay, that there can be anything deeper than love."[79] Dearborn rightly admits, however, that MacDonald stresses not only the fatherly but also the motherly attributes of God.[80] Parenthood, one could say, lies at the heart of MacDonald's theology. The many motherly and grandmotherly figures in his stories emphasize the wisdom and motherly attributes of God without minimizing other qualities, such as God's holiness.[81]

Just as the relationship between the Father and Son is marked by love, so is God's relationship with his created order marked by love. It is love that motivates God's action in creating and redeeming the world. MacDonald writes: "The being of God is love, therefore creation. I imagine that from all eternity he has been creating."[82] For MacDonald, it is love that motivates God's redemptive and sanctifying work in the world:

> For love loves unto purity. Love has ever in view the absolute loveliness of that which it beholds. Where loveliness is incomplete, and love cannot love its fill of loving, it spends itself to make more lovely, that it may love more . . . There is nothing eternal but that which loves and can be loved, and love is ever climbing towards the consummation when such shall be the universe, imperishable, divine.[83]

---

79. George MacDonald, *Unspoken Sermons*, 299. See also MacDonald's beautiful description of the love between Father and Son in his sermon "The Creation in Christ." Ibid., 421–22, esp. 429.

80. Dearborn, *Baptized Imagination*, 113–14. This is an important focus in MacDonald's work and provides a significant contribution to a balanced feminist perspective, as his emphasis on the maternal aspects of God does not happen at the expense of his paternal attributes. It is also an expression of MacDonald's belief that women are not to be seen as the weaker sex. This emphasis manifests itself not only in all the motherly figures in his stories; MacDonald also pays considerable attention to the female figures of Scripture and writes poetry on many "Gospel Women." See George MacDonald, *Poetical Works*, 1:221–47.

81. A beautiful example is the great-great-grandmother in *The Princess and the Goblins* and *The Princess and Curdie* or the beautiful lady North Wind in *At the Back of the North Wind*.

82. George MacDonald, *Unspoken Sermons*, 299. See also MacDonald's sermon "The Consuming Fire" where he argues that it is love that has motivated God to redeem and sanctify his creation. Ibid., 18–27.

83. Ibid., 18. See also Gerold, *Gotteskindschaft*, 272f.

Not only must the relationship between the Father and the Son be understood in terms of love, but all of God's actions in creating and redeeming are always and only motivated by his ever-enduring love for his creation.

Jesus Reveals the Father

God's love towards his creation finds form in his revelation of himself and his desire to be known by his creation.[84] MacDonald emphasizes over and over again that Christ did not come to conceal but to reveal. Jesus came to reveal the Father, and he can do so because he is his son and because he is one with the Father. Gerold goes so far as to say that "MacDonald's theology is wholly concentrated on the Father as he is revealed by the Son"; revelation in Christ is at the heart of MacDonald's Christology.[85] It is important for MacDonald to stress that Christ reveals the Father in and through his close and loving relationship with the Father.

> He has shown us the Father not only by doing what the Father does, not only by loving his Father's children even as the Father loves them, but by his perfect satisfaction with him, his joy in him, his utter obedience to him. He has shown us the Father by the absolute devotion of a perfect son.[86]

Christ rests in his relationship with the Father. His trust and utter obedience comes out of this intimate and loving union with the Father and culminates in his death on the cross. The primary place, then, where Christ reveals the love of the Father is at his death on the cross.[87]

For MacDonald, however, it is important not to stop at the idea that God the Father revealed himself in Christ but that Christ reveals the Father *to his creation*. The greatest tragedy of the whole human affair, according to MacDonald, is that humanity fails to see God as a loving Father.[88] Consequently, we find in his theology an emphasis on human receptivity: "The Father knows the Son and sends him to us that we may know him; the Son knows the Father, and dies to reveal him. The glory

---

84. Gerold, *Gotteskindschaft*, 70–71.

85. Ibid., 55, 57–58, 366. Translation mine. See also George MacDonald, *Unspoken Sermons*, 36. Dearborn looks at MacDonald's understanding of the atonement in light of Christ as the true revelation of the Father. Dearborn, "Prophet or Heretic," 101, 130–36.

86. George MacDonald, *Unspoken Sermons*, 490.

87. George MacDonald, *Hope/Miracles*, 152–53.

88. George MacDonald, *Unspoken Sermons*, 276.

of God's mysteries is—that they are for his children to look into . . . the eternal child alone can reveal him."[89] The reception of this revelation by humanity or the lack thereof is an important aspect of his understanding of revelation.[90]

MacDonald further argues that God's ultimate purpose in revealing himself to his children is not only that they might know the Father and the Son but also that they might partake in this intimate union between Father and Son. Mankind's participation in the divine life and union with God is the ultimate goal of God's revelation.[91] This is why MacDonald calls Jesus "the inexhaustible, the ever unfolding Revelation of God."[92] Like Coleridge, then, he emphasizes that revelation cannot be reduced to an abstract and static concept but must be understood in relational terms.[93] God seeks to be in intimate relationship with his creation. MacDonald writes:

> God is not a God that hides, but a God that reveals. His whole work in relation to the creatures he has made—and where else can lie his work?—is revelation—the giving them truth, the showing of himself to them, that they may know him, and come nearer and nearer to him, and so he have his children more and more of companions to him.[94]

Only God can initiate this participation in the divine life. MacDonald argues that God makes himself known by the Holy Spirit to each person individually, drawing them to himself and making them into his friends and companions. While MacDonald does not develop the role of the Holy Spirit in the same way as he develops the role of Christ and the Father in his understanding of revelation, the Holy Spirit nevertheless plays an important role as he draws people into this intimate union and speaks to each person individually.[95] It is the Holy Spirit that enables each person to "take and eat" that which is revealed in Christ:

89. George MacDonald, *Hope/Miracles*, 152.

90. Gerold's recent PhD thesis on MacDonald's anthropology is an exploration of and significant contribution to this dimension of MacDonald's theology. Gerold, *Gotteskindschaft*, chs. 5–19.

91. George MacDonald, *Unspoken Sermons*, 491.

92. Ibid., 36.

93. For a similar argument, see Gerold, *Gotteskindschaft*, 82.

94. George MacDonald, *Unspoken Sermons*, 593. See also idem, *Paul Faber*, 216–17.

95. George MacDonald, *Unspoken Sermons*, 37, 282. See also idem, *Seaboard*

> The Son of God *is* the Teacher of men, giving to them of his Spirit—that Spirit which manifests the deep things of God, being to a man the mind of Christ. The great heresy of the Church of the present day is unbelief in this Spirit. The mass of the Church does not believe that the Spirit has a revelation for every man individually—a revelation as different from the revelation of the Bible, as the food in the moment of passing into living brain and nerve differs from the bread and meat.[96]

While the "bread and meat" is central to this facet of revelation, the focus is now how this food is received and digested by each believer. It is a sort of *lectio divina*, a spiritual reading of Scripture. For MacDonald, then, it is crucial to emphasize that God's desire is to make himself known in such a way that every person should not only know of him but come to know him in a personal way by ingesting his word deeply.

The Transformative Power of Revelation

In order for humanity to see God and partake in the divine life, they must become like Jesus as he exemplifies the true humanity. God's revelation in Christ brings about the transformation of the believer. MacDonald writes:

> He will work until the same likeness is wrought out and perfected in us, the image, namely, of the humanity of God, in which image we were made at first, but which could never be developed in us except by the indwelling of the perfect likeness. By the power of Christ thus received and at home in us, we are changed—the glory in him becoming glory in us, his glory changing us to glory.[97]

Just as Christ's revelation of the Father culminates in his obedience even unto death on the cross, so does the transformation of the believer culminate in following Christ by dying to oneself. We quote MacDonald once more:

Parish, 40–41; *Orts*, 28, 194. MacDonald argues that "a wise imagination, which is the presence of the spirit of God, is the best guide that man or woman can have." It must be pointed out though that MacDonald's development of his pneumatology is relatively weak in comparison to his understanding of the Father and the Son. Thus MacDonald will often not use capital letter to describe the Spirit of God. Gerold argues similarly. Gerold, *Gotteskindschaft*, 55, 77.

96. George MacDonald, *Unspoken Sermons*, 37.

97. Ibid., 455, see also 45.

> Christ died to save us, not from suffering, but from ourselves; not from injustice, far less from justice, but from being unjust. He died that we might live—but live as he lives, by dying as he died who died to himself that he might live unto God. If we do not die to ourselves, we cannot live to God, and he that does not live to God, is dead.[98]

Not only his sermons but also most of MacDonald's stories look at this transformative process where fallen humanity is brought back to live life as God intended it.[99] Unlike Coleridge, then, MacDonald has a rather clear idea of what this transformation into "companions of God" entails. We must become like Christ, who exemplifies the true humanity: life as God intended it.[100] Transformation is the necessary result of God's revelation. It is within this central concept of transformation that one has to place MacDonald's repeated use of the symbol of death, and particularly death to self, as the way one is transformed into the likeness of Christ. MacDonald's *Lilith*, as we shall see, in particular hovers around this very important symbol.

In sum we can say that truth for MacDonald must never be reduced to a system or an idea but must be understood as something far more encompassing, capturing the whole person, being fundamentally a relational reality in which the person of Christ reveals himself to humankind, engaging them with all of who they are, capturing not just aspects but the essence of life.[101] For MacDonald truth in its deepest sense engages the person with all of their heart, mind, soul, and strength.[102] This profoundly personal and integrated understanding of truth, revelation, and transformation is a concern that MacDonald carries throughout his life

98. Ibid., 490, 433.

99. Just a few examples in which MacDonald portrays this transformative process in character developments are the characters Anodos in *Phantastes,* Hugh Sutherland in *David Elginbrod*, Alec Forbes in *Alec Forbes*, Robert Falconer in *Robert Falconer*, Nanny in *At the Back of the North Wind*, Reverent Clement Sclater and Mrs. Sclater in *Sir Gibbie*, Curdie in *The Princess and Curdie*, Mr. Vane in *Lilith*, and Margret McLear and James Blatherwick in *Salted with Fire*. While the characters depicted in these stories show a great variance in regard to their maturity, all of them grow towards Christ-likeness.

100. The primary places where MacDonald draws his understanding of Christ's true humanity from are of course the Gospels and Epistles of the NT as most of his sermons are based on these texts.

101. See MacDonald's essay "A Sketch of Individual Development" in George MacDonald, *Orts*.

102. George MacDonald, *Unspoken Sermons*, 69.

and writing career and is pivotal for understanding his view of the role of creation, Scripture, and stories in the revelatory process.

The Incarnate Christ as Creator and Revealer

It is significant for understanding MacDonald's view of the role of Scripture, the parabolic, and language in the revelatory process, that Christ as the revealer must not be seen in opposition to creation but as the one who comes to fulfill the created glory.[103] This is an important corrective to Federal Calvinism, as it tended, in the words of Dearborn, "toward a radical schism between nature and grace, creation and Creator."[104] MacDonald reflects on this in his poem "Of the son of man":

> And in these lines my purpose is to show
> That he who left the Father, though he came
> Not with art-splendor or the earthy flame
> Of genius, yet in that he did bestow
> His own true loving heart, whate'ver we name
> The best in human art, without the shame
> And that whate'ver of Beautiful and Grand
> The Earth contains, by him was not despised,
> But rather was so deeply realized . . .[105]

The reason MacDonald can make such an affirmation is his understanding of Christ as the creator. In his sermon "The Creation in Christ" based on the Johannine prologue, MacDonald takes the pre-existence of Christ and Christ as creator seriously. Jesus is the eternal child of the eternal Father and was with the Father in the beginning.[106] The world was created by Jesus, as John 1:3 affirms: "All things were made through him, and without him was made not one thing."[107] Creation must be understood as an expression of God's love; creation reflects the love between the Father and the Son. MacDonald writes: "[L]ove is the heart and hand of his

---

103. Ibid., 428. Coleridge was an important inspiration for MacDonald in this regard. Thus he writes about Coleridge's poetry: "[W]e find in him what we miss in Wordsworth, an inclined plane from the revelation in nature to the culminating revelation in the Son of Man" (George MacDonald, *England's Antiphon*, 307). See also Gerold, *Gotteskindschaft*, 68–69.

104. Dearborn, *Baptized Imagination*, 74. See also Hein, *Victorian Mythmaker*, 77.

105. George MacDonald, *Poetical Works*, 2:270.

106. George MacDonald, *Unspoken Sermons*, 417, 426.

107. Ibid., 419. Translation of Scripture by George MacDonald.

creation... The love that foresees creation is itself the power to create."[108] The beauty found in creation is an expression of the love and beauty of God: "I believe that God is absolutely, grandly beautiful even as the highest soul of man counts beauty, but infinitely beyond that soul's highest idea—with the beauty that creates beauty, not merely shows it, or itself exists beautiful."[109] In his essay on Wordsworth's poetry he argues further: "God is the first of artists . . . he has put beauty into nature, knowing how it will affect us, and intending that it should so affect us; that he has embodied his own grand thoughts thus that we might see them and be glad."[110] MacDonald understands the primary principle of creation not to be the Fall but the love of God and thus the givenness and goodness of creation.[111] Creation is shot through with meaningful patterns, correspondences, and beauty.

While the beauty and patterns of creation are not capable of revealing God in and of themselves, they serve as "clothing" whereby God makes himself known in Jesus, and we shall discuss this dynamic in more detail below. The gap between the transcendent and immanent, the uncreated and created, God and the world, cannot be bridged by the created order. MacDonald emphasizes this throughout his work: "Use all the symbols that we have in nature, in human relations, in the family—all our symbols of race and tenderness, and loving-kindness . . . but you can never come up to the thought of what God's ministration is."[112] MacDonald's Romantic outlook on creation is therefore wedded with a firm insistence that God is "other" from his creation. Dearborn puts it this way: "Here is immanence without pantheism, and harmony without loss of God's transcendence."[113]

For MacDonald, then, God's revelation does not begin with Christ's Incarnation but with Christ's creation of the world. The Incarnation is

---

108. Ibid., 421. See also idem, *Orts*, 246; *First and Final*, 72.

109. George MacDonald, *Unspoken Sermons*, 534. This does not mean for MacDonald that everything that appears beautiful must automatically reflect God. See the discussion of Diamond and North Wind about beauty in idem, *North Wind*, 21–22. See also the character of Lilith in *Lilith*. She is beautiful in appearance but evil in character. Her beauty is what leads Mr. Vane astray.

110. George MacDonald, *Orts*, 246–47; see also 254, 256.

111 See also Dearborn, *Baptized Imagination*, 74.

112. George MacDonald, *Orts*, 302, 256. See also idem, *Unspoken Sermons*, 417, 464; *Hope/Miracles*, 153–54.

113. Dearborn, *Baptized Imagination*, 75.

the culmination and climax of God's revelation.[114] Christ the creator and Christ the revealer are inextricably intertwined for MacDonald.[115] Creation is the living organism, the theatrical space where God has stepped onto the scene in human form to reveal and redeem and to allow his creation to respond creatively and obediently to him.[116] Only Christ can reveal the Father, and he does so not in opposition to creation but by deeply realizing the "theatrical space" that he created with the Father in the beginning of the world. In what way Jesus realizes the potential of creation is the concern of the next section.

The Revelatory Dimension of Creation

MacDonald discusses the role of creation in revelation throughout his work but in more detail in his sermon called "The God of the Living," based on Luke 20:38; the sermon "The Voice of Job," based on Job 14:13–15; "The Truth," based on John 14:6; and his discussion of Wordsworth's poetry.[117] The ultimate purpose of creation is to be in relationship with the Creator. The flowers of the field, the sky above, the water, the mountains, our human bodies, in short everything that exists has the potential of becoming a means of God's revelation.[118] MacDonald repeatedly insists that any knowledge of the world and God can only happen within the context of the created order and not outside and apart from it. Our bodily senses, for example, are the only way in which we can perceive reality at all. He argues:

> No thought, human or divine, can be conveyed from man to man save through the symbolism of the creation. The heavens and the earth are around us that it may be possible for us to speak of the unseen by the seen; for the outermost husk of creation has correspondence with the deepest things of the Creator. He is not a God that hideth himself, but a God who made that he might reveal; he is consistent and one throughout. There are things with which an

---

114. MacDonald, *England's Antiphon*, 307.

115. For a similar argument see Gerold, *Gotteskindschaft*, 68f.

116. MacDonald employs the metaphor of the theatre in order to speak about the human imagination in light of God's imaginative work. George MacDonald, *Orts*, 3–4. Especially in his sermons MacDonald discusses carefully Jesus' use of symbols from creation in order to speak about the Kingdom of God.

117. These sermons are found in volumes 1, 2, and 3 of *Unspoken Sermons* and show MacDonald's continual emphasis on the role of creation in the revelatory process.

118. For a similar argument see Hein, *Harmony Within*, 45.

> enemy hath meddled; but there are more things with which no enemy could meddle, and by which we may speak of God. They may not have revealed him to us, but at least when he is revealed, they show themselves so much of his nature, that we at once use them as spiritual tokens in the commerce of the spirit, to help convey to other minds what we may have seen of the unseen. The heavens and the earth are around us that it may be possible for us to speak of the unseen by the seen.[119]

There are three important observations in this passage to which we would like to draw attention. First, while MacDonald does not deny the fallen state of creation, he still insists that creation is capable of providing the visible material by which we might be able to speak about the "unseen" or "non-physical" world. Second, for MacDonald there exists a deep correspondence between the physical (macrocosm/outer world) and the inner world (microcosm) of a person. The physical world provides the language and pattern that is then transferred and used symbolically to speak about the non-physical world. All words that belong to the inner world of man are originally poetic words. Like Lakoff and Johnson, then, MacDonald articulates an account of metaphor/symbol that is central to the way we engage with reality. Third, while the discovery of the correspondence between the macrocosm and microcosm was a common project in the Romantic movement and is an expression of the Romantic desire to see the world in a more holistic manner,[120] it is important for our discussion that MacDonald places his theory of correspondence and his understanding of the symbol within a thoroughly theological framework, moving the emphasis from the finder of these correspondences to the one who created them:

> For what are the forms of which a man may reveal his thoughts? Are they not those of nature? For the world around him is an outward figuration of the condition of his mind; an inexhaustible storehouse of forms whence he may choose exponents—the

---

119. MacDonald, *Unspoken Sermons*, 439. See also 161, 199–200, 463; idem, *Hope/Miracles*, 298. While MacDonald focuses on the revelatory side of creation, he does not neglect the "dark" or fallen side of creation. He deals with it in some detail in *At the Back of the North Wind*, where Diamond watches a ship sink due to a storm. George MacDonald, *North Wind*, chapter 6.

120. See Kremer, *Romantik*, 63. Klauck, *Allegorie*, 139. As an example of early Romantic reflection on correspondence see Novalis, *Novalis*, 2:232ff. See also Roder's discussion of Novalis in this regard: Roder, *Novalis*, 390–92. The influence of Novalis on MacDonald in this regard is quite possible but beyond the limitations of this book.

crystal pitchers that shall protect his thought and not need to be broken that the light may break forth. The meanings are in those forms already, else they could be no garment of unveiling. God has made the world that it should serve his creature."[121]

But not only does the physical world serve as a "storehouse" to provide clothing for man's interior life such as thoughts and feelings, this "storehouse" has a deeper function still.

We have suggested above that for MacDonald creation serves as the "theatrical space" in and by which God reveals himself to his creatures. Everything within the created order has the potential for becoming the means by which God reveals himself.[122] MacDonald's minute attention to Jesus' use of symbols from creation for his proclamation of the Kingdom of God is central to his understanding of revelation in Christ. Christ the creator and Christ the revealer are brought together in Jesus' employment of symbols. Christ created the world in such a way that it might serve him to reveal the Father. Unlike the natural correspondence between visible and invisible *created* things, however, the symbols by which we may speak of God are revealed rather than discerned.

It is surprising then that MacDonald does not take his argument to its logical and climactic conclusion. He stresses the fact that the human body and the world around us is indispensable for any knowledge of the world and especially the divine, but he fails to reflect on the theological significance of God taking on human form. MacDonald discusses extensively how Jesus uses the symbols from creation, but he does not reflect on the importance that God himself took on fleshly form in Jesus and the implications thereof for the significance of creation in revelation.[123] God had to take on human form in order to reveal himself. It could be argued that the humanity of Christ is itself the supreme "created" symbol. A consideration of the Incarnation would have strengthened MacDonald's argument considerably. We must now turn to discuss MacDonald's understanding of the symbol, allegory, and Scripture in order to understand his view of story and the parabolic in particular as a literary space where God reveals himself to his creation.

121. George MacDonald, *Orts*, 5. See also 8–9, 24, 42.

122. George MacDonald, *Unspoken Sermons*, 161. MacDonald writes: "It is by the body that we come into contact with Nature, with our fellow-men, with all their revelations of God to us."

123. MacDonald does begin such reflections but does not them develop them in any way. See his brief comment in George MacDonald, *England's Antiphon*, 279.

George MacDonald's Understanding of the Symbol, Allegory, and Scripture

In discussing MacDonald's theological view of the symbol, allegory, and Scripture, we must note that MacDonald employs the term symbol to speak about the nature and function of language in general and that he uses the term in a rather broad and embracing manner, quite differently to our usage of the term metaphor in chapter 2. As we have already suggested, however, MacDonald's understanding of the symbol ties in closely with contemporary discussions of metaphor.

Many readers of MacDonald have wondered whether his view of the symbol tends towards a Neo-platonic or Platonic view of correspondence.[124] While some of his statements concerning the symbol examined in isolation might lead to such a conclusion, a consideration of his Christology (as laid out above) and his strong belief in the Incarnation makes it more difficult to uphold such a position. It is true that MacDonald saw a high correspondence between the physical and spiritual worlds, and some of his statements might lead one to think that his view of the world was platonic in the sense that this world is a mere ladder that serves to ascend to higher spheres. A more careful look at his argument, however, shows that MacDonald's concern was not to devalue the material world by relegating it to the status of a ladder.[125] Rather, he sought to recover a theological understanding of the material world in the face of the dangers that came with the Industrial Revolution. MacDonald saw, in rather prophetic way, a worldview emerging that was purely empirical and void of any sense of wonder and awe. In *Ronald Bannerman's Boyhood* MacDonald paints a vivid picture of this development:

> ... what more machines are there now? More than I can tell. I saw one going in the fields the other day, at the use of which I could only guess. Strange, wild-looking, mad-like machines, as the Scotch would call them, are growling and snapping, and clinking and clattering over our fields, so that it seems to an old boy as if all the sweet poetic twilight of things were vanishing

---

124. The following scholars tend towards a Platonic view of the symbol in MacDonald: Prickett, *Victorian Fantasy*, 170; Prickett, "Two Worlds"; Kegler, "Resakralisierung"; Kegler, "Silent House"; Marshall, "Allegory"; Riga, *Platonic Imagery*.

125. MacDonald does use the imagery of the ladder when he talks about the limitations of the symbol, but his point is that no symbol will be able to capture the reality it seeks to depict. It merely serves to approach mystery. See George MacDonald, *Unspoken Sermons*, 454–55.

> from the country; but he reminds himself that God is not going to sleep, for, as one of the greatest poets that ever lived says, *he slumbereth not nor sleepeth*; and the children of the earth are his, and he will see that their imaginations and feelings have food enough and to spare.[126]

MacDonald's primary concern, then, was the recovery of a sense of wonder for God's creation and, as we shall see, to show that God created the world and placed correspondence into his creation so that we might speak of the unseen by the seen.[127]

George MacDonald's Understanding of the Symbol

The starting point for a theological reflection on language begins for MacDonald with the realization that all of our human and finite language falls short of depicting infinite realities. He understands the symbol of God as Father as the most important by which we approach the mystery of God. And yet, even this highest of all symbols cannot fully capture the glorious meaning it seeks to depict.

> Jesus is the son, because God is the father—a statement imperfect and unfit because an attempt of human thought to represent that which it cannot grasp, yet which it so believes that it must try to utter it even in speech that cannot be right . . . The true heart will remember the inadequacy of our speech, and our thought also, to the things that lie near the unknown roots of our existence.[128]

In a discussion of 2 Cor 3:18, a crucial biblical text for MacDonald in general, he reiterates his insistence that the symbolic language Paul employs must fall short of that which it seeks to communicate. MacDonald translates the text as follows: "But we all, with open face beholding as in a glass the glory of the Lord, are changed into the same image from glory

---

126. George MacDonald, *Ranald*, 63. Other references to a merely material and at times greedy approach to creation are found in MacDonald's description of city of Gwyntystorm in *The Princess and Curdie* and Bulika in *Lilith*. He repeatedly reminds his audience in his *Unspoken Sermons* that a merely scientific understanding of creation is insufficient to understand reality in its fullest sense. See idem, *Unspoken Sermons*, 468.

127. For similar argument in regard to F. D. Maurice see Morris, *F. D. Maurice*, 170.

128. George MacDonald, *Unspoken Sermons*, 417.

to glory, even as by the spirit of the Lord."[129] MacDonald is trying to come to terms with the Greek word *katoptrizomenoi*, which he first translated as "changed." He rightly contends, however, that the most appropriate English word for translating this is "to mirror." MacDonald recognizes the limitations of this symbol while insisting that the symbol is the best way to speak about such spiritual realities, as they are open and suggestive in nature. We quote him at some length:

> It is but according to the law of symbol, that the thing symbolized by the mirror should have properties far beyond those of leaded glass or polished metal, seeing it is a live soul understanding that which it takes into its deeps . . . Unlike its symbol, it can hold not merely the outward visual resemblance, but the inward likeness of the person revealed by it; it is open to the influences of that which it embraces, and is capable of active-co-operation with them . . . Paul's idea is, that when we take into our understanding, our heart, our conscience, our being, the glory of God, namely Jesus Christ as he shows himself to our eyes, our hearts, our conscience, he works upon us, and will keep working, till we are changed to the very likeness we have thus mirrored in us; for with his likeness he comes himself, and dwells in us . . . But we must beware of receiving this or any symbol *after the flesh*, beware of interpreting it in any fashion that partakes of the character of the mere physical, psychical, or spirituo-mechanical. The symbol deals with things far beyond the deepest region whence symbols can be drawn. The indwelling of Jesus in the soul of man, who shall declare![130]

The symbol of the mirror is limited in its ability to capture the idea that Christ dwells in the believer by his Spirit and that somehow the believer is transformed into his likeness. And yet, by systematically exploring the symbol's field of meaning MacDonald seeks to come closer to the mystery of which Paul speaks.[131] It is the task of the theologian, according to

---

129. Ibid., 448.

130. Ibid., 455–56. See some of the many other places where MacDonald speaks of the limitations of language in regard to the theological discourse: George MacDonald, *Unspoken Sermons*, 23, 116, 163, 164, 377, 454–57; idem, *Orts*, 194. It is quite impossible for Diamond to describe what he sees when he is taken up by North Wind in *At the Back of the North Wind*. See esp. ch. 6. Mr. Vane in *Lilith* feels equally inhibited to talk about his experiences in the world of the seven dimensions. George MacDonald, *First and Final*, 74.

131. MacDonald explores the meaning of this symbol in a variety of ways, drawing from both 1 Cor 13:9–13 and 2 Cor 3:18. The mirror plays a significant role in

MacDonald, to recognize that the most appropriate ways to speak about God are the revealed and thus "given" scriptural symbols and figures taken from nature and human customs and to explore these symbols in a logical manner. The biblical writers are our prime examples in using symbols to speak about that which cannot be captured in language at all. MacDonald argues:

> I use the word mysticism as representing a certain mode of embodying truth, common, in various degrees, to almost all, if not all, the writers of the New Testament . . . A mystical mind is one which, having perceived that the highest expression of which the truth admits, lies in the symbolism of nature and the human customs that result from human necessities, prosecutes thought about truth so embodied by dealing with the symbols themselves after logical forms. This is the highest mode of conveying the deepest truth; and the Lord himself often employed it, as, for instance, in the whole passage ending with the words, 'If therefore the light that is in thee be darkness, how great is the darkness!'[132]

Here his view of the symbol draws close to Soskice's view of metaphor: "Metaphor should be treated as fully cognitive and capable of saying that which may be said in no other way."[133] MacDonald warns the interpreter that any logical exploration of a symbol must not leave the symbol behind lest the original breath and depth of the symbol gets lost.[134] Symbols to MacDonald also have the capacity to awaken things in a person that underlie thought, and this dimension is not properly captured with a logical exploration of a symbol's field of meaning.

---

both *Phantastes* and *Lilith*. See Soto's introductory article on the role of the mirror in *Phantastes*. Soto, "Mirrors," 27–47.

132. George MacDonald, *Unspoken Sermons*, 67, 376.

133. Soskice, *Metaphor*, 44. This is in contrast to McGillis, for example, who argues that MacDonald understands symbols in contrast to logic and the intellect. McGillis bases his view on a misquoted passage where MacDonald addresses the danger of logic leaving behind poetry. McGillis concludes from this that for MacDonald poetry leaves logic behind. This conclusion is, however, a complete misunderstanding of MacDonald's point here. He does not espouse an emotive theory of the symbol but recognizes that the symbol does not just address the intellect of a person. See George MacDonald, *England's Antiphon*, 232; McGillis, "Fantastic Imagination," 93.

134. George MacDonald, *England's Antiphon*, 232.

The Necessity of Variety in Symbols

Considering the fact that all symbols fall short of capturing the spiritual reality and inevitably fall even shorter to capture the infinite reality they seek to depict, MacDonald further argues that it is necessary to employ a whole range of symbols to approach the mystery they seek to convey. Because symbols only reveal in part, they hide certain other aspects of the reality of which they seek to speak, and it is of importance that one will not stay with just one symbol.[135] Once more MacDonald uses Jesus as his example to demonstrate this point. In his sermon called "The Salt and the Light of the World," MacDonald shows how Jesus employs a whole range of symbols such as salt, light, and the lamp to speak about the role of his disciples in the world. Taking each symbol as far as it will serve him, Jesus supplements them with others.[136] In order to picture Christ and what it means to follow him, one needs endless and sometimes even opposing symbols such as God as a door, a shepherd, the way, and a rock to approach this great mystery.[137] MacDonald expresses this dynamic in a more poetic image in "The Golden Key." Tangle, at the end of her long journey to the country where the shadows fall, encounters a child playing with balls:

> He was playing with balls of various colours and sizes, which he disposed in strange figures upon the floor beside him. And now Tangle felt that there was something in her knowledge which was not in her understanding. For she knew there must be an infinite meaning in the change and sequence and individual forms of the figures into which the child arranged the balls. Flashes of meaning would now pass from them to Tangle, and now again all would be not merely obscure, but utterly dark . . . For seven years she had stood there watching the naked child with his coloured balls, and it seemed to her like seven hours, when all at once the shape the balls took, she knew not why, reminded her of the Valley of Shadows . . .[138]

MacDonald, borrowing the imagery of the balls from Novalis, stresses that it is by contemplating the great variety of symbols used in Scripture

---

135. Ibid., 187. See also Flynn and Edwards, *Pulpit*, 66–67.

136. George MacDonald, *Hope/Miracles*, 163–64.

137. George MacDonald, *Unspoken Sermons*, 363. MacDonald does not explain in what way such symbols are opposing one another, but what is important for our discussion here is that these symbols depict rather different aspects of the nature of God.

138. George MacDonald, *Fairytales*, 139–40.

that one is able to penetrate deeper into the knowledge of God.[139] The story continues with the child telling Tangle to follow the serpent who shows her the way, and one of the last things we know of Tangle is that she sits in a hall with seven columns that have the color of the rainbow, reminding one of Prov 9:1 where Wisdom's feast is celebrated: "Wisdom has built her house, she has hewn her seven pillars." Tangle, by contemplating the great variety of symbols (balls) used by the child, has entered the hall of wisdom.[140]

Jesus, Correspondence, and the Tension between Similarity and Dissimilarity

As mentioned above, for MacDonald there exists a deep correspondence between the finite and the infinite world. God placed these correspondences there when he created the world, and Jesus now reveals them in his proclamation of the Kingdom of God. Just as the Matthean Jesus proclaims "I will open my mouth in parable, I will utter things hidden since the creation of the world" (Matt 13:35, quoting Ps 78:2), so does MacDonald see Jesus uncovering and revealing correspondences between the physical and infinite, thereby revealing the Father and his Kingdom. By taking images from creation and applying them symbolically to speak about his Father's business, Jesus is the ultimate poet. It is by embracing Jesus in faith that we can also embrace his words and the correspondences he reveals in faith.[141] MacDonald exclaims: "Great poet-king, I thank thee for the word."[142]

MacDonald carefully discusses Jesus' use of symbols to speak about the Kingdom of God. The symbol of water is one important example. In his sermon called "The Truth," he shows how both the Jewish wisdom tradition and Jesus use the symbol of water to speak about spiritual thirst. There exists a deep correspondence between the physical reality of water and its ability to quench a person's thirst and the spiritual reality of God and his ability to quench a person's spiritual longing. A scientific

---

139. MacDonald explicitly mentions that he has borrowed the "geometrical figures" of the balls from Novalis. Novalis uses the symbol of the balls in *Hymns to the Night* as well as his fragments. See Novalis, *Novalis*, 1:150; ibid., 2:91, 101.

140. The connection to Proverbs was first made by Aiura, "Recurring Symbols," 31.

141. See here his sermon "The Higher Faith" in George MacDonald, *Unspoken Sermons*, 34–44.

142. George MacDonald, *Rampolli* (March 19), 209.

understanding of water will never do to discover its deepest meaning. MacDonald explains:

> Is it for the sake of the fact that hydrogen and oxygen combined form water, that the precious thing exists? Or has God put the two together only that man might separate and find them out? He allows his child to pull his toys to pieces; but were they made that he might pull them to pieces? . . . There is no water in oxygen, no water in hydrogen: it comes bubbling fresh from the imagination of the living God, rushing from under the great white throne of the glacier. The very thought of it makes one gasp with an elemental joy no metaphysician can analyze. The water itself, that dances, and sings, and slakes the wonderful thirst—symbol and picture of that draught for which the woman of Samaria made her prayer to Jesus—this lovely thing itself, whose very wetness is a delight to every inch of the human body in its embrace—this live thing which, if I might, I would have running through my room,[143] yea, babbling along my table—this water is its own self its own truth, and is therein a truth of God. Let him who would know the love of the maker, become sorely athirst, and drink of the brook by the way—then lift up his heart—not at that moment to the maker of oxygen and hydrogen, but to the inventor and mediator of thirst and water, that man might foresee a little of what his soul may find in God. If he becomes not then as a hart panting for the waterbrooks, o let him go back to his science . . .[144]

There is a deep correspondence between the physical and spiritual, and it is only by the visible that we are able to speak about the invisible. To miss the spiritual dimension of creation as revealed by Christ is to give way to a reduced and merely scientific view of the world, void of wonder and awe for the creator. MacDonald discusses many other symbols of Jesus like the father, salt, light, and darkness. In all of them he detects a likeness that Jesus reveals by choosing them to speak about his Father's business.

---

143. MacDonald uses that very image of water running through the room in *Phantastes*, where Anodos suddenly discovers water running from his basin through his room. George MacDonald, *Phantastes*, 9.

144. George MacDonald, *Unspoken Sermons*, 469. MacDonald's scriptural references here are to Ps 42 and John 4. The symbol of water, like the mirror, is explored throughout MacDonald's work; *Phantastes* and *Lilith* are yet again two primary examples.

Similarity, Dissimilarity, and the Advancement of Understanding

Similarity between the vehicle and the tenor is not the only aspect that MacDonald recognizes in the function of the symbol. He realizes that there is tension involved in using certain kind of symbols. With some symbols, the recognition of similarity is more difficult as the correspondence must be discerned between things that seem dissimilar at first sight. This is true for many symbols, but with some symbols the dissimilarity seems greater than with others. MacDonald recognizes that Jesus uses some symbols in a variety of ways that seem to contradict one another, as with the symbol of the leaven. It is used in the parable of the leaven to speak positively about how the Kingdom of God advances. Elsewhere, however, it is used by Jesus to warn the disciples about his opponents, the Pharisees and Herod, and is therefore associated with sin.[145] The expected and natural correspondence breaks down. It is here that MacDonald draws out an aspect of the symbol that is quite familiar to our discussion of metaphor.

MacDonald points out in Paul's use of the symbol of the mirror in 2 Cor 3:18 that Paul had to discover "the same principle in things that look unlike; to embody things discovered, in forms and symbols heretofore unused, and so present to other minds the deeper truths to which those forms and symbols owe their being."[146] By placing the idea of mirroring into interaction with the idea of God dwelling and transforming a person, Paul is able to push further into the reality of God's transformative presence in the believer. By arranging a thought and symbol in a way as it has never been done before, new understanding is brought to the fore.[147] MacDonald makes a similar argument for the way the author of Hebrews re-uses the OT symbol of God as the "consuming fire" to advance our understanding of God's purifying presence in the world.[148] Like Soskice, then, MacDonald emphasizes that symbols are often active in advancing

---

145. Ibid., 205–6. See also idem, *Paul Faber,* 215.

146. George MacDonald, *Unspoken Sermons,* 448. See also idem, *Phantastes,* 75–76, where he describes the symbolic process as follows: "[C]ombine two propositions, both apparently true, either at once or in different remembered moods, and to find the point in which their invisibly converging lines would unite in one, revealing a truth higher than either and differing from both."

147. George MacDonald, *Orts,* 21. Prickett argues similarly in "Two Worlds," 27–28.

148. George MacDonald, *Unspoken Sermons,* 22.

one's understanding of the subject matter of which they seek to speak. While MacDonald does not discuss the tension between similarity and dissimilarity in any detail, his varied use of symbols shows that he is quite aware of this dynamic. He employs many symbols, where the primary intention is to show the similarity. He also uses, however, a significant number of symbols where the tension between similarity and dissimilarity is of primary importance, thereby creating a sense of surprise.

The symbol of the serpent in "The Golden Key" (1866), briefly mentioned above, will be a helpful example to demonstrate MacDonald's use of subversive symbols. The predominant theological idea connected with the serpent is that of Genesis, which portrays the serpent as the tempter and devil. MacDonald's own traditional Calvinist background and context with its heavy emphasis on the utter depravity of humanity and sin in general would most likely connect the serpent with temptation and sin. MacDonald, however, uses the serpent in a positive manner in "The Golden Key" and later also *Lilith*. The serpent, in Genesis portrayed as leading Eve and Adam astray, now shows Tangle the right way, and she is explicitly told to trust and follow the serpent.[149] The tension between similarity and dissimilarity is much stronger here than in many other symbols that MacDonald employs and reminds one of the dynamic of the Parable of the Leaven discussed in chapter 2. MacDonald, like Jesus, subverts traditional values by using conventional imagery in an unconventional way. What appears as bad and sinful might actually prove to be instrumental in leading one on the right path. MacDonald was not coy in disturbing traditional Victorian sensibilities. The use of subversive symbols serves MacDonald to challenge convention and draw his audience

---

149. Ibid., 141. A similar dynamic is happening in *Lilith* where "the worm-thing . . . white-hot, vivid as incandescent silver, the live heart of essential fire" (a snake), creeps out of the fire and enters Lilith's body to purify her: "[T]he creature had passed in by the centre of the black spot, and was piercing through the joints and marrow to the thoughts and intents of the heart" (George MacDonald, *First and Final*, 317). The citation of Heb 4:12 in this passage associates the snake with the word of God. The dynamic here is therefore similar to that of the leaven. Like the leaven, the serpent was primarily associated with sin in the Bible, but not always. In Num 21:8 God commands Moses to lift up a bronze serpent which has healing powers. The Matthean Jesus also uses the serpent in a positive manner when he tells his disciples to be wise as serpents (Matt 10:16). See Aiura, "Recurring Symbols," 32. Aiura also recognizes the subversive use of imagery here. See Erskine, *The Brazen Serpent* (1831) for another example of the positive use of the serpent imagery in a theological context. MacDonald shows this awareness and appreciation of tension in symbols in George MacDonald, *England's Antiphon*, 243.

back to the heart of the gospel message. *Lilith*, as we shall see, cannot be understood apart from this subversive approach to the symbol.

The Loss of Vitality in Symbols and the Need to Recover Vitality

MacDonald was well aware of the fact that while symbols have this ability to reveal and advance understanding, they can also lose this capacity due to commonness of use. Similarly to our discussion of the relationship between metaphor and literal language, he recognizes that words are "live" things and can change their function and be employed to various ends.[150] Once a symbol has been used regularly for a certain purpose, it ceases to be heard as a symbol and becomes literal language. MacDonald writes:

> All words, then, belonging to the inner world of the mind . . . are originally poetic words. The better, however, any such word is fitted for the needs of humanity, the sooner it loses its poetic aspect by commonness of use. It ceases to be heard as a symbol, and appears only as a sign. Thus thousands of words, which were originally poetic words owing their existence to the imagination, lose their vitality, and harden into mummies of prose.[151]

There is a profound understanding here that language is not static but a living reality, dependent upon contextual use. Language can lose its revelatory power. It is the poet's task to recognize this dynamic and recover the depth of meaning first expressed by a symbol.[152] We can see in MacDonald's work, especially in his sermons, a continual effort to understand and recover the symbolic meaning of what now appears only as a sign, such as Paul's use of the mirror, the consuming fire of Hebrews, or Jesus' employment of the symbol of the leaven. This in turn serves MacDonald as the

---

150. George MacDonald, *Orts*, 318.

151. Ibid., 9. This understanding of language MacDonald borrowed from English Romanticism. The influence of Coleridge on MacDonald's understanding of language should not be missed here: "For if words are not THINGS, they are LIVING POWERS by which the things of most importance to mankind are actuated, combined and harmonized." Samuel Taylor Coleridge, *Aids to Reflection*, xvii quoted in Prickett, *Words*, 201–2.

152. See here MacDonald's discussion of Shakespeare, who is an important example for MacDonald of a poet who recovered vitality for scriptural passages that had lost their power due to commonness of use. George MacDonald, *Orts*, 81–83. See also Flynn and Edwards, *Pulpit*, 27–28. Here he speaks of the problem of over-familiarity as the "crust of custom."

foundation for continuing in this tradition, finding new or recovering old symbols by placing them into strange contexts so that they might continue to serve as means of revelation. God's consuming fire finds a new context in *The Princess and Curdie* where Curdie has to put his hands into the fire of flaming roses. In *Lilith* the serpent comes out of the fire and enters Lilith's body to probe her thoughts. MacDonald employs the symbol of the mirror in *Phantastes* and *Lilith*, which resembles but is also different from Paul's employment of the symbol of the mirror. The symbols of the king, father, son, daughter, princess, light, darkness, water, bread and wine, the mountain and the ladder, and upward and downward movement for spiritual development are a few more examples of MacDonald's attempt to recover old symbols primarily taken from Scripture.[153]

While being the editor of *Good Words for the Young*, MacDonald is asked by an imagined reader why his stories are always about princesses. He writes:

> 'Because every little girl is a princess!'
> 'You will make them vain if you tell them that.'
> 'Not if they understand what I mean.'
> 'Then what do you mean?'
> 'What do you mean by a princess?'
> 'The daughter of a king.'
> 'Very well; then every little girl is a princess, and there would be no need to say anything about it, except that she is always in danger of forgetting about her rank, and behaving as if she had grown out of the mud. I have seen little princesses behave like the children of thieves and lying beggars, and that is why they need to be told they are princesses. And that is why, when I tell a story of this kind, I like to tell it about a princess. Then I can say better what I mean, because I can give her every beautiful thing I want her to have.'[154]

The symbol of the princess becomes a means by which MacDonald seeks to re-echo the idea that we are children of God and are called to live in light of our identity in God.

It seems that it was MacDonald's life-long effort to convert "mummies of prose" into new forms so as to recover and thereby continue the Jesus

---

153. See Airua's careful discussion of MacDonald's recurring use of the symbol of water, fire, moon, lights, fire, symbols of height and depth in Aiura, "Recurring Symbols," 80–128.

154. George MacDonald, "Goblin," 1.

tradition of revealing the Father in surprising ways. For MacDonald "The echoes of the word of truth gather volume and richness from every soul that re-echoes it to brother and sister souls."[155] This re-echoing, as he puts it, is the work of the poet as he has to find new images from creation and use them symbolically to speak about these old truths. MacDonald writes:

> Is not this a new form to the thought—a form which makes us feel the truth afresh? And every new embodiment of a known truth must be a new and wider revelation. No man is capable of seeing for himself the whole of any truth: he needs it echoed back to him from every soul in the universe; and still its centre is hid in the Father of Lights.[156]

MacDonald sees the need to "re-echo" the symbols with which we have grown too familiar and have therefore ceased to function as a symbol. He emphasizes that this capacity to make such connections comes from an imaginative engagement with the world. MacDonald argues that "it is the working of poetic imagination divinely alive, whose part is to foresee and welcome approaching truth."[157] It is no surprise, then, that for MacDonald the imagination also plays a central role in this recasting of scriptural truth.

Considering MacDonald's belief that the symbols of Scripture need to be re-echoed for new generations in order capture their original depth of meaning, he seems to imply that poetry and stories that do re-echo scriptural truth also serve as means of revelation. In a letter to his father, MacDonald writes: "The life, thoughts, deeds, aims, believes of Jesus have to be fresh expounded every age."[158] Good poetry, he argues elsewhere, "makes us feel afresh the truth which . . . [it] sets forth anew. In them some of the facts of our Lord's life and teaching look out upon us as from clear windows of the past."[159] It is in *England's Antiphon*, MacDonald's survey of and commentary on English religious poetry, that he seems to set forth an understanding of poetry, which suggests that somehow poetry is "revelatory" in a similar way to Scripture. Reed-Nancarrow even argues that MacDonald here demonstrates his belief in "progressive revelation."[160] MacDonald introduces the book as follows:

155. MacDonald, *Orts*, 21.
156. Ibid., 22. See MacDonald's praise of Shakespeare as such a poet in ibid., 79ff.
157. George MacDonald, *Unspoken Sermons*, 448. See also idem, *Orts*, 22.
158. Greville MacDonald, *MacDonald and Wife*, 185.
159. George MacDonald, *England's Antiphon*, 240.
160. Reed-Nancarrow, "Remythologizing," 43.

> In the worship of [Jesus] a thousand truths are working, unknown and yet active, which, embodied in theory, and dissociated from the living mind that was in Christ, will as certainly breed worms as any omer of hoarded manna. Holding the skirt of his garment in one hand, we shall in the other hold the key to all the treasures of wisdom and knowledge.[161]

These comments suggest that MacDonald understands poetry ("the key to all treasures") in close proximity to the revelatory nature of Scripture. He praises George Herbert, for example, as a poet who serves to express truth and brings forth revelation:

> [T]he nature of things . . . demanded of a poet . . . [are] Truth, Revelation—George Herbert offers us measure pressed down and running over . . . The heart of poetry is indeed truth, but its garments are music, and the garments come first in the process of revelation . . . The music goes before the fuller revelation, preparing the way.[162]

This ongoing process of "re-echoing" and "revealing" truth in poetry raises the question of what place it has in relation to Scripture. Can we dispose of Scripture once we have found new ways of expressing old truths? In what relation do these "new revelations" stand to God's revelation in Scripture? We shall discuss the role of Scripture following our discussion of allegory, to which will now turn.

Allegory and How it Differs from the Symbol

For MacDonald the allegorical mode has an important place in literature but must be seen as one among a variety of literary modes and should not be employed excessively.[163] MacDonald values Dante's *Divine Comedy* and

---

161. George MacDonald, *England's Antiphon*, 6

162. Ibid., 174–75. MacDonald describes Milton's poetry similarly. In his poetry Milton "calls upon Voice and Verse to rouse and raise our imagination until we hear the choral song of heaven, and hearing become able to sing in tuneful response," ibid., 199. See also ibid., 223.

163. Ibid., 54. Because allegory was often looked down upon in his time, MacDonald refers to his more allegorical stories as parables, and when discussing MacDonald's understanding of the parables of Jesus one must differentiate between his comments on allegory and when he actually speaks about parables of Jesus. See idem, *Adela Cathcart*, 427: "[O]ur host then read the following parable, as he called it, though I daresay it would be more correct to call it an allegory. But as that word has so many wearisome associations, I, too intend, whether right or wrong, to call it a parable."

Bunyan's *Pilgrim's Progress* greatly, and he employs the allegorical mode to various degrees in his writings. He acknowledges that his fairytales have allegory in them, and he calls his short story "The Castle" an allegory.[164]

He insists, however, that his fairytales are not strict allegory and should therefore not be decoded like an allegory. He writes: "A fairytale is not an allegory. There may be allegory in it, but it is not an allegory. He must be an artist indeed who can, in any mode, produce a strict allegory that is not a weariness to the spirit. An allegory must be Mastery or Moorditch."[165] When discussing the transition from medieval miracle plays to morality plays in his study of English religious poetry, MacDonald sees a degeneration in the use of the allegorical mode. With the morality plays, and MacDonald mentions *The Castle of Perseverance* as an example, the allegorical correspondence is so high and moralistic that it has lost greatly in poetic expression.[166]

In his discussion of medieval literature in *England's Antiphon*, we find a few more comments that shed light on MacDonald's understanding of allegory. He discusses the medieval poem *The Pearl* and decodes its allegorical elements:

> The poem sets forth the grief and consolation of a father who has lost his daughter . . . The father calls himself a jeweller; the pearl is his daughter. He has lost the pearl in the grass; it has gone to the ground, and he cannot find it; that is, his daughter is dead and buried . . . The poet, who is surely the father himself, cannot always keep up the allegory . . . But the allegory helps him out with what he means notwithstanding.[167]

Consonant with our discussion in chapter 2, MacDonald understands allegory as a story with a set of elements that correspond to elements of the reality that it seeks to depict.

What then distinguishes the allegorical mode from the other symbolic modes that MacDonald employs so freely in his fairytales? In his essay "The Fantastic Imagination," he addresses this question in some detail. For MacDonald the difference lies in the control the author exerts upon the interpretation of a given symbol. With allegorical elements,

---

164. George MacDonald, *England's Antiphon*, 37, 54; idem, *Adela Cathcart*, 427.

165. George MacDonald, *Orts*, 317. This has not kept interpreters from decoding some of his fairytales. See here Marshall, "Allegory," 62. Another example here is Lewis' allegorical interpretation of *Lilith*. Hooper, *Letters*, 2:118–20.

166. George MacDonald, *England's Antiphon*, 54.

167. Ibid., 37.

the author's control on the meaning is high, and the correspondence is clear. With "symbol" the author exerts less control on its meaning, and the symbol is therefore more suggestive and open in nature.[168] Various aspect of the symbol will resonate with different readers. It evokes things within a person like music rather than giving the reader one specific idea like a geometrical figure would do.

MacDonald continues his argument by anticipating from his readers the question of polyvalence and arbitrariness of meaning in symbols. If symbols are so open and suggestive, can readers then not find in them whatever they want?[169] MacDonald recognizes this tension but insists that because God has made the world in such a way that it unveils layers and layers of meaning, the suggestive symbols of creation and human custom will always mean more than an author intended precisely because he is finally not the author but only the finder of such symbols. MacDonald writes:

> A genuine work of art must mean many things . . . One difference between God's work and man's is, that, while God's work cannot mean more than he meant, man's must mean more than he meant. For in everything that God has made, there is layer upon layer of ascending significance . . . it is God's things, his embodied thoughts, which alone a man has to use, modified and adapted to his own purposes, for the expression of his thoughts; therefore he cannot help his words and figures falling into such combination in the mind of another as he had himself not foreseen.[170]

We must note here that MacDonald does not argue for arbitrary meaning in symbols but links the suggestive nature of the symbol and its ability to waken various things in different readers back to God the creator who put certain correspondences into his creation. What might be revealed through a person's employment of his symbols is not in the complete control of the author precisely because he is not the author but only finder of these symbols. Having discussed MacDonald's understanding of the symbol and allegory, we shall now briefly discuss his understanding of Scripture before turning to his understanding of the parabolic.

168. George MacDonald, *Orts*, 320. See Prickett, who argues similarly in *Victorian Fantasy*, 159.

169. George MacDonald, *Orts*, 320.

170. Ibid., 317, 320. It is noteworthy that he makes the exact same argument in his earlier essay on the imagination. See Ibid., 5, 20.

George MacDonald's Understanding of Scripture and Its Role within the Revelatory Process

Like Coleridge, George MacDonald's understanding of Scripture is formed against the notion of verbal inspiration and the infallibility of Scripture. It is worthwhile quoting MacDonald here at some length in order to get a sense for both the Victorian context and MacDonald's response to it. In a letter MacDonald writes quite dramatically:

> The Bible is to me the most precious *thing* in the world, because it tells me his story . . . *But the common theory of the inspiration of the words, instead of the breathing of God's truth into the hearts and souls of those who wrote it, and who then did their best with it, is degrading and evil*; and they who hold it are in danger of worshipping the letter instead of living in the Spirit, of being idolaters of the Bible instead of disciples of Jesus . . . It is Jesus who is the Revelation of God, not the Bible; that is but a means to a mighty eternal end. The book is indeed sent us by God, but it nowhere claims to be his very word. If it were—and it would be no irreverence to say it—it would have been a good deal better written. Yet even its errors and blunders do not touch the truth, and are the merest trifles-dear as the little spot of earth on the whiteness of the snowdrop. Jesus alone is The Word of God.[171]

As we have shown above, MacDonald reiterates throughout his work that the truth can only be found in Jesus Christ. He emphasizes this point more strongly than Coleridge. While the Bible plays a significant role in how God reveals himself, for MacDonald the Bible per se is not revelation. It guides us to the truth but it can never encompass the truth. We quote MacDonald once more:

> Sad, indeed, would the whole matter be, if the Bible had told us *everything* God meant us to believe. But herein is the Bible itself greatly wronged. It nowhere lays claim to be regarded as *the* Word, *the* Way, *the* Truth. The Bible leads us to Jesus, the inexhaustible, the ever unfolding Revelation of God. It is Christ 'in whom are hid all the treasures of wisdom and knowledge,' not the Bible, save as leading to him.[172]

---

171. George MacDonald in a letter to an unnamed lady quoted in MacDonald, *MacDonald and Wife*, 373. See also idem, *Unspoken Sermons*, 435. Here he discusses the danger of "word-worship" in more detail.

172. George MacDonald, *Unspoken Sermons*, 36–37.

MacDonald's view of the Bible is in line with his understanding of language in general. Language and symbols can never encompass the truth. While they reveal in part, they also hide other aspects of the reality of which they seek to speak.[173] The Bible, as a series of words and symbols, can never be exhaustive in things pertaining to God, and to expect the Bible to contain all truth is to do it great harm and misunderstand its place within God's revelation in Christ.

MacDonald, like Coleridge, understands truth and God's revelation in Christ fundamentally in personal and relational terms. While he would certainly affirm that God's revelation can be grasped cognitively, a merely intellectual and rational approach is insufficient and distorts the nature of what truth in Christ means. "Intellectual greed," as MacDonald calls it at some point, is in danger of eclipsing a relational understanding of truth and its demand for participation and transformation into Christ-likeness.[174] The role of the Bible is therefore not only to lead into a better intellectual understanding of Christ but also to move the reader to partake and practice that which is revealed.[175] This emphasis on knowing and living the truth is woven throughout his *Unspoken Sermons* and is closely linked to his understanding of revelation and the role of Scripture therein. It is Christ's congruency in speaking and living his words that is to be the believer's model. God's revelation in Christ is not a system or theological concepts to be mastered; it is a person to be encountered and a life to be modeled after. MacDonald points out Jesus' parables in particular as a means by which the hearer is not merely informed intellectually but challenged to practice that which is revealed by them.[176] With Coleridge, then, MacDonald would affirm that Scripture serves to make people "into friends of God," but unlike Coleridge, MacDonald does not seek to find a proof for Scripture's divine authority in human experience. We cannot have proof of God or Scripture's divine authority. Both Christ and Scripture have to be received in faith.[177]

---

173. Flynn and Edwards, *Pulpit*, 66–67.

174. George MacDonald, *Orts*, 322; idem, *Unspoken Sermons*, 259–60; Flynn and Edwards, *Pulpit*, 144–45, 148, 156.

175. George MacDonald, *Unspoken Sermons*, 67–69; see also 79–80, 371, 403, 449.

176. Ibid., 259.

177. Flynn and Edwards, *Pulpit*, 66–67, 71. MacDonald devotes a whole sermon on Heb 11:1 and the significance of faith in things pertaining to God.

Revealed Symbols as Trajectories

MacDonald believes that Scripture is given by God and therefore has divine authority, but he does not believe Scripture to be infallible. He does uphold that the biblical writers were inspired as they pondered and wrote down what they saw and heard.[178] MacDonald, like Coleridge, seeks to hold the divine and human side of Scripture in tension. This is not only true for its divine/human authorship but also for how Scripture employs symbols from nature and human custom to speak about God.

Scripture contains symbols, and MacDonald's interpretation of biblical passages is often concerned to probe the field of meaning of a given symbol and its limits, followed by theological reflections about the symbol's significance for understanding the nature of God and his Kingdom.[179] In his sermon "The Consuming Fire," based on Heb 12:29, MacDonald traces the usage of the symbol of "fire" and "consuming fire" in the OT and NT. He recognizes that the author of Hebrews builds on the OT usage and employs an old symbol in a new context, thereby advancing our understanding of how God works in this world.[180] What is significant in his discussion of the re-employment or re-echoing of this symbol within the Bible is that for MacDonald the biblical symbols must not be superseded but only be unfolded.[181] They serve as trajectories on which an interpreter can continue to unfold its meaning for new generations. For MacDonald, then, the Bible plays a pivotal role in revelation, as Scripture is the foundation upon which theological reflection must be built.

Similar to Coleridge, however, there is still a certain amount of ambiguity left as to how the Bible differs from other writings such as Shakespeare, for example, whom MacDonald held in great esteem. It is helpful to realize that one important reason why Shakespeare is so important for MacDonald can be found in Shakespeare's creative reflection upon biblical texts and images. After discussing several passages in Shakespeare's

---

178. See his discussion on the Gospel of John. Just because this Gospel is later and shows forth a greater degree of reflection upon the tradition does not mean for MacDonald that it is less accurate. George MacDonald, *Unspoken Sermons*, 435.

179. A few examples are his sermons "The New Name," "The Mirrors of the Lord," and "Abba, Father!" in his *Unspoken Sermons*. For a similar approach in NT studies see Hans Joachim Klauck who implements his understanding of metaphor in a similar way in his exegesis of the Marcan parables and metaphors. Klauck, *Allegorie*. See especially part D.

180. George MacDonald, *Unspoken Sermons*, 22.

181. Ibid., 25.

works that resonate with biblical texts, MacDonald comments on Shakespeare's ability to reinvest with vitality biblical passages with which his audience was all too familiar and which had lost their impact due to commonness of use. MacDonald writes:

> What is remarkable in the employment of these [biblical] passages, is not merely that they are so present to his mind that they come up for use in the most exciting moments of composition, but that he embodies the spirit of them in such a new form as reveals to mind saturated and deadened with the *sound* of the words, the very visual image and spiritual meaning involved in them.[182]

Not only does MacDonald here betray his concern for the centrality of Scripture in evaluating other literature but also the high value he places on a writer's ability to reinvest vitality into Scriptural truth that has been dulled by over-familiarity. He is particularly aware that Shakespeare reflects upon various biblical passages without using the words of Scripture themselves, thereby giving a fresh vision of an old truth, and he concludes that Shakespeare's "mode of writing historical plays is more after the fashion of the Bible histories than that of most writers of history."[183] For MacDonald, then, Shakespeare was an important model as he reflected theologically on biblical texts in his plays.

It is clear from this discussion that for MacDonald, Scripture plays a pivotal and indispensable role in leading to Christ, who is the only true revelation of the Father. His repeated insistence betrays his commitment to the Bible as a central means by which God reveals himself. MacDonald writes:

> The one use of the Bible is to make us look at Jesus, that through him we might know his Father and our Father, his God and our God. Till we thus know Him let us hold the Bible as the moon of our darkness, by which we travel towards the east; not dear as the sun whence her light cometh, and towards which we haste, that, walking in the sun himself, we may no more need the mirror that reflected his absent brightness.[184]

---

182. George MacDonald, *Orts*, 81.

183. Ibid., 83.

184. George MacDonald, *Unspoken Sermons*, 37. The imagery reminds one of Ps 119:105, where God's word is described as a light onto one's path.

The symbolism of Scripture, then, cannot be superseded but must always be unfolded for new generations so as to discover its meaning anew. The fact that MacDonald gives Scripture and the symbols used therein a central place in his writing betrays his attitude towards and anchorage in the Bible as given by God.

It is no surprise, then, that MacDonald not only prefers the symbols of creation and basic human custom to what he calls "man-made" symbols but also relegates man-made symbols to a lower level of revelation. He argues: "It is the temple of nature and not the temple of the church, the things made by the hands of God and not the things made by the hands of man, that afford the truest symbols of truth."[185] While this preference for "natural" symbols raises the questions of the relative value of such man-made symbols as the temple, the altar, and the pulpit, for example, MacDonald finds the theological basis for such a strict differentiation in Jesus' life and proclamation:

> What was his place of prayer? Not the temple, but the mountain top. Where does he find symbols whereby to speak of what goes on in the mind and before the face of his father in heaven? Not in the temple; not in its rites; not on its altars; not in its holy of holies; he finds them in the world and its lovely—lowly facts; on the roadside, in the field, in the vineyard, in the garden, in the house; in the family, and the commonest of its affairs—the lighting of the lamp, the leavening of the meal, the neighbour's borrowing, the losing of the coin, the straying of the sheep. Even in the unlovely facts also of the world which he turns to holy use, such as the unjust judge, the false steward, the faithless labourers, he ignores the temple.[186]

It is to Jesus' parables that MacDonald turns to discuss the nature of the truest symbols. The symbolic use of images from creation is not only

---

185. George MacDonald, *England's Antiphon*, 187. MacDonald criticizes George Herbert for using too many "artificial" symbols. MacDonald recognizes that the cross is not a natural symbol, but he argues the symbol of the cross is first of all not a symbol of a truth but of a historical fact, which is the outcome of the greatest truth. Rolland Hein has shown MacDonald's preferred use of natural symbols in his adult novels and how these function as means of revelation. Hein, *Harmony*, 46–47. See also Ankeny, *Story*, 36, 41–42. She discusses MacDonald's use of natural symbols in *Sir Gibbie* and *At the Back of the North Wind*. Swiatecka argued that MacDonald primarily uses the term "symbol" for the symbols of nature, the Bible, and the sacraments of the Eucharist and Baptism. Swiatecka, *Symbol*, 165.

186. George MacDonald, *Hope/Miracles*, 53.

central but indispensable in MacDonald's understanding of how Jesus reveals himself and explores more profoundly the mystery of God's Kingdom. Jesus' parables are a primary example of how this happens. It is to MacDonald's understanding of the parabolic that we must now turn, having outlined both MacDonald's Christological understanding of revelation and the role of symbols and Scripture therein.

George MacDonald's Understanding of the Parabolic as a Literary Space for Revelation and Spiritual Formation

MacDonald's symbolic understanding of Scripture always places Scripture in the context of Jesus, who reveals the Father in and through the language taken from creation. In considering MacDonald's understanding of the "parabolic," we must keep in mind this relational understanding of Revelation. Scripture, including the parabolic, serves this main purpose: to reveal Christ and his kingdom and somehow move the reader/hearer into a deeper understanding of it. But how does one come to a deeper understanding of the truth that is found in the person of Jesus Christ? MacDonald saw story as a profound way by which one could come to know Christ more fully, and he developed a decidedly theological understanding of story and the "parabolic" in particular. The purpose of his fiction was not mere entertainment or illustration of spiritual truth. Rather, his pastoral concern in writing Christian fiction focused on the spiritual formation of his literary audience.

While MacDonald's stories are quite different from the parables of Jesus in some ways, there are important strands in his fiction that bear striking similarities to the way Jesus taught his disciples in and through parables. In what follows we seeks to trace this "parabolic" dimension of his writing.

As we have suggested earlier, MacDonald is not a systematic thinker, and his understanding of the "parabolic" is much more fluid than our definition provided in chapter 2. Nor does he use terms like "symbol" or "parable" in a systematic fashion.[187] Many of his comments about story, fairytales, the imagination, and language are relevant for his understanding of the "parabolic" and will therefore be drawn into our discussion here.

---

187. Sometimes he even uses the term to speak about allegory. See his comments on this in George MacDonald, *Adela Cathcart*, 187, 427.

The "Parabolic" and Participation

MacDonald's understanding of story and the "parabolic" in particular is profoundly participatory. His fiction exists to draw the reader into the story, make the reader/hearer part of the story, and transform the reader. How does that happen? Literal language, called by MacDonald "mummies of prose," has lost the ability to reveal because of common usage and over-familiarity. Literal language has a way of washing over people without touching them while poetic language works upon the reader in profound ways. For MacDonald all language relating to the immaterial conditions of humanity including emotional, mental, moral, and spiritual aspects of reality are originally poetic words with an intrinsic vitality, and they have a revelatory quality. They reveal insofar as they put us in touch with things beyond the material world. Once they have lost this revelatory quality due to commonness of use, they need to be reinvested with this original power to reveal aspects of our lives that are real but unseen. In creating fiction where old symbols are used in a surprising way, MacDonald sees the possibility of reawakening the reader to old truths, and in his case, Christian truth with which his Victorian audience was all too familiar but without power to transform their lives.

For MacDonald the way one uses words in such stories is also important. Words can be used in a more scientific manner, putting forth information, or they can be used like music, arranged carefully in order to impress and awake things within a person. Stories have the capacity to address a person on a deeper level than the mere intellect, what MacDonald calls "the power that underlies thoughts."[188] The meaning of these words is not easily reducible to one idea or fact and moves the reader much like music does. They impress the reader without being exact in its meaning and thereby invite the reader to be drawn in, to participate, to wonder, to think, and to become receptive. These kinds of symbols, poems, and parables demand participation in order to be understood properly.

MacDonald explains this dynamic quite well when he discusses the nature of parable in *Adela Cathcart*. This is a story about a young lady ridden with a deep melancholy, and it is through communal story telling

---

188. George MacDonald, *Orts*, 319, 320. C. S. Lewis, in his introduction to *Phantastes*, gives witness to this effect in MacDonald's own stories. When he first read *Phantastes*, he states that "[it] did nothing to my intellect . . . What it actually did to me was to convert, even to baptise . . . my imagination" (*Phantastes*, xi).

that she finds healing. In one of the story telling sessions, the company discusses the nature of parable:

> 'What do you mean by *a parable*, Mr. Henry?' interrupted Mrs. Cathcart...'
> 'I mean a picture in words, where more is meant than meets the ear...'
> 'Why not speak in plain words then?'
> 'Because a good parable is plainer than the plainest words. You remember what Tennyson says—that
> "truth embodied in a tale
> Shall enter in at lowly doors"?'
> 'Goethe,' said the curate, 'has a little parable about poems, which is equally true about parables—
> "Poems are painted window-panes.
> If one looks from the square into the church,
> Dusk and dimness are his gains—
> Sir Philistine is left in the lurch.
> The sight, so seen, may well enrage him,
> Nor any words hence forth assuage him.
> But come just inside what conceals;
> Cross the holy threshold quite—
> All at once, 'tis rainbow-bright;
> Device and story flash to light;
> A gracious splendour truth reveals.
> This, to God's children, is full measure;
> It edifies and gives them pleasure."'[189]

This seemingly casual conversation about parable reveals MacDonald's profound understanding of language and the parabolic in particular. First, in parable and poetic words that deal with the divine, the meaning (tenor) far exceeds the material and physical reality of the word employed (vehicle). Second, in parable "truth shall enter in at lowly doors." Parabolic speech is indirect, employing language that appears secular but has deeply Christian meaning. It confronts the reader not directly but indirectly. It hits us and speaks to us in unexpected ways: *parabolē*. Just before this dialogue on parable, Adela, the main character of the story, complains to Mr. Armstrong about his story telling: "It seemed to me that there was nothing Christian in the story. And I cannot help feeling that a clergyman might, therefore, have done better." Mr. Armstrong responds:

---

189. George MacDonald, *Adela Cathcart*, 272. MacDonald quotes this poem again in his discussion of Browning's "Christmas Eve" in idem, *Orts*, 195.

George MacDonald's Theological Rationale for Story and the "Parabolic"

"'I allow that in words there is nothing Christian,' answered Mr. Armstrong; . . . 'But I cannot allow that, in spirit and scope, it is anything other than Christian, or indeed anything but Christian. It seems to me that the whole might be used as a Christian parable.'"[190] The tension that is created by a clergyman telling a "secular" story causes the "patient" to wonder, to ask questions, to come alive, and to participate. This is the third point of MacDonald's discussion on parable. A parable invites the hearer/reader into its narrative, and only as one enters does the story "flash to light" and reveals its meaning to the hearer turned participant. True revelation only happens when one participates in the meaning of the story. Form and content are intricately intertwined in parable. They perform the pastoral and priestly function of inviting the hearer to enter imaginatively, participate, and embrace the "full measure" of the "gracious splendour" that is truth revealed and received as it is being pondered, grasped, and actively embraced.[191] Parable, for MacDonald, is sacred space, and its primary purpose is to move the hearer to become a faith-filled and faithful participant and encounter God in life-changing ways.

But why do parables only uncover their meaning as one participates? Why do symbols have this capacity to wake things up and work within a person in such a unique way? Symbols to MacDonald, as we discussed earlier, are open and suggestive in nature, and new connections are suggested by the symbol, but these connections have to be discerned by the hearer/reader. In this way symbols and consequently parables do not just inform about facts but demand a high level of engagement and in this address a person's moral and spiritual attitudes, seeking to bring about revelation and transformation. Both the fairytale and the parable have this possibility of revelation and transformation. MacDonald writes about the fairytale:

> A fairytale, a sonata, a gathering storm, a limitless night, seizes you and sweeps you away . . . To one, the cloudy rendezvous is a wild dance, with a terror at its heart; to another, a majestic march of heavenly hosts, with Truth in their centre pointing their course, but as yet restraining her voice. The greatest forces lie in the region of the uncomprehended. I will go farther.—The best thing you can do for your fellow, next to rousing his conscience, is—not

---

190. George MacDonald, *Adela Cathcart*, 270–71.
191. George MacDonald, *Orts*, 196–97.

to give him things to think about, but to wake things up that are in him; or say, to make him think things for himself.[192]

Why would a writer with such an important message as George MacDonald want to "restrain" the voice of truth in his stories? When one pilgrims through MacDonald's parabolic fiction, one cannot but stop and wonder what all these strange symbols ought to mean: how is the golden key of "The Golden Key" related to the keys that Peter receives in the Gospels (Matt 16:18)? It is a symbol for faith, and if so, what does having faith in God mean when one journeys through the wilderness? Why does Mossy hold the golden key and not Tangle? Why does a snake lead Tangle along the way and show her the path to wisdom when traditionally the snake stands for deceit and temptation? Why do rocks, water, and fire play such important roles in "the Golden Key"? Do they somehow speak of Christ as our rock, our living water, and our consuming fire? Why is Jesus not mentioned in the story? What do the symbols of the night and the day symbolize in "The Day Boy and the Night Girl," and how do they speak to us about the way we come to understand God and our Christian journey in this world? Why does George MacDonald create a fiction that centers around the theme of a cosmic funeral in *Lilith*? The posture that MacDonald seeks to create in his readers is that of wonder, of thinking for oneself, of reconsidering familiar ideas and symbols in a rather unfamiliar context, urging the reader to ask what these symbols might mean and how they might be connected to one another.

It is true, MacDonald demands a high level of engagement from his readers, and those who want to figure it all out and extract three spiritual laws shall be utterly frustrated by his stories. But does the call of Jesus to follow him not also demand a high level of personal engagement? The form of MacDonald's parabolic stories drives home this spiritual truth: the Christian faith calls for profound participation. MacDonald, in his use of symbols, defies "intellectual greed" and invites his readers to come with a posture of trust. His readers need to learn to enter and participate rather than control the meaning of the story by figuring out its exact and precise meaning. The reader is called upon to make connections and gain understanding whilst not being able to figure out the whole story and therefore remain in a posture of trust in the face of the unknown.

---

192. Ibid., 319.

It is within this context of the unique function of symbols and how they work upon the reader in transformative ways that one has to understand MacDonald's comment about Jesus' parables:

> There is a thing wonderful and admirable in the parables, not readily grasped, but specially indicated by the Lord himself—their unintelligibility to the mere intellect. They are addressed to the conscience and not the intellect . . . They are strong and direct but not definite. They are not meant to explain anything, but to rouse a man to the feeling, 'I am not what I ought to be, I do not the thing I ought to do!'[193]

Parables by the nature of their genre invite the hearer to participate. For MacDonald, however, parables demand participation in a dual sense. Participation in the narrative of the parable should lead to participation in that which is revealed about the Kingdom of God in the parable. Parables thus offer to MacDonald "a greater depth of expression" as Paula Elizabeth Reed-Nancarrow put it,[194] in that they seek to move the hearer/reader from the position of a spectator to active participation. MacDonald's pastoral concern in writing parabolic fiction is not to win the reader over by "logical conviction."[195] There is of course a place for this, but this is not his pastoral concern in writing parabolic stories. Rather, his concern is to move the reader to a deeper understanding of old and known truths by creating imaginative worlds in which the reader stumbles across familiar symbols in unfamiliar contexts and is thereby challenged to ponder them in new ways.

Shock Reinvested

The underlying assumption in MacDonald's thinking and writing in Christian fiction is that language is "living." He understands language as emerging out of Christ's created world, and he sees it as part of God's wider revelation in Christ. In this way MacDonald affirms the importance of

---

193. George MacDonald, *Unspoken Sermons*, 259. The turn to conscience as an important inward capacity for discerning moral responsibility, and behavior was an important aspect of nineteenth-century theology. See Horrocks, *Laws*, 168–70. Pelikan, *Doctrine*, 158–59, 186. Thus MacDonald distinguishes a merely intellectual knowledge of God from a knowledge that discerns and feels a responsibility to live out the moral demands pressed upon a person by the parables.

194. Reed-Nancarrow, "Remythologizing," 38.

195. George MacDonald, *Orts*, 321.

language and its ability to communicate/reveal, but he also recognizes its limitations. He does not locate truth in language per se; rather, he places its possibility for partaking in the revelatory process into a much larger context because for MacDonald language is limited in its ability to capture reality, especially spiritual truths.

And as we have discussed earlier, he also argues that language and symbols in particular can lose their vitality and their power to communicate. As a consequence language continually needs to be reinvested with the revelatory power that it once had. For him this loss of power is mainly due to commonness of use and therefore over-familiarity with the symbols.[196]

For this reason MacDonald understands his role as a writing pastor to be that of the poet: for every new generation the truth of Christ must be expressed in fresh ways so as to continue the revelatory power of the original symbols that Jesus employed. MacDonald's view of the language and the parabolic corresponds to our discussion of parable in chapter 2, where we sought to demonstrate that many parables lose their ability to communicate due to the reader's over-familiarity with the metaphors used and historical distance from the world to which they constantly refer. MacDonald recognizes this dynamic within the interpretive process, and as we have shown in our discussion of the symbol, it seems that it was MacDonald's life-long attempt to write parables, fairytales, poetry, and stories in which the symbols of the gospel would be rescued from their fate as "mummies of prose" and be reinvested with the vitality that they once had.

Shocking Revelations: Parables and Subversion

The recovery of "mummies of prose" finds expression in the nature of MacDonald's subversive writing. He reverses the common and familiar use of traditional themes and symbols in many of his stories, and this should be understood as part of his parabolic strategy. MacDonald employs subversive symbols, characters, and structures in his fairytales, fantasy stories, and his realistic fiction.[197] We have already discussed his

---

196. George MacDonald, *Unspoken Sermons*, 8–9.

197. John Pennington has devoted his entire PhD thesis to tracing subversive themes and structures in George MacDonald's fairytales and fantasies. Pennington, "Subversion." See also Airua's discussion of MacDonald's subversive use of symbols. Aiura, "Recurring Symbols," 80–128, esp. 120. Jack Zipes includes some of MacDonald's stories as an example of subversive fairytales. See Zipes, *Fairy Tales*, 97–133.

subversive structure in "The Light Princess." While we will discuss MacDonald's employment of subversive symbols in *Lilith* in some detail in the next chapter, it will be helpful here to give a few examples of MacDonald's subversive use of symbols and characters in order to demonstrate the importance of this literary strategy in his writing.

In the realistic novel *Sir Gibbie*, for example, it is the son of a drunkard who becomes the Good Samaritan, and it is Mr. Sclater, a Calvinist pastor, who is the self-righteous Christian. As mentioned before, in "The Golden Key" a snake, quite contrary to its traditional and strong association with the Fall in Genesis, leads onto the path of wisdom. In *Lilith* it is a snake that enters Lilith's body and seeks to bring healing. In *Salted with Fire* it is the young theology student James Blatherwick who seduces the innocent girl Isy and becomes the Prodigal Son. All these instances remind one of the theme of reversal in Jesus' parables.

An important reversal of imagery can also be seen in MacDonald's use of spatial symbols. Traditionally, upward movement is used to speak about spiritual progression while downward movement is used to speak about moral and spiritual decline. MacDonald himself uses these symbols in this way. The little princess Irene in *The Princess and the Goblins* has to ascend on long and windy stairs to enter the great-great-grandmother's chambers. Stairs play an important part in *Robert Falconer*, and Robert's spiritual growth is accompanied by images of his ascent of stairs and time spent in the garret. It is on top of the stairs that Robert meets Miss Mary St. John who becomes like God's hand to him. Mr. Vane in *Lilith* also has to ascend the stairs of his own house where he discovers a mirror in the garret that will eventually lead him into the world of the seven dimensions. The little boy Diamond in *At the Back of the North Wind* first encounters the lady North Wind in his little loft above the horse stable.[198]

It is in the story *At the Back of the North Wind* that we find a reversal of ideas as MacDonald uses spatial symbols subversively. Diamond, longing to see the beautiful lady North Wind again, dreams that he is looking for lady North Wind but cannot find her. The stars invite him to come up and Diamond asks:

> 'How can I come up?' shouted Diamond
> 'Go round the rose-bush. It's got its foot in it', said the first voice.

---

198. MacDonald plays with the symbols of upward and downward movement in many of his stories, such as "The Light Princess" and "The Golden Key."

> Diamond got up at once, and walked to the other side of the rose-bush.
> There he found what seemed the very opposite of what he wanted–a stair down into the earth. It was of turf and moss. It did not seem to promise well for getting into the sky, but Diamond had learned to look through the look of things.[199]

Diamond's spiritual progression is now expressed by a downward movement. The way forward is no longer the way upward but the way downward into the dark. As Diamond goes down the stairs, a stream is flowing upwards towards him. Thus Diamond, while descending, is also moving up a steam.[200] He who wants to go up must first go down.

This subversive use of spatial symbols is enhanced in this story by the ideas that MacDonald brings together in the person of North Wind. The icy and violent North Wind who sinks ships and chills people to the bone is also a beautiful, kind, and wise lady who shows Diamond the way.[201] While it is hard to pin down the identity of lady North Wind as she seems to serve multiple functions in the story, she does personify death. The personification of death was quite common in Victorian Britain, but it was done primarily in conjunction with negative images such as the horseman on the pale horse in Rev 6 or death as the son of Satan in Milton's *Paradise Lost*. The depiction of death as a skeleton stooping over the deathbed was also very popular.[202] William Blake depicts death more positively as a door in his engraving "Death's door," an image of which MacDonald was very fond.[203] Awareness of death was an all-pervading reality in Victorian times and more particularly in MacDonald's own life. By bringing into interaction the idea of the harsh reality of death with the beautiful and kind lady North Wind, MacDonald subverts Victorian sensibilities of seeing death as a destroyer or a mere stepping-stone to life beyond this world. For him death has a positive and even beautiful work to do in people's lives.[204] The

---

199. George MacDonald, *North Wind*, ch. 25, "Diamond's Dream," 244.

200. Ibid., 244.

201. Ibid., ch. 6.

202. A famous Victorian example is Punch's cartoon of the Hungry Forties entitled "The Poor Man's Friend" (1845). Wheeler, *Death*, 26.

203. See Greville MacDonald on the influence of Blake in *MacDonald and Wife*, 552–55.

204. See Davis, who provides a range of examples of the theme of death in Victorian literature. Davis, *Victorians*. While Dearborn discusses the nature of good death in MacDonald, she lacks any engagement with MacDonald's negative view of death. Gerold is the one who provides a more comprehensive discussion of MacDonald's positive

cross of Christ demands that our upward journey towards God is marked by a downward movement with Christ. Suffering and death are not meaningless but must be understood and embraced in light Christ. MacDonald understood the power of subversive symbols in directing his readers to live into this profound truth of the gospel.

For MacDonald, then, the 'parabolic' stories he wrote were never meant merely to inform people. They were meant to challenge a person to live more fully according to the newly ushered in Kingdom as revealed in these stories. They were meant "to rouse a man to the feeling, 'I am not what I ought to be, I do not the thing I ought to do.'"[205]

What these 'parabolic' stories do in MacDonald's understanding is challenge the hearer's worldview and provide a fresh and renewed vision of Christ's kingdom. For MacDonald, an interpreter of the biblical text needs to understand the subversive use of language and its purpose to surprise the listener into a new reality. The question of what this new reality entails is crucial for the interpretive process. MacDonald warns teachers not to leave the "house empty" but to use every possibility of teaching for a new vision of the truth:

> Convince a man by argument that the thing he has been taught is false, and you leave his house empty, swept, and garnished; but the expulsion of the falsehood is no protection against its re-entrance in another mask, with seven worse than itself in its company. The right effort of the teacher is to give the positive—to present, as he may, the vision of reality, for the perception of which, and not for the discovery of falsehood, is man created.[206]

What MacDonald appears to achieve in much of his writing is a fresh and startling vision of the Christian life. A vision that would on the one hand break down certain kind of preconceived ideas but also fill those "swept rooms" with new visions of what it means to live the Christian life in a Christ-like manner in the particular context and conditions of his Victorian culture. MacDonald's insistence that "all growth that is not toward God is growing to decay" emphasizes that the Christian life must remain a life directed towards Christ, always growing towards him.[207]

---

and negative attitude towards death. Dearborn, "Prophet or Heretic," 272ff. Gerold, *Gotteskindschaft*, Chapter 11. Kegler, in her brief discussion on death, is also more nuanced. Kegler, "Resakralisierung," 95–97.

205. George MacDonald, *Unspoken Sermons*, 259.

206. George MacDonald, *England's Antiphon*, 171.

207. MacDonald asserts this in the voice of the monk Julian in his first published

For this purpose, the pastor must embrace his/her priestly calling as a poet, recovering Jesus' poetic use of symbols from creation to continue to reveal that which has been hidden since the foundation of the world.

Conclusion

We have argued in this chapter that MacDonald's understanding of language, the symbol, and the parabolic must be understood within his wider theological framework, especially his Christology, his understanding of revelation, and the roles of language and the Bible in how Jesus reveals the Father in and through creation.

MacDonald believes that it is by imaginatively participating in stories and 'parabolic' stories in particular that God provides a space and Christ reveals himself to his people, seeking to transform them into his likeness. Parables serve as a catalyst to open up new levels of understanding Christ and his Kingdom as the hearer is challenged to participate, figure out meaning, and thereby undergo a transformative experience.

For MacDonald, however, symbols are especially prone to lose this revelatory dimension and are therefore always in need of being reinvested with vitality. It was an important concern for MacDonald to continue this shocking and subversive dimension of Jesus' proclamation of the Kingdom of God. By employing subversive imagery, he sought to continue the revelatory function of these biblical symbol and parables.

This theological understanding of the symbol and the parabolic has shaped MacDonald's view and writing of story more widely. Only by understanding the theological significance that MacDonald places on the symbol can one understand the depth of theological meaning that stands behind MacDonald's own careful use of symbols in his stories. None of his stories, however, have the exact form of Jesus' parables. His parables, fairytales, and fantastic stories are usually much longer and draw on a

---

poem "Within and Without" (1855), in George MacDonald, *Poetical Works*, 1:13. The way that Julian experiences this growth is wholly different from what he expected. In *Adela Cathcart* MacDonald reflects on Christ as the true child and the necessity that we all must grow into his likeness. Adela, the protagonist of the story, is ill, and the cure that the new doctor prescribes her is listening to stories and parables. Idem, *Adela Cathcart*, 20, 50, 57, 69. See also Ankeny, *Story*, 114–15, where, after discussing the relationship between author, text, and reader in MacDonald's novels, she comes to similar conclusions: "Ultimately, the exemplary author points readers to God, whose presence is both hope and home, and thereby becomes a 'high priest' who makes known to readers that God is present everywhere."

wide range of traditions, especially Dante's *Divine Comedy*, Bunyan's *The Pilgrim's Progress*, and the genre of the German *Kunstmärchen* (artistic fairytale). On a surface level his fantastic stories seem quite different to Jesus' parables. And yet, we seek to show that the parabolic mode is an important strand in his stories, and *Lilith* shall serve as our test case. There are some striking similarities between the parables and MacDonald's fantastic stories, and by drawing out these similarities we hope to understand MacDonald's theological and pastoral intent in writing Christian fiction. It is to a discussion of *Lilith* that we must now turn.

5

Patterns of Subversion and Promise
Lilith

LILITH, FIRST WRITTEN IN 1890, is MacDonald's last fantastic novel. It is often considered to be his most difficult and disturbing piece of writing. He revised his first draft several times over a period of five years and completed the final version in 1895. The editing process for this novel was intense and long, and Richard Reis argues that of all the manuscripts we have of MacDonald's works, none shows so much careful re-writing as the *Lilith* manuscripts.[1] This gives us some indication that *Lilith* is a well thought out piece of writing with its imagery carefully and purposefully chosen. George MacDonald's son, Greville, called it "the Revelation of St. George" and emphasized the spiritual dimension of the book. He argues that *Lilith* was his father's "last urgent message." Interestingly, he writes that his father "was possessed by a feeling—he would hardly let me call it a conviction, I think—that is was a mandate direct from God, for which he himself was to find form and clothing." Greville suggests in relation to *Lilith* that his father's fiction became "a vehicle for re-stating the Gospel in its original beauty."[2] According to MacDonald's son Greville, then, *Lilith* has a deeply theological and pastoral concern.

While MacDonald's earlier works, such as *Phantastes*, deal more explicitly with the importance of the imagination and art for theology, *Lilith* presupposes these arguments and focuses more heavily on the nature of evil, the prevalence of disobedience, the importance of obedience,

---

1. Reis, *George MacDonald*, 94.
2. Greville MacDonald, *MacDonald and Wife*, 547–48.

the function of sorrow, and the Christian mystery that new life can only come through some kind of death experience. No Christian jargon or familiar language is used in the novel to approach this great mystery and its consequence for those who are willing to participate. Woven throughout the story is MacDonald's insistence that reality is fundamentally theological that includes the empirical. This is in contrast to an exclusively empirical view of reality; a view that gained increasing popularity during the late Victorian period.

Lilith is one of MacDonald's most difficult books. No other of his novels has caused as much confusion and bewilderment. As one reads through the extensive secondary literature on *Lilith*, one can find as much bewilderment in commentary as Mr. Vane himself, the protagonist of the story, experiences as he is trying to make sense of the world of the seven dimensions that he encounters.[3] It seems that "bewilderment" is a response that MacDonald intentionally seeks from his readers. Why did MacDonald write such a disturbing piece of fiction at the end of his literary career? Why did he erase so many of the overt references to Christ and God in his final version of *Lilith*? Is *Lilith* a Christian theological statement and if so, to what extent? The lack of references to God seems to make it quite difficult to read *Lilith* in specifically Christian terms and seems to open up interpretation to a much broader, possibly still religious but much less decidedly Christian reading. Some scholars have suggested precisely this. And yet, there might be a different answer to this important question. When applying the category of the "parabolic" to *Lilith*, the lack of overt references to God, rather than diminishing the theological import of the novel, now might become of particular theological importance. Could it be that MacDonald's employment of parabolic patterns reminiscent of Jesus' parables serves him for a decidedly Christian theological agenda?

Another important issue is the question of the role of paradox in the book. Does paradox, as some suggest, exist in the novel for its own sake, or is it somehow linked to the absence of direct references to God and part of MacDonald's parabolic strategy? A third issue is the question of what MacDonald's metaphors of death, sleep, the house of the dead, night, and dream seek to convey. Rolland Hein suggests that Eve's house is the "atonemaker" and concludes that there is therefore no logical place for Christ in the book.[4] But what does the house of the dead actually

3. For a careful discussion of secondary literature on *Lilith* see Kreglinger, "Christian Fiction," 220–32.

4. Hein, "Faith and Fiction," 237–38.

signify? Many have recognized the central importance of the theme of death in particular, but no in-depth study has been made of what the metaphors of death, the house of the dead, sleep, night, and dream seek to suggest and *how* they are interrelated. A more careful investigation is needed in order to come to terms with these crucial metaphors in *Lilith*.

In what follows we shall revisit the assumption that death in *Lilith* simply means death to self.[5] By exploring MacDonald's extensive use of metaphors in terms of the category of the "parabolic," a new perspective opens up to the reader. A careful consideration of how metaphor functions in parable sheds light on MacDonald's use of the metaphor of death in particular and helps unfold the theological significance of this central and crucial metaphor in *Lilith*.

This discussion of the parabolic dimensions of *Lilith* will serve as the foundation for then looking at the influence of Novalis. We contend that the function of the metaphors of the night and dream are similar to the way Novalis employed them and serve MacDonald to complete the theological argument he began with the metaphor of death.

Parabolic Patterns in Lilith

The genre of *Lilith* is hard to define. The term "mythopoeic" has become popular to capture the complex nature of MacDonald's fantasy writing.[6] W. H. Auden rightly recognizes the difficulty in trying to define such "mythical creations."[7] MacDonald himself just called it "A Romance," Glen Cavaliero calls it "a mythopoeic psycho-drama,"[8] and Stephen Prickett a "death romance." No doubt MacDonald mixed a wide range of genres and styles to create his last fantastic work.

In *Lilith* MacDonald weaves together many different modes of writing such as the German *Kunstmärchen*, the German *Bildungsroman*,

---

5. The idea of death to self seems to be a conflation of two Pauline metaphors taken from Ephesians and Romans. In Eph 4:22 Paul speaks about laying aside the old self and putting on the new self. In Rom 6 he speaks metaphorically of death in sin and dying to sin on the one hand and becoming alive to God through baptism, employing the metaphors of being buried and resurrected with Christ.

6. It seems that C. S. Lewis first employed this term to describe MacDonald's writing. In his preface to the MacDonald anthology he writes: "What he does best is fantasy-fantasy that hovers between the allegorical and the mythopoeic" (Lewis, *George MacDonald*, 14).

7. Auden, "Afterword," 83.

8. Cavaliero, *Supernatural*, 98.

romance, the Gothic novel, myth, and fantasy. The aim here, however, is not to come to terms with the complexity of *Lilith's* genre; rather, we seek to pay attention to one strand in particular that has received hardly any attention in MacDonald scholarship. We seek to draw out parabolic patterns in *Lilith*.

Earlier in the book we looked at Jesus' parables and traced certain patterns: Jesus' parables are often short narrative fiction used to speak about something other than the ostensive subject matter, the Kingdom of God. We noticed that despite this clear theological subject matter, God is never explicitly mentioned in the parables. This strategy, we argued, serves to create negative space in which to explore new understanding of God. The parables usually begin by creating a familiar world and/or using a familiar (allegorical) code in order to invite the reader to participate in the story. This also serves to establish the story amidst that which is known in order to explore unknown territory. At some point in the story, however, a twist or turn occurs where the story's familiarity with the world of the audience is purposefully disturbed and broken down. The hearer is confronted with something unexpected. This usually happens through the introduction of a metaphor or the use of subversive examples, such as the Good Samaritan. In this way the parables challenge a certain worldview or cultural code and urge the audience to embrace a new or more comprehensive understanding of reality. The parables are also deeply rooted within a Jewish frame of mind and make use of the Old Testament. This Old Testament usage is often not straightforward and generates a considerable amount of tension within the parable. In the following we shall trace each of these parabolic elements in *Lilith*.

The first and most fundamental aspect of the novel's nature is that *Lilith* is a narrative fiction that seeks to speak about something other than what seems immediately ostensive. While *Lilith* is much longer than Jesus' parables, it shares with parables this important dimension: it invites the reader to decode its imagery to a certain degree. This is foundational for understanding certain parabolic pattern at work in the novel. Mr. Vane's journey into the world of the seven dimensions is somehow descriptive of his spiritual and moral development. The crucial and also most difficult question in regard to *Lilith* is to discern to what extent individual characters and symbols have a deeper meaning. If one had to locate *Lilith* on a scale of correspondence between the story and its subject matter, one would probably have to locate it somewhere between C. S. Lewis' *The Lion, the Witch and the Wardrobe*, where there is a fairly high degree of allegorical correspondence between the characters of the story and the gospel story, and Tolkien's *Lord of the Rings*, where there are similarities but no direct correspondences. Tolkien insisted that his story exists first and foremost for its own sake and was not supposed to be "about" something else. Wider patterns of reality are brought into particular expressions and should not be decoded.

Tracing Parabolic Patterns in Lilith

The fact that there are hardly any overt references to God/Christ in the final version of *Lilith* is striking and has provoked much debate. What were MacDonald's intentions in removing these references in the final version of *Lilith*? Rod McGillis' conclusion that *Lilith* should therefore not be read as a Christian document is quite radical. Rolland Hein and Jennifer Sattaur suggest that Christ's work was not essential for MacDonald's theology as portrayed in *Lilith*, and David Robb sought to see the omission of direct references as a sign of MacDonald's Calvinist belief in the distance between God and man.[9] Indeed, MacDonald's frequent and creative use of both allegorical and metaphorical elements in *Lilith* is striking and has inspired many different interpretations of the book. The lack of clear references to God/Christ together with the amount of open and suggestive metaphors used in *Lilith* seem to indicate a shift away from a theological frame of reference and invite a much broader and polyvalent interpretation.

If *Lilith* is to be seen within the parabolic tradition, however, then the lack of overt references to God are not only an important but a *necessary* part of MacDonald's parabolic strategy and are of theological import. Rather than minimizing the role that God and more specifically Christ plays within the story, the lack of overt references might serve MacDonald as negative space by which he seeks to explore and recover for the reader a deeper understanding of how God works in the world. When Mr. Raven refuses to give Mr. Vane clear directions for how to get home, he explains: "you and I use the same words with different meanings. We are often unable to tell people what they *need* to know, because they *want*

---

9. For specific references, see my discussion of secondary literature in Kreglinger, "Christian Fiction," 220–32. Dearborn has convincingly shown in her doctoral thesis that MacDonald distanced himself from this specific Calvinist point of view and stressed instead the loving presence of God. See Dearborn, "Prophetic or Heretic," 100–150. Gerold argues similarly. Gerold, *Gotteskindschaft*, 55–105.

to know something else, and would therefore only misunderstand what we said" (71).[10] Mr. Vane himself acknowledges shortly after that he finds it hard to put into words what he sees and experiences in the world of the seven dimensions (73–74). MacDonald seems to shy away from using literal and familiar language to speak about his most important concerns in *Lilith* lest the reader attaches the wrong notions to a familiar word used. It is no use for Mr. Raven to use the word "home" with Mr. Vane; he would only misunderstand Mr. Raven's intention in using this word. It is for this reason, we suggest, that MacDonald avoids direct references to God and Christ in *Lilith*. His late Victorian audience would attach to such direct references meanings that MacDonald himself seeks to circumvent. While late Victorian society was rapidly moving away from a theological worldview, it was still saturated with Christian jargon. By avoiding familiar language about God and Jesus, we shall see, MacDonald can take his readers by surprise and help them to probe more fully into a reality that MacDonald held to be of utmost importance.[11] There are, however, some other indicators that further tie *Lilith* to an explicitly Christian theological interpretation.

The number of direct citations, references, and allusions to the Bible remaining in the final version of *Lilith* are striking and deserve more attention than they have received. Rolland Hein and Tim Martin have provided a careful but not exhaustive list of these references and allusions.[12] From Genesis to Revelation MacDonald refers to the Bible consistently throughout *Lilith*, the allusions becoming more obvious in the final chapters of the novel.

This raises the question of the importance of these biblical allusions. Are they mere echoes that serve to embellish the narrative or are they significant signposts, essential to the way we interpret *Lilith*? If certain dimensions of *Lilith* are indeed to be understood as parts of a parabolic strategy by which MacDonald seeks to confront his readers with a more profound understanding of the gospel for his own time, then we do have to take those biblical citations and allusions more seriously. The task,

---

10. George MacDonald, *Lilith*, 71. For the rest of the chapter, references to *Lilith* will be indicated parenthetically in the main text.

11. MacNeice also mentions this parabolic strategy in *Lilith* and concludes that MacDonald's choice to omit direct references is more commendable than Goethe's overt references in the second part of *Faust*, as they seem unsatisfactory and take away from the effect of the story. MacNeice, *Varieties*, 98.

12. Hein, *Harmony*, 103–5. Martin, "Checklist."

however, is not only to acknowledge their presence in the novel, which has been done to a limited extent, but to ask what role these citations and allusions play and how far they determine the meaning of the book. Even in the late Victorian period, MacDonald's readership would still have been very familiar with the Bible and its imagery. This is in contrast to a modern readership and explains, in part, the lack of attention to MacDonald's use of Scripture in *Lilith*.

Could it be possible that the biblical allusions serve as part of MacDonald's parabolic strategy? Many allusions in *Lilith* connect the characters and their actions to similar characters and actions in the Bible and suggest a degree of allegorical correspondence between the two. MacDonald creates such connections with Mr. Vane, Lilith, and Mara, for example. These connections are based on similarity and familiarity. Allegorical correspondence serves to anchor the story in a familiar world and function like allegorical elements. A few examples shall suffice to show this dynamic. When Mr. Vane is invited to sleep in the house of death, Mr. Raven describes him as being "neither weary nor heavy laden" (45), an apparent reference to Matt 11:28 where Jesus proclaims himself to be the only way to the Father.[13] Mr. Vane does not want to lie down and replies: "Let me first go home . . . and come again after I have found or made, invented, or at least discovered something!" (45). This is a comment reminding the informed reader of the disciple's response to Jesus' invitation to follow him in Luke 9:61: "Lord, I will follow thee; but let me first go bid them farewell, which are at home at my house." The Raven's wife can only give "to him who asks" (47–48), an allusion to Jesus' saying in Luke 11:9 "And I say unto you, Ask, and it shall be given you; seek, and ye shall find; knock, and it shall be opened unto you." Mr. Raven also explains to Mr. Vane that "the business of the universe is to make such a fool of you that you will know yourself for one, and so begin to be wise" (41), evoking 1 Cor 3:18, where Paul urges, "Do not deceive yourselves. If any of you thinks he is wise by the standards of this age, he should become a 'fool' so that he may become wise."

With such allusions and citations from Scripture, MacDonald somehow ties Mr. Vane's journey to that of the disciples. Mr. Raven, Mr. Vane's self-announced guide in the world of the seven dimensions, shows

---

13. "Come unto me, all ye that labour and are heavy laden, and I will give you rest" (KJV). Unless otherwise indicated, all references to the Bible in this chapter are taken from the King James Version as this is the version with which MacDonald and his audience would have been most familiar.

Mr. Vane "the way," and this theme continues throughout the book.[14] The theme of "the way" is reminiscent of the Gospels, particularly the Gospel of Mark, where the theme of "the way" is very important. The term "way" is used twenty-two times in the Gospel of Mark and closely connected to the theme of discipleship.[15] Not only is Jesus on the way from Galilee to Jerusalem and back to Galilee, but he also sends his disciples "on the way" (Mark 6:8). Three of MacDonald's Unspoken Sermons are on the middle section of Mark 8—10, a very important section dealing with Christ, the cross, and the disciples' struggle to accept that Jesus must die.[16] These three sermons show how closely MacDonald wrestled with the interaction between Jesus and his disciples and their struggle to follow Jesus on "the way" to the cross.[17] Somehow, Mr. Vane's struggle to follow Mr. Raven to the house of the dead is tied to the disciples' struggle in the Gospel of Mark to embrace that Jesus must go to the cross and die.

14. Mr. Vane takes the way that Mr. Raven had gone (24), Mr. Raven exclaims: "This is the way" (30), Mr. Vane wants Mr. Raven to show him the way home (36), Mr. Raven "immediately . . . led the way" (37), Mr. Vane is on the way (299, 303), and the lady of sorrow leads the way (333). Adam, another face of Mr. Raven, continues to lead the way through the door of death (339). The way Mr. Vane has to go is difficult (350) and in deep shadow (351). The theme of "the way" is also prominent in the *Pilgrim's Progress*, one of MacDonald's favorite books, and it might well have inspired MacDonald to weave this theme into his novel *Lilith*. The influence of the Marcan account seems more likely, however, as the theme of "the way" is so closely linked with Jesus' and the disciples' journey to the cross, thus showing similarity to Mr. Vane's journey to the house of death.

15. John the Baptist is reported to proclaim "Prepare ye the way of the Lord" (Mark 1:3). It is by "the way" that Jesus asks his disciples "who do people say that I am?" and continues to predict his death and resurrection, but the disciples do not understand (Mark 8:27-33). Instead, they dispute among themselves "by the way" who should be the greatest (Mark 9:34). In contrast to the disciples, who seem to be blind to Jesus' teaching, a blind man received his sight from Jesus and follows him "on the way" (Mark 10:52). And finally, Jesus "teachest the way of God in truth" (Mark 12:14). See Ernst Best here who traces the connection between "the way" motif and discipleship in Mark's Gospel. Best, *Following Jesus*.

16. The importance of the theme of "the way" in the Gospel of Mark is commonly acknowledged. See Marcus, *Way of the Lord*, 29-47. Swartley, *Scripture Traditions*, 96-115.

17. The first one is "The child in our midst" based on Mark 9:33-37, the second is "The hardness of the way" based on Mark 10:24, and the third is "The cause of spiritual stupidity" based on Mark 8:21. In his sermon on self-denial, MacDonald emphasizes that Jesus is not only the way, but the leader in the way. George MacDonald, *Unspoken Sermons*, 363. While these sermons were written much earlier in MacDonald's writing career (1867), it seems clear that he intentionally revisited this subject in *Lilith*.

David Robb rightly recognizes the allegorical nature of the character of Mara. The name Mara (Hebrew: *mara'* meaning "bitter") is taken from the book of Ruth 1:20 where *mara'* expresses Naomi's grief in the face of severe suffering: "And she said unto them, Call me not Naomi, call me Mara: for the Almighty hath dealt very bitterly with me." Robb concludes that the Little Ones' fear of Mara "is an allegory of the human instinct to shun pain and sorrow."[18] This connection is further supported by the close affiliation between Mara's house and the house of mourning in Eccl 7:1–5. The presence of Mara and her house in the story serve MacDonald to emphasize the important role that sorrow and suffering play on one's spiritual pilgrimage and that we must not run away from facing sorrow. In *The Hope of the Gospel* he writes: "Perhaps the greater part of the energy of this world's life goes forth in the endeavour to rid itself of discomfort." At another point he argues "suffering is *for* the sinner, that he may be delivered from his sin."[19] For MacDonald, the experience of suffering is not meaningless but carries potential for spiritual growth if embraced with a posture of faith.

The character of Lilith is primarily based on the Lilith legend of the Jewish Kabala, but MacDonald also connects her identity to Mark 9 and uses Pauline imagery to speak of her nature and destiny. Lilith is the one who offends the Little Ones (Mark 9:42), and because of her sin her hand has to be cut off (Mark 9:43). Lilith is a slave of sin (235) and will be saved by childbearing (234), both Pauline images.[20] Lilith, according to the Lilith legend, lives in rebellion and disobedience to God, and the references to Mark suggest that she is the embodiment of sin. Both Mara and Lilith play clear roles within the story. The allegorical correspondence between the vehicle and the tenor is clear and direct and without strain.

We have suggested here that MacDonald's employment of biblical imagery and allusions serves as part of his parabolic strategy. Primarily, but not always, these references and allusions serve to anchor the story in a world with which the late Victorian audience was still very familiar. Not all references to the Bible in *Lilith*, however, are straightforward or suggest such a clear allegorical correspondence. There are allusions to the Bible in *Lilith* that create more tension and jolt and demand a much higher imaginative engagement from the reader. They are more "metaphorical"

---

18. Robb, *God's Fiction*, 104. See also Broome, "Science-Fantasy," 279.
19. George MacDonald, *Hope/Miracles*, 10, 21.
20. Rom 6:20; 1 Tim 2:14.

than "allegorical" in terms of our earlier analysis of these terms. MacDonald's employment of the metaphor of death, as we shall argue, is one such example. Before investigating his use of the metaphor of death as part of his parabolic strategy, we shall discuss how MacDonald further creates a familiar setting in order draw the reader into the story.

Familiarity as Invitation

Like a parable *Lilith* opens in a rather ordinary and, for the Victorian reader, familiar setting, aiding the reader to find an entry point into the novel. The protagonist of the story is an Oxford graduate, grown up an orphan and now heir to a large house and estate that he is to manage. As he is without relations and any significant relationships, he spends much of his time in his own library pursuing his interests in the physical sciences, but he also has a notable interest in metaphysics and the relation between them (7–8).[21] We have already noted in our discussion of *The Light Princess* the Victorian fascination with empiricism and metaphysics. Not quite so revolting as Mr. Casaubon of George Eliot's *Middlemarch*, he is an intellectual of his own day, well read and educated but somewhat lost and desultory in his studies and theoretical musings about the world. Rolland Hein captures Mr. Vane's personality well when he writes:

> Vane, the protagonist, is a late nineteenth-century man as MacDonald understood him: proud, more scientifically and materially oriented than Anodos, an intellectual to whom spiritual realities are simply 'metaphysical' speculations, noumena about which he is curious only as he perceives them affecting the physical world. Such people need to confront the demanding verities of the world of the spirit, be made to see how foolish by comparison the self-confident attitudes of scientific rationalism are.[22]

The protagonist of the story is a rather ordinary figure and one of the simplest characters in the plot. Certainly in comparison to Mr. Raven he seems a rather flat character with only one name assigned to him. His name, "Mr. Vane" ("Mr. Fane" in the first version of *Lilith*) denotes, according to the OED, a weathercock, which turns readily with the wind.

---

21. It is noteworthy that while Mr. Vane is portrayed as an orphan and isolated individual in the final version, the first draft portrays him with a number of siblings and his father merely as having disappeared rather than dead. The search for his father is what leads him into the other world (407–22).

22. Hein, "Great Good," 124.

Figuratively speaking it suggests someone who is unstable and changes constantly with the fashion of the day. The image also resonates with Paul's description of the immature believer in Eph 4:14 as someone "tossed to and fro, and carried about with every wind of doctrine." Ephesians in general is an important book for understanding both some of the imagery and theology of *Lilith*, and we shall discuss this influence shortly.

Mr. Vane is basically a "good" person. His behavior is decent and predictable. His intentions are good. He wants to help the Little Ones. He takes pride in his rights as a self-sufficient and independent individual (33). He is an orphan both relationally and spiritually speaking, thus reflecting his time quite well. Davis, in his introduction to the Victorian age, points out how secularized culture had become by the mid-nineteenth century. He describes this age from John Henry Newman's perspective:

> The Victorian world was to Newman a sort of Dickensian orphan: 'a boy of good make and mind, with the tokens on him of a refined nature, cast upon the world without provision, unable to say whence he came, his birthplace or his family connections' (*Apologia Pro Vita Sua*, pt. 7). Would the boy try to reclaim his lost inheritance as a child of God or . . . reject all fathers, earthly and heavenly, in the movement towards secular adult autonomy?[23]

It is striking that Mr. Vane himself, once he has entered the world of the seven dimensions, acknowledges being just such a person. When asked by Mr. Raven who he is, he suddenly realizes: "Then I understood that I did not know myself, did not know what I was, had no grounds on which to determine that I was one and not another" (21–22).

MacDonald creates a character and setting in Mr. Vane and his circumstances with which a late nineteenth century Victorian reader of a certain social standing would quite easily identify. We would suggest that just as the ordinary and everyday setting of the parables of Jesus served to draw the contemporary audience into the world of the parable, so did MacDonald seek to draw in his contemporary audience by creating a world with which the Victorian reader would be familiar. Both the insertion of references/allusions to the Bible and the creation of a familiar world engender a sense of familiarity and seem to serve this purpose. The parabolic twist and subversion does not come in the person of Mr. Vane himself. The surprise comes in the form of another important character and the use of metaphors relating to some sort of death experience.

---

23. Davis, *Victorians*, 100.

Subversive Metaphors and Other Disturbing Factors

MacDonald's fascination with death in *Lilith* is remarkable. But what kind of death does he mean? We suggest here that his employment of the image of death must be understood within the wider context of other related metaphors in *Lilith*. MacDonald's use of the metaphor of death, as we shall see, would have been disturbing and subversive in its Victorian context. The relationship between the vehicle and its tenor is opaque, complex, and not easily grasped. It demands a high imaginative engagement from the reader in making the connections that MacDonald here suggests. With this metaphor MacDonald deliberately seeks to de-familiarize his readers. He compels them to re-consider and abandon held beliefs about the nature of reality and draws them into an attentive configuration and embrace of reality as he understands it. MacDonald seems to rely directly on Paul's use of the metaphor of death in Ephesians and Romans, and this metaphor and its entailments, we suggest, has to be understood in relation to his use of the metaphors of sleep, night, and dreams, borrowing the ideas associated with these metaphors from Novalis.

The Metaphor of Death and Its Entailments in Lilith

Many George MacDonald scholars have pointed out the importance of death in *Lilith*. Colin Manlove argues, "*Lilith* is wholly organized by the theme of death and resurrection."[24] Hein thinks that in *Lilith* "spiritual death to the self, symbolized by sleep, is essential to being and doing."[25] For Prickett death in *Lilith* becomes "the symbol for the greater reality of human dependency on God."[26] Robb goes so far to say that death in *Lilith* "is the utter abandonment of self—the complete negation of identity."[27] Jeff McInnes suggests more generally about MacDonald's work that "some kind of death is needed" in order to turn from evil.[28] While all of these assertions are helpful, none of them quite capture the importance of the metaphor in *Lilith*, which is much more complex and suggestive. We

---

24. Manlove, *Modern Fantasy*, 79.
25. Hein, "Lilith," 219.
26. Prickett, *Victorian Fantasy*, 201.
27. Robb, *God's Fiction*, 107.
28. While McInnes does not deal with *Lilith* in particular, he rightly recognizes that for MacDonald a turn from evil cannot be accomplished without the help of Christ. He refers to "The Light Princess" and *Unspoken Sermons* in particular to support his argument. McInnes, "Shadows and chivalry," 230, 360–62.

have argued in chapter 2 that metaphors bring into interaction two ideas in a surprising and subversive way and thereby force the hearer/reader to make new connections. In the following we shall explore how MacDonald sought to do this with the metaphor of death. As this metaphor is rather important and complex, we shall devote a careful discussion to it in order to grasp its significance with *Lilith*.

Awareness of death was an all-pervading presence in Victorian society, and Michael Wheeler argues that the deathbed and the grave are the two loci of visual and literary association with death in the nineteenth century.[29] Social and literary conventions relating to the deathbed included among other things the visit from a doctor or priest, confession, the laying out of a corpse in a darkened room, and the closing of a coffin. Death was also commonly referred to as sleep and the grave as a bed. Wheeler argues that this interchange of terminology has to be understood within the context of the Victorian belief in the eschatological hope of the resurrection from the dead. Coleridge in *Aids to Reflections* calls the grave "thy bed of rest" that "thy Saviour has warmed . . . and made it fragrant."[30] William Blake's engravings for Blair's poem "The Grave" suggest similar ideas. His engraving called "Death's door," which served MacDonald as a book plate, synchronizes the moment of death and resurrection by picturing a stooped man entering into death's door while the resurrected young man sits on top of the door.[31] Blake's engraving called "The Counsellor, King, Warrior, Mother and Child in the Tomb" depicts the dead as sleeping on a bed, and Roderick McGillis has rightly pointed out that MacDonald might have had this engraving in mind when he describes the house of the dead and its sleepers in *Lilith* (52–53).[32] Many of these common images relating to physical death such as sleep, bed, the coffin, the grave, and the graveyard are used in *Lilith*. None of them are used in a familiar way, however, and two seeming dissimilars are brought together, creating a sense of jolt for the reader.

---

29. Wheeler, *Death*, 25–27.

30. Ibid., 25–28, 55, 65–66. While some mocked belief in the hope of the resurrection, it was still an important part of many Victorians' faith. Thomas Hardy, in his poems "The Levelled Churchyard," dated 1882, mocks the hope in the resurrection, and in "In Death divided," a poem of the 1890s, he questions the common belief of reunion with one's loved ones by omitting the subject altogether. Wheeler, *Death*, 67.

31. Wheeler, *Death*, 298.

32. McGillis, "Fantastic Imagination," 366–67.

The Raven

MacDonald introduces the metaphor of death through the character of Mr. Raven. Understanding the character and role of Mr. Raven is crucial for exploring the meaning of death in *Lilith*. The question of Mr. Raven's identity is a difficult one and often neglected.[33] McGillis rightly points out that "Mr. Raven is intent on breaking down old categories of thought" by putting things in paradox and riddle.[34] Prickett recognizes that somehow Mr. Raven's office is linked to a Pauline understanding of death and life.[35] Raeper argues that the raven functions as symbol of death.[36] MacDonald employs a range of metaphors to speak about Mr. Raven, and we contend that MacDonald purposefully created a character whose identity cannot be fully grasped and who will remain in a certain amount of obscurity. His names and roles evoke various associations within the reader, some of them seemingly contradictory. To interpret Mr. Raven in an allegorical manner would be to resolve a tension that MacDonald purposefully creates.

Mr. Raven first appears to Mr. Vane as an ancient librarian, thereby connecting to the very familiar world of Mr. Vane consisting of books and ideas. He appears suddenly, seemingly out of nowhere and without invitation in Mr. Vane's library. Intrigued by the appearance of this mysterious figure, Mr. Vane decides to find out his identity. He follows the ancient librarian to the attic of his own house where he leaves his familiar world and stumbles into a completely new and strange world, gaining access through a mirror that stands in his attic.

It is at this point that the librarian's form changes. He appears no longer as an ancient librarian but an old raven with strikingly manlike appearance, reminiscent of the librarian (22–23). This change of appearance at this stage of the story is significant. The first encounter with the mysterious character in his strange world is with that of a raven, a bird traditionally seen as an evil omen, a symbol for impending death and

---

33. Even McGillis, in his most extensive discussion of *Lilith*, does not discuss this very important character in any significant way. A notable exception here is Broome, "Science-Fantasy," 253–56.

34. McGillis, "Phantastes and Lilith," 36, 48.

35. Prickett, *Romanticism and Religion*, 235. It was C. S. Lewis who first suggested that MacDonald relies on a Pauline understanding of death, mentioning among other passages Rom 6. See Hooper, *Letters*, 1:246. Hobbis also suggests this connection. Hobbis, "That Night," 244.

36. Raeper, *George MacDonald*, 373.

disaster. The OED describes a raven as mischievous and thievish, a bird of ill omen and mysterious character.[37]

In Edgar Allan Poe's poem "The Raven," the bird is a messenger of despairing and dark news. The poem, written in 1845, caused quite a sensation in England.[38] The Raven appears to a lover who laments the loss of his beloved maiden. He listens to the lover's complaint and queries, and when the grieving lover asks him whether he will be reunited with his beloved, the Raven responds with "Nevermore." The raven is depicted as an agent who intensifies the despair and sorrow by dashing the lover's hope of resurrection reunion with his beloved.

In light of such associations, it is no surprise that Mr. Vane would be suspicious of Mr. Raven. Startling as this encounter is for Mr. Vane, it is even more surprising that Mr. Raven now announces himself to be Mr. Vane's guide by firmly telling him that he needs to follow him. He specifically and repeatedly tells him "This is the way" (30), and we have already pointed to the connection here with Mark's Gospel, where Jesus repeatedly seeks to lead the disciples "on the way."

The Raven's persona is further developed in the novel, when Mr. Raven announces that he is a sexton at a certain graveyard/cemetery. The office of a sexton would of course further enhance the notion of death in relation to the character of Mr. Raven, as the task of a sexton was to ring the church bells and dig graves for upcoming funerals. Mr. Vane is confronted with someone who not only has the air of death around him but also by someone who prepares the grave and the dead for burial. The description of the sexton's cottage and his cemetery evoke all those very common associations of the Victorian deathbed and the grave scene. Human forms are laid out in a darkened room on beds, covered with sheets (50–51). Even the door to Mr. Raven's cottage is no normal door but the lid of a coffin (44), reinforcing the notion of death surrounding Mr. Raven's person, home, and occupation. This use of imagery in the novel is rather disconcerting and unsettling as it becomes clear that Mr. Vane, a young and healthy person with the best prospects for a comfortable and successful life and who therefore should have nothing to do with death at this point in his life, is to join the sleepers in the cemetery. He is to share in their death. Mr. Vane is filled with dread and is left wondering what all this means.

---

37. In the first version of *Lilith*, he is Mr. Rook rather than Mr. Raven, creating very similar associations.

38. Wheeler, *Death*, 148.

MacDonald, however, does not leave the reader in the dark about the metaphor's possible meaning. We have already shown how MacDonald, by inserting allusions and references to the Gospels, somehow ties Mr. Vane's journey to that of Jesus and his disciples. He further clarifies matters by providing other and more constructive images in connection with Mr. Raven's occupation. The first action that Mr. Vane sees Mr. Raven perform in the world of the seven dimensions is that of plunging his beak into the sod and pulling out a worm (rather than a caterpillar), throwing it into the air where the worm turns into a butterfly (31). According to Wheeler this imagery was quite popular in the Victorian time as a way to approach the complex and mysterious subject of death and resurrection.[39] MacDonald himself reflects on the butterfly as a metaphor for the Christian hope of resurrection from the dead.[40] And yet, in *Lilith* it seems more likely that MacDonald uses the metaphors of the worm and the butterfly in a slightly different way, not speaking about physical death and resurrection. Considering that Dante's Purgatory features quite prominently in *Lilith*, MacDonald's usage might compare to Dante's. In Canto X of *Purgatorio* Dante writes,

> O Christians, arrogant, exhausted, wretched, whose intellects are sick and cannot see, who place your confidence in backward steps, do you not know that we are worms and born to form the angelic butterfly that soars, without defences, to confront His judgement?[41]

This is further supported by MacDonald's usage of the butterfly metaphor in the latter part of *Lilith* when Vane has returned to the Little Ones. He explains about the Little Ones:

> Most of them would have nothing to do with a caterpillar, except watch it through its changes; but when at length it came from its retirement with wings, all would immediately address it as Sister Butterfly, congratulating it on its metamorphosis—for which they used a word that meant something like *repentance* and evidently regarding it as something sacred. (264)

For MacDonald then, it seems that this metaphor is suggestive of human transformation in light of the Christian concept of repentance.

39. Ibid., 183.

40. George MacDonald, *Annals*, 516–17. He also uses this metaphor in idem, *Diary of an Old Soul*, December 14.

41. Dante Alighieri, *Divine Comedy*, 262.

Mr. Raven as the sexton seems have a more constructive side to his vocation: he is responsible for the transformation of worms into butterflies. Mr. Raven asserts: "That is the business of a sexton. If only the rest of the clergy understood it as well!" (32). This statement is very important. It links his vocation as sexton to that of a priest.[42] Broome argues that MacDonald's description of the Raven as "purply black" also suggests a spiritual office.[43] In the world of the seven dimensions, the sexton/priest serves to facilitate this process of transformation, and he does so as someone who prepares people for death and burial. MacDonald here closely intertwines the process of spiritual transformation with a certain kind of a death. But what sort of a death is it?

As Mr. Vane is brought into the cemetery and sees all the sleepers lying in the still and ice cold chamber of the dead he wonders: "I thought at first their sleep was death, but I soon saw it was something deeper still—a something I did not know" (52). The reader, together with Mr. Vane, is left to wonder what this death means. Mr. Vane is told that those sleeping are healing in their sleep (54), and he wonders: "Are they not dead?" (54). It is important that Mr. Raven refuses to give Mr. Vane a straight answer to this question lest he misunderstand: "'I cannot answer you,' he replied in a subdued voice. 'I almost forget what they mean by *dead* in the old world. If I said a person was dead, my wife would understand one thing, and you would another.'" (54) It becomes clear that someone coming from Mr. Vane's world does not easily grasp the death experienced in Mr. Raven's cemetery, and MacDonald resists providing an easy or quick explanation. Nevertheless, when Mr. Vane is terrified by the invitation to lie down and sleep in the chamber of death, Mr. Raven seeks to calm him: "Be of good comfort; we watch the flock of the great shepherd" (57). Borrowing and adapting the famous image from the Gospel of John, MacDonald now links Mr. Raven's vocation to that of Jesus, the good, or as MacDonald puts it, the "great shepherd." This merging of the images of the raven and sexton with that of a priest and shepherd as a facilitator of human transformation is powerful and very

---

42. The role of a priest/clergyman was an important question for MacDonald in later life. A culturally acceptable occupation, it drew people that were wholly unqualified for this vocation. In his last novel, MacDonald discusses and critiques clergymen who might be well-educated but have no moral/spiritual awareness of themselves or others and are thus unable to preach the gospel with integrity. See the character James Blatherwick in George MacDonald, *Salted with Fire*.

43. Broome, "Science-Fantasy," 255.

close to MacDonald's theological understanding of the role of the priest. It clarifies that what Mr. Vane is to learn about death is somehow linked to the "great shepherd."

Another hint from Mr. Raven to Mr. Vane provides further clues to death's nature in this "other" world, hints that Mr. Vane will not grasp until much later. Mr. Raven explains: "Your sexton looks at the clock to know when to ring the dead-alive to church; I hearken for the cock on the spire to crow: '*Awake thou that sleepest, and arise from the dead!*'" (55). This last phrase is the only quotation from the Bible given in cursive writing and singles it out from other quotations and references in *Lilith*. It is a direct quotation from Eph 5:14. We shall argue next that MacDonald employs the metaphor of death as it is found in Ephesians and merges it with Paul's use of death in Rom 6. By looking at Paul's use of this metaphor, we shall arrive at a better understanding of its significance in *Lilith*.

Death in Ephesians

We have already suggested that Mr. Vane in name and character reminds one of Paul's description of the immature believer in Eph 4 who is "tossed to and fro . . . by every wind of doctrine." Other parallels between the Ephesians and *Lilith* further support our argument that MacDonald might indeed be drawing his idea of death from this epistle. Mara describes Lilith as an evil person, in league with "the Prince of the Power of the Air," a direct allusion to Eph 2:2. This "Prince of the Power of the Air" works in the children of disobedience (Eph 2:3), and it becomes clear that both Lilith and Mr. Vane are unwilling to obey. When Mr. Raven tells Mr. Vane the story of his first wife Lilith, he explains that she refused to be one with him and bear him children, implying her refusal to accept his headship (233). Mr. Raven predicts that even Lilith will be saved by her childbearing (234). The author of Ephesians admonishes the wives to submit to their husbands (Eph 5:22), and Paul argues that Eve (and women in general) will be saved through childbearing (1 Tim 2:15). Several times the Ephesians are reminded that once they were dead in sin obeying the Prince of the Power of the Air (Eph 2:1, 5) but were made alive in Christ (Eph 2:5). Mr. Raven accuses Mr. Vane of being dead (248), and Mr. Vane is led astray by Lilith who is in league with the Prince of the Power of the Air. Lilith's hand is cut off by a sword that brings healing (345–46), reminding one of the sword in Eph 6:17 (and Rom 13:4; Rev 1:16; 2:12) symbolizing the word of God. The Ephesians are admonished to live wisely and not foolishly: "See then that ye walk circumspectly, not as fools, but as wise" (Eph 5:14–15). It is clear that Mr. Raven attempts to teach Mr. Vane that he is indeed a fool and needs to learn to be wise (22, 25, 34, 41).[44] And finally the believers of Ephesus are admonished to turn away from sin and be wise: "Wherefore he saith, Awake thou that sleepest, and arise from the dead, and Christ shall give thee light" (Eph 5:14).

This is one of the exceptional places, where MacDonald cites a whole sentence from Scripture in *Lilith*, and it is important to notice that MacDonald does not quote the latter part of this verse, "and Christ shall give thee light," even though it is clear that in Ephesians this fragment, possibly stemming from an old hymn, forms a unity within the argument of the book.[45] The fact that MacDonald does not cite the last part of this verse fits well with our argument that he purposefully seeks to avoid direct references to Christ. This negative space, we argue, serves MacDonald to surprise the reader into a renewed understanding of familiar yet not fully grasped spiritual realities.

The meaning of the metaphor of death in chapter 5 of Ephesians is dependent on its earlier use in chapter 2. The author here reflects on the pre-Christian condition of the believers:

> You were dead through the trespasses and sins in which you once lived, following the course of this world, following the ruler of the power of the air, the spirit that is now at work among those who are disobedient . . . But God, who is rich in mercy, out of the great love with which he loved us even when we were dead through our trespasses, made us alive together with Christ. (Eph 2:1–5)[46]

The metaphor of death is used to speak about both life without God and life in sin. Andrew Lincoln and A. J. M. Wedderburn explain the meaning of the metaphor of death here as follows:

> In 2.1–10 the writer, viewing his readers' past from the perspective of their present participation in resurrection life, reminds them that their pre-Christian existence can only be regarded as

---

44. Mr. Vane's journey is that of one who slowly recognizes that he has been a fool and needs to learn to be wise. This theme is brought to a climax when Mr. Raven confronts Mr. Vane about his unwillingness to listen to him and obey. The most foolish thing that Mr. Vane has ever done, according to Mr. Raven, "was to run from our dead" (248).

45. See Lincoln and Wedderburn, *Pauline Letters*, 87, 109, 144.

46. For our discussion of the biblical text outside of *Lilith*, we shall use once more the New Revised Standard Version.

a state of death. This living death was characterized by trespasses and sins, which had caused death in the first place, and associated with the trespasses and sins were the forces of the world, the devil and the flesh . . . The writer then turns to God's decisive action in the past which has reversed his readers' condition. This divine reversal, launched on the basis of his rich mercy and great love, involved making the readers alive with Christ, raising them up and seating them with Christ in the heavenly realms. The readers are reminded that what God did for Christ (see 1.19–21) he has done for all believers. What God accomplished for Christ he accomplished for him as representative of a new humanity, seen as included in him so that believers are to view themselves as participants in the events of Christ's resurrection and exaltation."[47]

The resurrection call in Ephesians is addressed to those who were once dead in sin and are now alive in Christ. The author uses the metaphor of death and sleep interchangeably to speak about those who were once dead in sin, and he uses the metaphor of waking and arising to speak about those who have embraced new life in Christ.[48] Sin can only be dealt with in Christ's death and resurrection. In 1:7 the author proclaims about Christ: "In whom we have redemption through his blood, the forgiveness of sins, according to the riches of his grace." Because Christ died and was resurrected from the dead, the believer can share in this new way of life. The resurrection call in Ephesians gives witness to this new life in Christ and invites believers to leave their old lives of sin behind and continue to embrace the new life available in Christ's death and resurrection.

Mr. Raven's resurrection call in the chamber of the dead clearly evokes Paul's resurrection call in Ephesians and is further substantiated by other parallels between *Lilith* and Ephesians, as we have shown. Just as the Ephesians were subject to the Prince of the Power of the Air, so is Lilith, the ultimate personification of evil and sin in *Lilith*, in league with the prince of the power of the air. The believers in Ephesians are called to put down the old man (Eph 4:22) and put on the new man (4:24), and Mr. Vane, when he finally understands Mr. Raven's identity towards the end of the story, realizes that Mr. Raven is "Adam, the old and the new man" (234). MacDonald here employs imagery from Ephesians to describe Mr. Raven's true identity. Mr. Raven is the personification of the

---

47. Lincoln and Wedderburn, *Pauline Letters*, 104.
48. Best, "Dead in Sin," 15–17.

true humanity by partaking in Christ's death and resurrection. While he partook of Adam's sinful nature (old man), he was also being made new in Christ, thus having a new nature (new man). MacDonald makes clear towards the end that Mr. Raven, in contrast to Lilith, was willing the repent (234).

The resurrection call in *Lilith* is addressed to those who have already taken their place among the sleepers, those who have accepted Mr. Raven's invitation to lie down in the chamber of the dead and sleep. The chamber of the dead then functions as a spatial metaphor for the place where people renounce their old way of life in death and sin (the old man) and embrace the new life made available in Christ's death and resurrection (the new man). Mr. Raven and his wife's invitation and hospitality extended to Mr. Vane to lie down in the ice-cold and frightening cemetery, we suggest, has to be understood as an invitation to enter into and partake in the greatest and most puzzling mystery: new life is made available to humanity through Christ's death and resurrection and his forgiveness of sins. By embracing and partaking in the sleep offered at the house of the dead, one mysteriously participates in Christ's death. Mr. Vane's partaking in the bread and wine and the fact that he needs to be forgiven before he can lie down in the chamber of the dead suggests the same context that the author speaks about in Ephesians (48, 348). MacDonald's references are subtle, but they do evoke these very same associations. It seems that MacDonald here seeks to approach the great Christian mystery and seeming paradox that new life comes out of death. He does so by employing the most paradoxical language. Form and content merge in the most profound way in *Lilith* and thus remind one of Jesus' use of parable to express the seemingly paradoxical nature of the Kingdom of God. MacDonald startles and disorients his audience in order to make them think for themselves and ponder anew this profound Christian mystery: What does it mean to participate in Christ's death?

It is clear, however, that Mr. Vane is not ready to hear the resurrection call. He refuses to lie down and sleep and therefore belongs to those who are still dead. Mr. Raven challenges him: "[T]hou who callest thyself alive, has brought into this chamber the odours of death, and its air will not be wholesome for the sleepers until thou art gone from it!" (57). In light of our discussion above it seems quite likely that Mr. Vane's state of death should be understood in the sense of Ephesians. Mr. Vane is one of those who are unwilling and afraid to embrace the new life that is offered to him. As long as he refuses to embrace this new life, he will remain dead in the sense that his life is lived without and apart from God and thus in the sin of the "old man." By using the metaphor of death in this suggestive manner, MacDonald is able effectively to speak about sin without having to use language to which the Victorian reader would immediately bring certain negative and even oppressive associations.[49] We suggest that this is also part of MacDonald's parabolic and pastoral strategy. Just like he seeks to avoid direct references to Christ, so does he avoid using the term "sin."

This interpretation is further supported by a later encounter between Mr. Vane and Mr. Raven after Mr. Vane has accomplished a great deal of mischief. When Mr. Raven confronts Mr. Vane regarding his foolish and useless behavior (by now Mr. Vane has brought Lilith the vampire demon back to life), his critique lies with Mr. Vane's general state of being dead and his unwillingness to die, rather than with one specific mistake. Mr. Raven speaks:

> "Mr. Vane" he said, "do you not know why you have not yet done anything worth doing?"
> "Because I have been a fool," I answered.
> "Wherein."
> "In everything."
> "Which do you count your most indiscreet action?"
> "Bringing the princess to life: I ought to have left her to her just fate."
> "Nay, now you talk foolishly! You could not have done otherwise then you did, not knowing she was evil! —but you never brought any one to life! How could you, yourself dead?"
> "I dead?" I cried.
> "Yes," he answered, "and you will be dead, so long as you refuse to die."
> "Back to the old riddling!" I returned scornfully.
> "Be persuaded, and go home with me," he continued gently. (247–48)

Mr. Raven here comes to the point more quickly. Mr. Vane no longer just has "the odours of death around him" but is in fact dead. It is noteworthy

---

49. One only needs to think of little Jane in *Jane Eyre*, who is taken into an orphanage and made to stand on a stool in humiliation, proclaimed to be a liar and sinner by pious Mr. Brocklehurst. Late Victorian society rejected and sought to move away from an oppressive and guilt-ridden spirituality that focuses on sin, God's wrath, and the punishment of hell. See Wheeler, *Death*, 184–96. Wheeler argues that hell came to be viewed as a state of being, a spiritual condition, rather than an actual place. Wheeler, *Death*, 218. It is striking that MacDonald seems to espouse a similar position in *Lilith* (144–47).

that Mr. Raven does not reprimand Mr. Vane for bringing Lilith back to life, which has terrible consequences in the novel. Instead, Mr. Raven stresses that the key problem with Mr. Vane is the fact that he is still dead. MacDonald's intention is, we suggest once more, to show that Mr. Vane is dead because he seeks to live his life without God and thus in sin. As a consequence he cannot understand the nature of evil and sin nor God's economy in dealing with sin. He still lives as the "old man" and is unwilling to embrace the new.

It is also important to note that MacDonald adds here another important dimension to the metaphor of death. Mr. Vane's problem is not only that he is dead; he also refuses to die. MacDonald here moves beyond the sense of death of Ephesians. While the metaphors of death and sleep in Ephesians are interchangeably used to speak about life lived in sin before salvation, in *Lilith* the metaphors of death and sleep are more complex. They cannot merely be equated with sin. It becomes clear that those who want to be woken have first to die. It is here that MacDonald introduces a usage of death that is seemingly drawn from Paul's letter to the Romans, a letter that the author of Ephesians relies on both in ideas and language.[50]

Death in Romans 6

As in Ephesians, so Paul argues in Romans that it is only in Christ that sin was dealt with successfully and completely. Just as sin entered through one man (Adam), so was sin overcome by one man (Christ). Through Christ's obedience and death are believers reconciled to God (Rom 5). Paul continues his argument in chapter 6 by reflecting on how this Christ event is worked out in daily living and how the believer is to view and deal with the old life of sin and death. We quote Paul at some length:

> What then are we to say? Should we continue in sin in order that grace may abound? By no means! How can we who died to sin go on living in it? Do you not know that all of us who have been baptized into Christ Jesus were baptized into his death? Therefore we have been buried with him by baptism into death, so that, just as Christ was raised from the dead by the glory of the Father, so we too might walk in newness of life . . . We know

---

50. As suggested before, the author of Ephesians knew Paul's letter to the Romans and draws both on wording and ideas from this letter. Lincoln and Wedderburn, *Pauline Letters*, 83–89.

> that our old self was crucified with him so that the body of sin might be destroyed, and we might no longer be enslaved to sin. For whoever has died is freed from sin. But if we have died with Christ, we believe that we will also live with him. We know that Christ, being raised from the dead, will never die again; death no longer has dominion over him. The death he died, he died to sin, once for all; but the life he lives, he lives to God. So you also must consider yourselves dead to sin and alive to God in Christ Jesus. Therefore, do not let sin exercise dominion in your mortal bodies, to make you obey their passions. No longer present your members to sin as instruments of wickedness, but present yourselves to God as those who have been brought from death to life, and present your members to God as instruments of righteousness. (Rom 6:1–13)

In this passage Paul seeks to help young Christians with the very practical question of how to deal with the still existing reality of sin. He uses the metaphor of dying to sin to speak about the radical disjunction between a life of sin and a life lived onto God. In doing so he traces an organic connection between the nature of Jesus' own "death" to sin on the cross and our daily "putting of sin to death" in our lives. For Paul, then, the only "coping mechanism" in combating a life of sin is anchored solely in Christ's death. James Dunn writes about this passage:

> Christ's death and resurrection has brought about a new stage in God's dealings with men . . . Christ has introduced a new era. As a freely embraced act of obedience . . . Christ's death marked the end of the realm and reign of sin, law and death. Consequently the implication is fairly clear, even before we move on from v. 2, that the dying to sin here spoken of is not something independent of Christ, but is somehow a sharing in his death, a sharing in his transition from one era to the other.[51]

The answer to overcoming a life of sin is thus only found in embracing and identifying with Christ's death. The metaphors that Paul employs to approach the mystery of the believer's participation in Christ's death are those of baptism and the funeral. While the metaphor of baptism is the more prominent one in Rom 6, it is the metaphor of the funeral that MacDonald appropriates in *Lilith*.

We have already discussed how prominently the deathbed and the Victorian funeral scene features in *Lilith*. Mr. Raven who is the sexton,

---

51. Dunn, "Salvation Proclaimed," 261.

the sexton's cottage, and the house of the dead all speak about a cosmic funeral, and Mr. Vane is to join in by taking the bed that is prepared for him (51–53). What is this cosmic funeral about? Prickett, for example, argues, "To 'die' in Mr. Raven's sense is something you *yourself* must do."[52] Prickett seeks to emphasize that Mr. Vane must move from second to firsthand experience; this is an important observation. And yet, there is more at stake here. Death in *Lilith* is not something that Mr. Vane must do. Rather, it is something in which he must participate.[53] This death only happens when Mr. Vane is willing to accept Mr. Raven's invitation and hospitality by following him into the chamber of the dead and lying down on the couch that is reserved especially for him. It is by ceasing to do things, by embracing an invitation and accepting Mr. Raven's hospitality that Mr. Vane dies. Just as a Christian can overcome a life of sin only by accepting Jesus' invitation to follow him and somehow receive the benefits of his death, so is Mr. Vane challenged to embrace the "magic" that happens in the house of death. Mr. Vane cannot produce this death and what follows; it is something that is given to him.

MacDonald's use of the metaphor of death and its entailments, such as the cosmic funeral, make most sense when they are understood within this Pauline sense of participation in Christ's death. MacDonald creatively reflects on the Pauline metaphor of being "buried with Christ" and "dying to sin" by writing a novel that is centered on the metaphor of death and its entailments of the funeral and the house of the dead. Something that is not of his doing happens to Mr. Vane when he finally lies down to sleep in the house of the dead. To neglect the importance of the house of the dead and what happens to those who embrace the sleep that is offered there is to miss an important dynamic that holds all of *Lilith* together. To understand death in *Lilith* as a mere death to self or something that Mr. Vane must do by himself is to miss the depth of this rich and complex metaphor and its entailments and how it is anchored within a matrix of references to the Gospels and Pauline metaphors. To die in *Lilith* means to die to sin, and the only way one is able to do this is by participating in Christ's death. MacDonald sought to approach this mysterious participation upon which Paul reflects by using the spatial metaphor of the house of the dead. It is significant that the house of the

---

52. Prickett, *Victorian Fantasy*, 201.

53. See here MacDonald's sermon "God's family" (1892) where he closely links the believer's death to sin to that of Christ's death and resurrection. George MacDonald, *Hope/Miracles*, 297.

dead reminds Mr. Vane of a cathedral nave (52). Mr. Raven, in his priestly office, tells Mr. Vane: "Every creature must one night yield himself and lie down . . . he was made for liberty, and must not be left as slave!" (361). This is another usage of Pauline imagery to speak of the life apart from Christ and in sin as a life in slavery. Paul writes in Galatians "So then, brethren, we are not children of the bondwoman, but of the free. Stand fast therefore in the liberty wherewith Christ hath made us free, and be not entangled again with the yoke of bondage" (Gal 4:31—5:1). Not only must Mr. Vane recognize that he is indeed dead, he must learn to be willing to die to this state of deadness by lying down. Mr. Vane must embrace Mr. Raven's invitation and follow him on the way that he shows him. But just as the disciples of Mark's Gospel struggle to follow Jesus on the way to the cross, so does Mr. Vane struggle to follow Mr. Raven's way and accept his invitation to lie down in the chamber of the dead.

Concluding Notes on Death in Lilith

We have sought to argue here that MacDonald's employment of the metaphor of death and its entailments serves as part of his parabolic strategy. The associations created by the Victorian deathbed and funeral scene are disturbing and subversive of a life that seems to have all the prospects of health, wealth, and learning. While these images permeated much of Victorian life, they were only appropriate in contexts of physical suffering, physical death, and grief over the loss of a loved one. Why should a well-educated and well-off young man of good health be buried? MacDonald here brings together two seemingly contradictory ideas and uses it to challenge the complacency of the Victorian idea of "good Christian people." In one of his sermons he writes:

> [T]he skin-diseases of the soul linger long after the heart is greatly cured. Witness the petulance, fastidiousness, censoriousness, social self-assertion, general disagreeableness of so many good people—all in the moral skin–repulsive exceedingly. I say *good* people; I do not say *very good*, nor do I say Christ-*like*, for that they are not.[54]

By employing the metaphor of death in this disturbing way, MacDonald challenges a complacent attitude towards life and God. As MacDonald continues to develop this complex metaphor, it becomes clear that the

54. Ibid.

death Mr. Vane is to die is linked to Mr. Raven's priestly role. Mr. Raven serves to facilitate spiritual transformation, and this transformation is linked to a Pauline understanding of death. Dying in the world of the seven dimensions, we have suggested, is participating in the cosmic funeral, a metaphor for participating in Christ's death. This is the only way one can leave behind the old life apart from God and in sin. MacDonald's parabolic strategy takes the reader from familiarity through subversion to a confrontation with a deeper understanding of the great mystery of the Christian faith: new life can only be found by participation in death, that is Christ's death. To reject this great mystery is to remain dead and in a state of nonbeing of which Lilith is MacDonald's prime example.[55]

MacDonald's choice in leaving out direct references to both Christ and sin creates negative space in which he seeks to confront his audience anew with old and familiar truth. MacDonald spoke into a time and culture that was still saturated with Christian language and jargon while rapidly moving away from the Christian faith. By avoiding direct references to Christ and sin and focusing on the metaphor of death, he seeks to prevent his audience from attaching too quickly certain ideas to them, and it gives him space to explore anew these realities for the reader in this parabolic and subversive way. John Docherty puts it this way:

> Much of *Lilith* . . . is devoted to a description of how Vane gradually comes to learn that the understanding of 'life' and 'death' possessed by those whom he sees on their cold beds is infinitely preferable to his own initial outlook . . . MacDonald . . . believes he is dealing with an absolutely crucial matter which is not readily comprehensible to most people. Therefore he is perfectly prepared to risk unbalancing his story to ensure that the concept is grasped by as many of his readers as possible.[56]

Docherty rightly recognizes that much of the novel is indeed concerned to explore the nature of a certain kind of death.

Our interpretation of the metaphor of death raises the question of the role of Christ's resurrection in *Lilith* and what happens to Mr. Vane in the house of the dead. While it makes sense that MacDonald will not refer to Christ directly because of his parabolic strategy, one needs to ask in what way the resurrection of Christ plays any role in the novel.

---

55. For a discussion of the character of Lilith as MacDonald's response to nihilism see Hobbis, "That Night," 32–48.

56. Docherty, "Worlds," 64.

Mr. Raven's resurrection call from Ephesians suggests that some kind of resurrection is to come. In the last part of this chapter, we seek to show that MacDonald now departs from Pauline imagery where the life of the resurrection is spoken of as "walking in the light" and "alive to Christ" (Eph 5:8, 14). MacDonald, we suggest, turns to Novalis and his metaphors of the night and dreams to continue his reflection upon the importance of Christ's death and resurrection for Mr. Vane's spiritual and moral development.

The Influence of Novalis: The Night and the Dreams that Come

The parameters of this book do not allow a discussion of MacDonald's employment of the early Romantic stylistic devices of the German *Kunstmärchen* to shape his last novel. The movement between two worlds, non-coherence in the plot, non-closure, and the arbitrary use of the world of the senses are a few examples of how MacDonald challenges and critiques a mere rational and empirical view of the world and thus appropriates the German *Kunstmärchen* genre and merges it with his parabolic strategy.[57] We must focus on a discussion of the influence of Novalis' metaphors of the night and dreams in *Lilith* and how they function to complement MacDonald's use of the metaphor of death.

MacDonald's Appropriation of Novalis' Night

We have shown that Novalis employs the metaphor of the night in *Hymns to the Night* in a subversive way to critique the Enlightenment overemphasis on reason and a mere rational understanding of the world. Novalis creates a reality in these hymns where the metaphor of the night rather than the light becomes central. This metaphor serves to suggest that the most important aspects of the Christian faith cannot be grasped on a merely rational basis; they have to be experienced by a turn towards the "holy, mysterious inexpressible night." Central for understanding Novalis' night is his belief that redemption is only found in Christ's suffering,

---

57. For a short but helpful introduction see Bergmann, "Roots." McGillis makes helpful suggestions in terms of MacDonald's employment of non-closure. McGillis, "Phantastes and Lilith." It is striking how much the movement between the two worlds in *Lilith* resembles that of Anselmus' journey in *Der Goldene Topf*. See Hoffmann, *Goldene Topf*.

death, and resurrection, and because of Christ's work, the night becomes "the mighty womb of revelation." The very places that one naturally would consider as dark such as suffering and the death of a beloved now become the very places where God reveals himself. Thus, the turn down into the night becomes the path that leads home, which Novalis closely connects with his "beloved Jesus."

In light of this context, it becomes significant that MacDonald does not follow Paul's use of the metaphor of the light to speak about participation in Christ's resurrection as the counterpart to the metaphor of death in and to sin. Rather, we suggest here, he follows Novalis in creating a setting where the night rather than the light is the predominant context for Mr. Vane's adventures. In contrast to Novalis, however, MacDonald stays with his parabolic strategy and does not reflect openly on the significance of Christ's death and resurrection for Mr. Vane's education in the world of the seven dimensions.

Mr. Raven and his wife's invitation to Mr. Vane strongly resonates with Novalis' imagery.[58] When they first invite Mr. Vane to lie down in the chamber of the dead, they realize that he is not ready: "He has not yet learned that the day begins with sleep! . . . Tell him he must rest before he can do anything!" (45). They lead Mr. Vane into the chamber of the dead where Mr. Vane sees many couches lined up in a long and cold room with a sleeper on each of them. He is taken to his own couch to lie down, and Mr. Vane is terrified. Mr. Raven tries to encourage him: "Do not be a coward, Mr. Vane. Turn your back on fear, and your face to whatever may come. Give yourself up to the night, and you will rest indeed. Harm will not come, but a good you cannot foreknow" (56). It is in this use of the metaphor of the night and giving oneself up to the night that one can see the influence of Novalis. MacDonald uses the same metaphor of the night but appropriates it for his own purposes. While the voice in *Hymns to the Night* is of someone who has recognized the importance of giving oneself up to the night and is able to embrace the goodness that comes, this same invitation in *Lilith* is consistently refused. Mr. Vane's story is that of someone who struggles to give himself up to the night. He wants to follow his own ideas.

While we sought to demonstrate earlier that the metaphor of death used in *Lilith* must be understood in relation to the gospel story and

---

58. The only other person who has suggested a possible connection here is Kegler, "Schlaf," 140. Kegler, however, does not discuss this influence in any detail, nor does she recognize Novalis' strong Christological associations with the night.

Pauline ideas of death, there are important indications that MacDonald's night is also closely related to the work of Christ. This is so because death and giving oneself up to the night are closely related in *Lilith*. In addition, there is one biblical reference of particular importance as it reoccurs in *Lilith* at very important turns in the story and suggests certain associations in relation to the night. When Mr. Vane first enters the sexton's cottage he asks for food and drink that will quench his thirst, and he is given bread and wine. Bread and wine are of course the central elements of the Eucharist, the sacrament where Christians enter the mysteries of Christ's death and resurrection. After Mr. Vane eats and drinks of it, he remarks: "the bread and wine seemed to go deeper than the hunger and thirst" (48). Towards the end of the novel, Lilith herself is offered bread and wine, and Eve tells her: "This food will help thee to die" (339), but Lilith refuses to eat of it (339). At the very end Mr. Vane is finally ready to lie down in the chamber of death, but Adam and Eve must first forgive him (348). After his final test Mr. Vane is served bread and wine once more, and he literally "partakes of it," liturgical language indicative of the Lord's supper (360). We would suggest that these references deliberately evoke associations of the Eucharist and further tie Mr. Vane's journey, and especially his lying down in the chamber of death and giving himself up to the night, to that of Christ's redemptive work in his death and resurrection.

The night is the primary context in which Mr. Vane journeys and slowly learns to surrender himself to Mr. Raven's invitation. This night is usually accompanied by the comforting presence of the moon, a symbol that MacDonald employs elsewhere to speak about the Bible.[59] Just

---

59. In his sermons "The Higher Faith," MacDonald discusses the importance and role of Scripture. He argues: "The one use of the Bible is to make us look at Jesus, that through him we might know his Father as our Father, his God and our God. Till we thus know Him, let us hold the Bible dear as the moon of our darkness, by which we travel towards the east; not dear as the sun whence her light cometh, and towards which we haste" (George MacDonald, *Unspoken Sermons*, 37). In *Lilith* there are several moons, but one moon in particular seems to accompany Mr. Vane in his journey. When Mr. Vane first meets the Raven's wife, her hands shine "with a white radiance, . . . like a moon-stone" (*Lilith*, 50). As they walk towards the cemetery, where Mr. Vane is to lie down, the moon rises: "The moon looked in at an opening in the wall, and a thousand gleams of white responded to her shine" (ibid., 51–52). The moon shines upon those lying in the chamber of the dead (52). The moon reads the faces of the dead and smiles (54), and Mr. Vane is told that the moon in the world of the seven dimensions is not like the moon in his world. The moon's beams "embalms the dead" (54). Mr. Vane is "left alone in the moonlight with the dead" (57). The moon accompanies Mr. Vane throughout his journey. As Mr. Vane enters the Bad Burrow, the moon is with him and brings him light and companionship: "She brought me light . . . The moon seemed to

as Novalis' night is the context where suffering becomes meaningful in light of Christ's death and resurrection, so is MacDonald's night the place where Mara, the lady of sorrow and suffering, sees perfectly: "I see badly in the day, but at night perfectly" (114). Suffering plays an important role in bringing Mr. Vane to the point of being willing to die (355). And just as Novalis critiques a mere rational understanding of reality, so does MacDonald critique a mere empirical view of the world.[60] Both Novalis and MacDonald argue in their own ways that the most important aspects of the Christian faith cannot be grasped on a merely rational and intellectual basis. They have to be experienced by turning towards the night and participating in what is revealed in this mysterious night.

There are also, however, important differences between the way Novalis and MacDonald treat the night. While Novalis' emphasis is on the mysterious transformation of suffering into new hope in light of Christ's death and resurrection, MacDonald's emphasis lies elsewhere. The night in *Lilith* is primarily the context where Mr. Vane learns that he is dead in sin and needs to die to sin in order to live. Michael Mendelson rightly points out that the night accompanied by the moon is juxtaposed with a night of terror.[61] Monsters of the bad burrow, dancers with skull faces, horse skeletons, and Lilith serve to paint the picture of a Gothic night that is not filled with the brightness of the moon but with the air of death. In *Lilith* the night also becomes "a mighty womb of revelation," but what is revealed to Mr. Vane is his own sinfulness and his need of forgiveness. The spiritual journey of Mr. Vane is that of increasing self-knowledge, coming to understand his own particular ways of sin and disobedience. The metaphor of the night is closely linked to the metaphor of death and sleep in *Lilith*.

---

know something, for she stared at me oddly. Her look was indeed icy-cold, but full of interest, or at least curiosity. She was not the same moon I had known on the earth; her face was strange to me, and her light yet stranger. Perhaps it came from an unknown sun! Every time I looked up, I found her staring at me with all her might! At first I was annoyed, as at the rudeness of a fellow creature; but soon I saw or fancied a certain wondering pity in her gaze: why was I out in her night?" (76). The moon starts to affect his brain (77). Lona explains to Mr. Vane that the moon came to take care of him and show him *the way* (110). Mr. Vane continues his travels attended by the moon (113), and Mara sees Mr. Vane "in the light of the moon" (114). Towards the end Mr. Vane sees Adam, and "He stood large and grand, clothed in a white robe, with the moon in his hair" (368). The moon of Mr. Vane's night reminds one of Ps 119:105, where the Psalmist prays: "Thy word is a lamp unto my feet, and a light unto my path."

60. See Kegler, "Resakralisierung."

61. Mendelson, "Conventions of Ascent," 204.

The hope of the resurrection only comes to Mr. Vane when he has finally surrendered and gone to sleep in the house of the dead without any knowledge of how he will wake. It is in his sleep/death of the night that dreams come to him. But what role do these dreams have and how are they related to all the other metaphors? We suggest that here, too, Novalis was a primary inspiration for MacDonald.

MacDonald's Appropriation of Novalis' Dream World

In the following, we seek to show that Novalis was an important inspiration for MacDonald's use of the metaphor of dreams in *Lilith*. As mentioned before, there are only two direct citations in *Lilith* where the author is actually named. The first one is taken from Thoreau and serves as a prelude to the story. The other is the Novalis quotation "Our life is no dream; but it should and will perhaps become one." With this quotation MacDonald closes the novel.

It is noteworthy that MacDonald only inserted this reference in the final version of *Lilith* and that the first version of *Lilith* is quite different from the final version in regard to the ending of the story. Mr. Fane of the first version leads the Little Ones into victorious battle, the Little Ones run into the kingdom of heaven (599), and Mr. Fane is taken back through a door into his own world and is given a comforter named hope (601). The ending is unambiguous and short. MacDonald employs no dream imagery here. In the final version the ending is much more complex, placing Mr. Vane not only into a state between dreaming and waking but also into a state in between hoping and doubting. This is an important change and deserves attention.

Novalis

In order to understand the possible influence of Novalis here, we will briefly recall Novalis' understanding of dream imagery and then proceed by suggesting how MacDonald employs it for his own purpose. For Novalis the symbol of dreams becomes a poetic device in order to open up his reader's vision for the divine. Novalis opposed a mere rational and scientific understanding of the world and sought to express a renewed and more profound vision of reality. Divine interventions still happen for Novalis and cannot be sufficiently encapsulated in a mere rational outlook. He sought to destroy such a one-sided rationality only in order to re-establish another rationality where both the rational and the spiritual dimension of reality are integral to one's understanding of the world. God still speaks and sends dreams, and the imagery of dreams becomes a poetic device to open up one's vision for God. The highest form of dreams happens in a synthesis of dreaming and waking as an expression of the integration of the physical with the spiritual rather than a mere transcending from the physical to the spiritual. In this synthesis the experience of the individual is integrated into the spiritual world created by the poet. Novalis also associates dreams with his longing for the "Golden Age," which he identifies in *Hymns to the Night* with Christian eschatology. Only in the future will the fulfillment of this dream come. We shall argue that it is precisely in these ways that MacDonald employs Novalis' imagery.

MacDonald's Context and his Usage of Dreams

The context into which MacDonald writes *Lilith* bears important similarities to that of Novalis. The nature of dreams and their source was a hotly debated issue during the Victorian era. We have already shown that the publication of *Essays and Reviews* contributed in a significant way to the questioning of traditionally held beliefs about Scripture and Revelation. The question of whether supernatural interventions in the laws of nature continue to happen became heavily disputed after its publication.[62] Nicola Brown, in her insightful article "What is the stuff that dreams are made of?" shows that the Victorian discussion on the nature of dreams is one example of how this debate took shape. Similarly to Novalis' context, there was a strong tendency towards explaining dreams empirically, either physically or psychologically, in order to combat superstition and supernaturalism among the uneducated and those influenced by Swedenborg. His book was translated in 1846, and he had claimed in his diaries to have conversed with angels and supernatural beings in his dreams.[63]

Unlike Novalis' context, however, there was also a great interest among Victorians in the supernatural, owing its debt to the Romantics and their interest in the transcendent. William Blake, for example was an important proponent of the supernatural origin of dreams.[64] Brown

---

62. N. Brown et al., "Introduction," 5–6.

63. N. Brown, "Dreams," 151–54, 160–61.

64. Ibid., 156. Of course, this interest in the supernatural varied greatly and took many different shapes, such as the occult, and is explored in some detail in the various

shows that John Anster Fitzgerald's painting *The Stuff That Dreams Are Made Of* (1845) gives voice to this deep uncertainty among the Victorians about the nature of dreams as the painting integrates references to both science and the supernatural.[65] Brown further argues that the Victorian debate over the nature of dreams became closely linked to debates over the nature of the human mind. She writes:

> At the centre of these debates was the problem of whether dreams and, by extension, the human mind are supernatural or material. Did dreams originate in the soul, and was consciousness spiritual, or were the workings of the mind physical and dreams merely a normal, if strange, form of mental functioning? Did dreams come from outside the dreamer, or were they all in his or his own mind?[66]

In light of this context, it is noteworthy that Mr. Vane in *Lilith* struggles with those very issues when he ponders the source of the dreams that he has received in the world of the seven dimensions. It shows how aware MacDonald was of the current debates of his time. Mr. Vane wonders:

> "Could God Himself create such lovely things as I dreamed?"
> "Whence then came thy dream?" Answers Hope.
> "Out of my dark self, into the light of my consciousness."
> "But whence first into they dark self?" Rejoins Hope.
> "My brain was its mother, and the fever in my blood its father."
> "Say rather", suggest Hope, "thy brain was the violin whence it issued, and the fever in thy blood the bow that drew it forth.— But who made the violin? And who guided the bow across its strings?" . . .
> Man dreams and desires; God broods and wills and quickens.
> When a man dreams his own dreams, he is the sport of his dream;
> When Another gives it him, that Other is able to fulfil it.[67]

MacDonald here firmly situated dreams, the human mind, and imagination within the context of God's created order. While he recognizes that not all dreams come from God, he affirms that some dreams do come from God. God still reveals himself, and one way he does so is by

---

essays in *The Victorian Supernatural*.

 65. Ibid., 167.

 66. Ibid., 159.

 67. George MacDonald, *First and Final*, 396. MacDonald makes a similar argument in his first essay on the imagination. See idem, *Orts*, 25.

supernatural intervention through dreams.[68] It is in the context of this understanding of revelation in dreams that one needs to understand the Novalis quotation of which MacDonald was so fond. "Our life is no dream, but it should and will perhaps become one" becomes now a metaphor for an understanding of life, where the spiritual dimension of reality becomes an integral part of life and which finds its ultimate fulfillment only in the future. A mere empirical understanding of the world is insufficient as it excludes the possibility of divine intervention. It is like "trying to live in the scaffold of the house invisible," as MacDonald puts it elsewhere.[69] Thus his employment of the metaphor of the dream serves to challenge a mere empirical view of the world and affirms a greater spiritual reality, the existence of which cannot be proven scientifically but has to be embraced in faith and held onto in hope even in the midst of the trials of life that will surely come.[70]

In between Dreaming and Waking as an Expression of MacDonald's Eschatology

It is once Mr. Vane has agreed to lie down and give himself up to the night that he receives his dreams. The dreams that come to him are visions of God and reconciliation. MacDonald's language in relation to God and his theological concerns now becomes more explicit. Mr. Vane finds himself "in the heart of God" (364), and he is confronted with all the people that he has wronged and becomes reconciled to them (364–65). He is now a true pilgrim (368). This experience is followed by another encounter with Adam (Mr. Raven) who is now "clothed in a white robe, with the moon in his hair" (368). Adam, like the believers in Rev 3 who overcome, is clothed in a white raiment (Rev 3:5, 18; 4:4).

---

68. Dreams are by no means the only way in which MacDonald affirms a positive view of revelation in *Lilith*. The only way in which the mirror in Vane's attic (and elsewhere) serves as a door into the world of the seven dimension is through the light that falls upon it (16). The "doorness" of a mirror depends on the light explains Mr. Raven elsewhere (65).

69. George MacDonald, *Orts*, 58.

70. The discussion between Mr. Raven and Mr. Vane in ch. 43, "The dreams that came," is about this very issue (*Lilith*, 369–75). It is noteworthy that Hobbis devotes a whole section in her thesis on comparing MacDonald's understanding of hope with that of Jürgen Moltman. She argues: "Hope has substance in *Lilith*, and affirms that 'Another' dreamed this dream and not himself; but he grounds that affirmation not in the strength of his imaginings but in Hope." Hobbis, "That Night," 243.

And yet, despite his glorious visions,[71] Mr. Vane finds himself wondering whether he is dreaming or awake: "To myself I seemed wide awake, but I believed I was in a dream, because he had told me so" (371). Consequently, Mr. Vane finds himself back in his own house (372), and he is afraid that he is separated from those of the region of the seven dimensions because he is awake and they are asleep. This is terrifying to him, as it would mean that he could not partake in the final waking (373). MacDonald now completely blurs the lines between Mr. Vane's state of waking and dreaming in the final chapters of the novel, and the novel ends with Mr. Vane at home, wondering whether the dream he dreamed was of his own making.

This, we suggest, is not an expression of MacDonald's lack of control over his imagery, his Platonic worldview, or that the reader is meant to be left in uncertainly.[72] Rather, MacDonald here employs Novalis' romantic strategy by elevating the state in between dreaming and waking as the true human state. It is an expression of MacDonald's eschatology.[73] The life offered in Christ's death and resurrection only finds its fulfillment in the future, and thus the Christian believer is left in an in between stage. The believer already partakes in Christ's resurrection, but this work of Christ will only be complete when he returns at the end of time. MacDonald expresses this reality in *Lilith* by placing Mr. Vane in a state between dreaming and waking. Waking in the world of the seven dimensions is a process (376) that must be continued in Mr. Vane's old world and only finds its

---

71. McGillis points out the parallels to Dante in those visions. McGillis, "Phantastes and Lilith," 50–51.

72. Wolff cannot make sense of MacDonald imagery here at all. He concludes: "Why should MacDonald feel it necessary to warn again of the vileness of people with unwholesome minds, in the very moment of the final triumph? Only, one is forced to conclude, because he had lost control of his imagery. On the one hand MacDonald paints the picture of a triumphant resurrection. On the other, evil is all about, even on the 'frontiers' of heaven itself." He concludes that the last chapters are bad art. Wolff, *Golden Key*, 368–69. Prickett argues that MacDonald's employment of dream imagery is "a new, existential gloss on the traditional Platonic belief that human life is but a dream of a greater reality." He also argues, relying on McGillis, that the reader is to be left in a state of uncertainty and ambiguity. Prickett, *Victorian Fantasy*, 199, 202. Prickett realizes that this might serve to suggest a more integrated vision of reality, but he misses the eschatological overtones.

73. Adelheid Kegler argues similarly here but sees this eschatological tension in terms of Romantic philosophy rather than Christian eschatology. Kegler, "Schlaf," 139. Karl Kegler at least recognizes MacDonald's appropriation of biblical imagery in the final section of *Lilith*. Kegler, "Eine Stadt," 86–88.

fulfillment in the final waking. Mr. Vane must await the fulfillment of the "other world" that he has begun to discover in the world of the seven dimensions. Until then, Mr. Vane is to wait in hope until "he" comes:

> The master-minister of the human tabernacle is at hand! ... something more than the sun, greater than the light, is coming, is coming ... He is coming, is coming, and the necks of all humanity are stretched out to see him come! Every morning will they thus outstretch themselves, every evening will they droop and wait- until he comes. (386)

Mr. Vane's last words are "I wait; asleep or awake, I wait," and the novel closes with the Novalis citation "Our life is no dream, but it should and will perhaps become one" (397–98).

Concluding Notes on Dreams in Lilith

MacDonald's employment of the metaphor of dreams, we suggest, forms a coherent whole with his employment of the metaphor of death. Just as the metaphor of death suggests MacDonald's belief that every true pilgrim must learn to partake in Christ's death, so does the metaphor of the dream suggest that as one participates in Christ's death, one will also partake in Christ's resurrection. Mr. Raven's call "Awake though that sleepest, and arise from the dead" (55) will continue "until the dawn of the day eternal" (380). Those who were willing to die to sin and partake in Christ's death by lying down to sleep are now called to wake into the life of the resurrection that is made available in Christ. The life of the resurrection in *Lilith*, however, does not find its consummation in this life.[74] It only comes in the world to come and leaves Mr. Vane in a state of waiting. By employing the metaphor of the dream and elevating the state in between dreaming and waking, MacDonald is able to capture the eschatological tension that comes with a life that seeks to partake in Christ's death and resurrection and awaits its consummation in the future.[75] Those who are willing to venture into this mystery must remember that "When

---

74. McGillis at least realizes the importance of a final consummation yet to come in *Lilith*. McGillis, "Phantastes and Lilith," 50. Kegler also recognizes this tension between expectation and consummation but does not connect it to Christ's death and resurrection. Kegler, "Schlaf," 139.

75. Of course, there are many other sources that MacDonald draws upon in this last section, most notably Dante. Due to our particular focus and the lack of space, we will not touch upon those.

a man dreams his own dreams, he is the sport of his dream; When Another gives it him, that Other is able to fulfil it" (396).[76] MacDonald, with Paul and John, affirms that even though Mr. Vane can only see through a glass darkly now, he must wait in hope and obedience until "the Truth himself, will come, and depart no more, but abide with him for ever" (1 Cor 13:12–13; John 14, 16; and *Lilith*, 371). That MacDonald changed the ending of final version of *Lilith* in a substantial way is significant. We have sought to show that it serves to give due justice to the wholly eschatological nature and implications of a Christian worldview.

Conclusion

We have begun our study of *Lilith* by pointing out how carefully MacDonald edited this novel over a period of five years and the common response of bewilderment to the novel among its readers. The strange imagery used and the lack of direct references to God has caused many an interpreter to assume that the novel is a departure from MacDonald's otherwise Christo-centric view of the world to a more broadly religious and possibly polyvalent perspective on reality. By interpreting the novel in light of the "parabolic," we have not only challenged but overturned this dominant view. These lack of references can now be seen as part of his parabolic strategy and thus serve a decidedly Christian theological agenda. A consideration of the parabolic is therefore not merely important because MacDonald adopts this genre but also because it fundamentally challenges MacDonald scholarship and shows that not only in content but also in form MacDonald stays close to the New Testament. Employing the parabolic in his fantasy then makes MacDonald more rather than less theological when compared with his other modes of writing.

With the category of the "parabolic," we have also sought to come to terms with MacDonald's complex matrix of metaphors, showing that the metaphors of death, the house of the dead, sleep, waking, and dreaming are carefully chosen and work together to speak about the implications of Christ's death and resurrection for the believer in concrete terms. Form and content in *Lilith* work together to press further into the mystery of the cross and its eschatological implications for the life of the believer. MacDonald's pastoral concern was always how Christian truth might be appropriated in the believer's life and his or her specific life circumstances.

---

76. MacDonald makes a similar argument in his first essay on the imagination. See George MacDonald, *Orts*, 25.

While the novel is indeed disturbing in its choice of metaphors, these serve to confront the audience with the gospel in a surprising fashion, invite them to make sense of these metaphors, and in this way challenge the readers to join Mr. Vane on his journey, embracing the night and that which will surely come.

Conclusion

WE HAVE SUGGESTED IN the beginning of this book that George MacDonald is primarily a theological thinker and writer. What sort of a theologian is MacDonald? His pastoral concern was for his audience to come to know God in personal and transformative ways. His focus was on the lived dimension of the Christian faith. The way he sought to minister to his Christian audience was through story. While MacDonald employed a wide range of literary styles, the "parabolic" is a dimension of his writing that has received surprisingly little attention.

The "parabolic" is an important genre both in Jesus' proclamation of the Kingdom of God and more subtly in MacDonald's fantasy and fairytale writing. Rather than serving as a nice illustrative story to an important theological point made elsewhere, the form of parabolic speech is crucial for the message that it seeks to convey. The form and content of Jesus' parables work together in a unique way to break open the reality depicted in parable. The genre of Jesus' parables is thus not an arbitrary means of figurative speech but a well-chosen tool for a provocative proclamation.

In these pages we have sought to come to terms with the form of Jesus' parables, in what way some of George MacDonald's fantastic stories might be invested with parabolic patterns reminiscent of Jesus' parables, and how this perspective can aid our understanding of MacDonald's works. There is considerable disagreement in MacDonald scholarship over the nature of his fantasy writing and to what extent it might be and/or contain Christian theology. By looking at MacDonald as a parabolic writer in the Jesus tradition, we shed new light on this important question.

Defining the genre of Jesus' parables is not easy, and there is in fact considerable confusion and disagreement amongst biblical scholars as to the nature of NT parables and how to interpret them. In particular, there is confusion over the relationship between metaphor, allegory, and parable. By discussing each category we have sought to bring clarity to this confusion and see how metaphor, allegory, and parable are related to one another. Building on this foundation, we have provided a working definition of NT parables. That many of the NT parables have a surprising and even shocking dimension to them is striking. In parables Jesus' proclamation of the Kingdom of God finds its perfect form. The tension of the new in the old, the discontinuity within the continuity, and the already not yet finds expression in a unique form that can hold these dimensions in tension without reducing them. The parables, by juxtaposing dissimilars, are the ideal means by which to proclaim the Kingdom of God and probe into its mystery that was once hidden and is now revealed. Form and content are intrinsically related in Jesus' parables. Precisely because of this surprising dimension, however, parables are particularly prone to lose this revelatory dimension due to over-familiarity with the metaphors used and unfamiliarity with the world and texts to which the parables refer. As a consequence parables no longer modify understanding of the subject matter in the way they once did. There is thus a great need to recover and refresh the shock-experience that many of Jesus' parables once had.

It is at this point that we introduce George MacDonald, who not only understood the dynamics of metaphorical language in general but the importance of parabolic speech in particular. MacDonald developed a decidedly theological understanding of language, story, and the parabolic within his larger understanding of Scripture and revelation. The context of Victorian Britain and Romanticism, both German and English, is crucial for understanding MacDonald in this regard. The rise of historical criticism and the advance of scientific discoveries in Victorian Britain challenged deeply held beliefs and raised important questions regarding the reliability of the Bible and revelation more generally speaking. The question of revelation was pushed to the side, and slowly but surely scientific inquiry and historical criticism emerged as the deciding factor for "accurate truth." MacDonald's response to this development included both the affirmation of the importance of science and a recognition of its limitations in capturing reality in its fullness, especially in things pertaining to God. For MacDonald the fullness of truth can only be found in Jesus Christ, who is revealed to us rather than being discovered by us.

The influence of German and English Romanticism on MacDonald is significant and has not been explored sufficiently in MacDonald scholarship. While both Novalis and Coleridge are commonly recognized as important influences, we explored these influences more fully. The influence of Novalis, and particularly his use of dream imagery and *Hymns to the Night*, on MacDonald is altogether unexplored territory in MacDonald scholarship, and our own work has sought to further understanding of this significant influence. Novalis is an important model for MacDonald as he employs poetics in order to recover and explore more fully Christian truth for his own time. His use of dream imagery is an important example in this regard. Novalis opposes a merely rational and scientific understanding of the world and employs the symbol of dreams to express a renewed and more comprehensive vision of the world, particularly his belief in God and divine intervention. For Novalis, the possibility of God's speech cannot be constrained to a time of old but must be contemplated in the present. MacDonald in *Lilith*, we bring to light later, employs Novalis' imagery of dreams to express similar concerns. Furthermore, in *Hymns to the Night* Novalis makes use of the subversive imagery of the night to probe deeper into the mystery of Christ's death and resurrection and its pastoral implications for Christian living. This usage of the night also sheds considerable light on MacDonald's use of subversive imagery in *Lilith*. For Novalis the role of the poet and priest are intimately connected, and this perspective shaped MacDonald's thinking in a significant way.

With Coleridge, MacDonald affirms that the imagination is much more fundamental to human life and action than previously acknowledged. According to both, the imagination is at work in all spheres of life both on a conscious and unconscious level. MacDonald explores the function of the imagination in human cognition and in creative, artistic expression, and like Coleridge he singles out the poet as his primary example. A careful reading of MacDonald's argument, however, also betrays a subtle but definite critique of Coleridge's Idealist tendencies. In doing so, MacDonald recovers a decidedly Christian framework for understanding the role of the imagination. The poet does not create the world in any primary sense, and therefore the poet's work must never been seen as a repetition of God's work; the poet is always and only a mere *Trouvère*, a finder rather than the maker. For MacDonald the poet seeks to discover new forms by which to recover and express old truths. It is here that we see an important link between MacDonald's understanding of the imagination and the loss of surprise and shock in parables. It is by the imagination that a poet is able to find new ways of recapturing old and forgotten truths, especially those of Scripture.

This can be seen in MacDonald's understanding of revelation. MacDonald emphasizes that Jesus reveals the Father not in opposition to creation. Rather, Christ must be seen as the one who comes to fulfill his created glory; he is both creator and revealer. MacDonald demonstrates this theological point by discussing carefully Jesus' employment of symbols from creation to speak about the Father. For him Jesus is the "great poet-King." In discussing MacDonald's understanding of symbol, allegory, and Scripture, we have shown that he was well aware of the fact that symbols are particularly prone to lose their vitality and are therefore always in need of being recovered as symbols in order to continue their revelatory nature. Poetics more widely speaking can therefore be "revelatory" insofar as it refreshes the revelatory nature of Scripture.

MacDonald's understanding of the parabolic must be considered within his wider understanding of revelation in Christ and Jesus' employment of symbols from creation to reveal the Father. Just as the symbol is particularly prone to lose its revelatory dimension, so by implication is the language of Scripture. The need to refresh the surprising and often subversive nature of Scripture is an important concern for MacDonald's own writing as he sought to recover the revelatory and transformative power of the Bible.

Focusing in on MacDonald's understanding of the parabolic, we brought to the fore his insistence that parable demands participation in order to be understood properly. By drawing the hearer/reader into the world of the story, MacDonald challenges the reader to become an active participant, to think for him/herself by making literary connections that are surprising and even shocking, and in the process of doing so embrace that which is revealed. Form and content of parabolic speech work together in a unique way to bring about the participation and transformation of the reader.

In the final chapter the insights gained from our discussion of the form of Jesus' parables guide our interpretation of *Lilith*. Discerning parabolic patterns opens up a unique perspective and helps solve many riddles in one of Macdonald's most difficult works. Novalis' employment of the metaphor of the night and dream also contributes to understanding the theological nature of *Lilith*, and MacDonald's use of these same metaphors. With this twofold cord in hand, we have challenged an important strand in MacDonald scholarship that sees his use of fantasy as a move away from a decidedly Christian and Christo-centric view to a more polyvalent, possibly still religious but less Christian perspective of reality. The lack of direct references to God and especially Christ has caused many an interpreter to suggest that Christ does not play any (significant) role in *Lilith*. On a surface level this option seems quite possible. The lack of references to Christ and MacDonald's use of highly suggestive metaphors seem to make it less likely to read *Lilith* in a decidedly Christian way. We have argued, to the contrary, that examining parabolic patterns in *Lilith* sheds new light on this very important question. The lack of overt references to Christ is no longer seen as indication that *Lilith* is less Christian but becomes now not only an important but also necessary part of MacDonald's parabolic strategy.

That our interpretation is a highly probable one is further supported by the fact that it can make sense of and see the connections between a whole range of key metaphors used in the novel. Considering that metaphors often have entailments, we have been able to offer an interpretation of the metaphor of death, the house of the dead, the cosmic funeral, Mr. Raven, and his vocations as sexton and priest that is coherent and logical and in line with MacDonald's overall Christo-centric view of the world. Interpreting the metaphors of the night and dreams in light of Novalis has further substantiated our argument as these metaphors complement the metaphor of death and its entailments and highlight the eschatological dimension of Christ's death and resurrection for the believer. Content and form work together in *Lilith* to approach one of the most difficult mysteries of the Christian faith. A willingness to enter into Christ's death and resurrection can only find its fulfillment in the future with Christ's second coming.

In this study, we have sought to further the dialogue between the study of the Bible and literature for Christian spirituality. Not only has this study brought to the fore how important the genre of parable is for the proclamation of the Kingdom of God but has also shed considerable light on George MacDonald as "spiritual theologian" whose intent in writing Christian fiction has always been a pastoral one: exploring and expressing the lived dimension of the Christian faith. For MacDonald an important pastoral incentive for writing fiction was to recover the gospel message for his very particular Victorian audience and move his audience from being spectators to becoming active and growing participants in the gospel of Jesus Christ. MacDonald knew the dangers of a cultural Christianity that had "tamed" the gospel into a system of beliefs one could hold at arm's length without allowing the death and resurrection of Christ to pierce and transform one's daily life. His concern in writing Christian fiction was to provide a literary space that would challenge his readership to be "questioned, judged, stripped naked and left speechless by that which lies at the center of their faith" as Rowan Williams put it so eloquently.[1]

While we have reached the end of this specific project, it is only a beginning for understanding MacDonald's fantasy and fairytales—and particularly their form—from a decidedly Christian perspective. George MacDonald was primarily a spiritual theologian whose intent in writing Christian fiction was for the formation and transformation for his literary parish. Ronald MacDonald, George MacDonald's son, captured beautifully this marriage of spiritual theology and imagination in storied form:

> Because his religion was his life, he could no more divide the religious from the secular than a fish separate swimming from water . . . I have heard of men whose whole lives were coloured by religion. But George MacDonald's life *was* religion . . . his imaginative faculty was a prism, falling through which the Great White Light was disparted into seventy times seven hues of human delight.[2]

---

1. Williams, *Wound*, 11.
2. Ronald MacDonald, "George MacDonald," 112–13.

Bibliography

Aiura, Reiko. "Recurring Symbols in the Fantasies and Children's Stories of George MacDonald." MLit, University of Aberdeen, 1986.
Amell, Barbara, editor. *The Art of God: Lectures on the Great Poets by George MacDonald*. Portland: Wingfold, 2004.
Ankeny, Rebecca. *The Story, the Teller and the Audience in George MacDonald's Fiction*. Lewiston, NY: Mellen, 2000.
Auden, W. H. "Afterword." In *The Golden Key*. New York: Farrar, Straus & Giroux, 1966.
Bailey, Kenneth. *Finding the Lost Cultural Keys to Luke 15*. St. Louis: Concordia, 1992.
———. *Jacob & the Prodigal: How Jesus Retold Israel's Story*. Downers Grove, IL: InterVarsity, 2003.
———. *Poet and Peasant: A Literary Cultural Approach to the Parables in Luke*. Grand Rapids: Eerdmans, 1976.
Balthasar, Hans Urs von. *Prometheus*. Heidelberg: Kerle, 1947.
Barbour, Ian G. *Myths, Models and Paradigms*. London: Harper & Row, 1974.
Barfield, Owen. "Either: Or." In *Imagination and the Spirit*, edited by Charles A. Huttar, 25–42. Grand Rapids: Eerdmans, 1971.
Bauckham, Richard, and Trevor Hart. *Hope against Hope: Christian Eschatology at the Turn of the Millennium*. Grand Rapids: Eerdmans, 1999.
Bauer, W., et al., editors. *Greek-English Lexicon of the New Testament and other Early Christian Literature*. 2nd ed. Chicago: University of Chicago Press, 1957.
Bergmann, Frank. "The Roots of Tolkien's Tree: the Influence of George MacDonald and German Romanticism upon Tolkien's Essay 'On Fairy-Stories.'" *Mosaic* 10 (1977) 5–14.
Berlin, Isaiah. *The Roots of Romanticism*. London: Chatto & Windus, 1999.
Best, Ernest. "Dead in Trespasses and Sin (Eph 2.1)." *JSNT* 13 (1981) 9–25.
———. *Following Jesus: Discipleship in the Gospel of Mark*. Sheffield: University of Sheffield, 1981.
Biser, Eugen. *Abstieg und Auferstehung: die Geistige Welt in Novalis Hymnen an die Nacht*. Heidelberg: Schneider, 1954.
Black, Max. *Models and Metaphors: Studies in Language and Philosophy*. New York: Cornell University Press, 1962.
Bohm, David. *On Creativity*. London: Routledge, 1996.
Broome, F. Hal. "The Science-Fantasy of George MacDonald." PhD diss., University of Edinburgh, 1985.

Brown, Francis, S. R. Driver, and Charles A. Brigges, editors. *A Hebrew and English Lexicon of the Old Testament*. Oxford: Clarendon, 1966.
Brown, Nicola. "What Is the Stuff That Dreams Are Made Of?" In *The Victorian Supernatural*, edited by Nicola Brown, Carolyn Burdett, and Pamela Thurschwell. Cambridge: Cambridge University Press, 2004.
Brown, Nicola, Carolyn Burdett, and Pamela Thurschwell. "Introduction." In *The Victorian Supernatural*, edited by Nicola Brown, Carolyn Burdett, and Pamela Thurschwell. Cambridge: Cambridge University Press, 2004.
Buber, Martin. *Ich Und Du*. Berlin: Schocken, 1936.
Carpenter, Humphrey. *Tolkien: A Biography*. London: Allen & Unwin, 1977.
Cavaliero, Glen. *The Supernatural and English Fiction*. Oxford: Oxford University Press, 1995.
Chadwick, Owen. *The Secularization of the European Mind in the Nineteenth Century*. Cambridge: Cambridge University Press, 1975.
———. *The Victorian Church*. 2 vols. London: Black, 1971–1972.
Cheyne, Alec. "The Bible and Change in the Nineteenth Century." In *The Bible in Scottish Life and Literature*, edited by David Wright, 192–207. Edinburgh: Saint Andrew, 1988.
Coleridge, Samuel Taylor. *Aids to Reflection*. London: Routledge, n.d.
———. *Biographia Literaria*. London: Dent, 1906.
———. *Confessions of an Inquiring Spirit*. New York: Chelsea House, 1983.
———. *The Works of Samuel Taylor Coleridge*. Ware, UK: Wordsworth, 1994.
Copleston, Frederick. *A History of Philosophy*. Vol. 7. London: Search, 1963.
———. *A History of Philosophy*. Vol. 8. London: Burns & Oates, 1966.
Cosslett, Tess, editor. *Science and Religion in the Nineteenth Century*. Cambridge: Cambridge University Press, 1984.
Crossan, J. D. *In Parables: the Challenge of the Historical Jesus*. New York: Harper & Row, 1973.
———. "Parable, Allegory, and Paradox." In *Semiology and the Parables*, edited by Daniel Patte, 264–71. Pittsburgh: Pickwick, 1976.
———. *The Power of Parable: How Fiction by Jesus became Fiction about Jesus*. New York: Harper Collins, 2012.
Dante Alighieri. *The Divine Comedy*. New York: Knopf, 1995.
Davis, Philip. *The Victorians*. Oxford English Literary History. New York: Oxford University Press, 2002.
Dawson, John David. *Christian Figural Reading and the Fashioning of Identity*. Berkeley: University of California Press, 2002.
Dearborn, Kerry. *Baptized Imagination: The Theology of George MacDonald*. Ashgate: Aldershot, 2006.
———. "Prophetic or Heretic: A Study of the Theology of George MacDonald." PhD diss., University of Aberdeen, 1994.
Docherty, John. "Worlds Beyond the Looking-Glass: Charles Dodgson's Second *Alice* and the Structural Elements of George MacDonald's *Lilith*." *Inklings: Jahrbuch* 13 (1995) 61–72.
Drummond, Andrew, and James Bulloch. *The Church in Victorian Scotland*. Edinburgh: Saint Andrew, 1975.
Dunn, James. "Salvation Proclaimed VI. Romans 6.1–11: Dead and Alive." *The Expository Times* 93 (1982) 259–64.

Edwards, Mark. "Origen on Christ, Tropology, and Exegesis." In *Metaphor, Allegory, and the Classical Tradition*, edited by G. R. Boys-Stones, 235–56. Oxford: Oxford University Press, 2003.

Engel, Manfred. "Träumen und Nichtträumen Zugleich. Novalis' Theorie und Poetik des Traumes zwischen Aufklärung und Hochromantik." In *Novalis und die Wissenschaften*, edited by Herbert Uerlings, 143–168. Tübingen: Niemeyer, 1997.

Engell, James. *The Creative Imagination*. Cambridge, MA: Havard Unviersity Press, 1981.

Erlemann, Kurt. "Wohin Steuert die Gleichnisforschung?" *Zeitschrift für Neues Testament* 2 (1999) 2–10.

Fishbane, Michael. *The Garments of Torah: Essays in Biblical Hermeneutics*. Bloomington: Indiana University Press, 1992.

Fletcher, Angus. *Allegory: the Theory of a Symbolic Mode*. London: Cornell University Press, 1964.

Flusser, David. *Die Rabbinischen Gleichnisse und der Gleichniserzähler Jesus, Teil 1: Das Wesen der Gleichnisse*. Bern: Lang, 1981.

Flynn, Joseph, and David Edwards, editors. *George MacDonald in the Pulpit*. Whitethorn, CA: Johannesen, 1996.

Frei, Hans. *The Eclipse of Biblical Narrative*. Chelsea: BookCrafters, 1974.

Frör, Kurt. *Wege zur Schriftauslegung: Biblische Hermeneutik für Unterricht und Predigt*. Düsseldorf: Patmos, 1967.

Frye, Northrop. *Anatomy of Criticism*. Princeton: Princeton University Press, 1957.

Gerold, Thomas. *Die Gotteskindschaft des Menschen: die Theologische Anthropologie bei George MacDonald*. Berlin: Lit, 2007.

Goodwin, Charles. "On the Mosaic Cosmogony." In *Essays and Reviews*. London: Green, Longman, & Roberts, 1861.

Green, J. H. "Introduction." In *Confessions of an Inquiring Spirit*. New York: Chelsea House, 1983.

Gunton, Colin E. *The Actuality of the Atonement: A Study of Metaphor, Rationality and the Christian Tradition*. Edinburgh: T. & T. Clark, 1988.

Harding, Anthony John. *Coleridge and the Inspired Word*. McGill-Queen's Studies in the History of Ideas. Montreal: McGill-Queen's University Press, 1985.

Hart, Trevor. *Creation, Creaturliness and Artistry*. Louisville: Westminster John Knox, forthcoming.

———. "Reformed Theology in Scotland." *Acta Theologica* 12 (1992) 63–87.

———. *Transfigured Flesh*. Louisville: Westminster John Knox, forthcoming.

Hays, Richard. *The Conversion of the Imagination: Paul as Interpreter of Israel's Scripture*. Grand Rapids: Eerdmans, 2005.

———. *Echoes of Scripture in the Letters of Paul*. New Haven: Yale University Press, 1989.

Hayward, Deirdre Christine. "George MacDonald and Three German Thinkers." PhD diss., University of Dundee, 2000.

Hein, Rolland. "Faith and Fiction: a Study of the Effects of Religious Convictions in the Adult Fantasies and Novels of George MacDonald." PhD diss., Purdue University, 1971.

———. *George MacDonald: Victorian Mythmaker*. Whitethorn, CA: Johannesen, 1999.

———. "A Great Good Is Coming: George MacDonald's Phantastes and Lilith." In *Journey to the Celestial City*, edited by Wayne Martindale, 119–28. Chicago: Moody, 1995.

———. *The Harmony Within: The Spiritual Vision of George MacDonald*. Grand Rapids: Eerdmans, 1982.

———. "Lilith: Theology through Mythopoeia." *Christian Scholar's Review* 3 (1973) 215–31.

Helmholtz, Anna Augusta. *The Indebtedness of Samuel Taylor Coleridge to August Wilhelm Von Schlegel*. 1969 ed. Reprint, Madison, WI: Folcroft, 1907.

Heschel, Abraham. *The Sabbath*. New York: Farrer, Straus & Giroux, 2005.

Herzog, William. *Parables as Subversive Speech*. Louisville: Westminster John Knox, 1994.

Hobbis, Faith Mary. "'That Night': Vane's Struggle for Christian Identity in George MacDonald's *Lilith*." PhD diss., University of Glasgow, 2001.

Hoffmann, E. T. A. *Der Goldene Topf*. Ditzingen: Reklam, 1993.

Holmes, Richard. *Coleridge Darker Reflections*. London: HarperCollins, 1998.

———. *Coleridge Early Visions*. London: Hodder & Stoughton, 1989.

Honig, Edwin. *Dark Conceit: The Making of Allegory*. Evanston, IL: Northwestern University Press, 1959.

Hooper, Walter, editor. *The Collected Letters of C. S. Lewis*. 3 vols. London: Harper Collins, 2000.

Horrocks, Don. *Laws of the Spiritual Order: Innovation and Reconstruction on the Soteriology of Thomas Erskine of Linlathen*. Carlisle, UK: Paternoster, 2004.

Jackson, Bernard. "The Jewish Background to the Prodigal Son: An Unresolved Problem." Unpublished paper given at the International SBL meeting. Summer 2006. Edinburgh.

Jeremias, Joachim. *Die Gleichnisse Jesu*. Berlin: Evangelische Verlagsanstalt GmbH, 1955.

Johnson, Kirstin Jeffrey. "Curdie's Intertextual Dialogue: Engaging Maurice, Arnold, and Isaiah." In *George MacDonald: Literary Heritage and Heirs*, edited by Roderick McGillis, 153–82. Wayne, PA: Zossima, 2007.

———. "Sacred Story." *Christian History* 86 (2005) 35–38.

Jones, Peter d' A. *The Christian Socialist Revival, 1877–1914 Religion, Class, and Social Conscience in Late-Victorian England*. Princeton: Princeton University Press, 1968.

Jowett, Benjamin. "On the Interpretation of Scripture." In *Essays and Reviews*, 330–433. London: Green, Longman, & Roberts, 1861.

Jülicher, Adolf. *Die Gleichnisreden Jesu*. Tübingen: Mohr/Siebeck, 1901.

Jüngel, Eberhard. "Metaphorical Truth." In *Theological Essays*, edited by J. B. Webster, 16–71. Edinburgh: T. & T. Clark, 1989.

Kasperowski, Ira. *Mittelalterrezeption im Werk des Novalis*. Tübingen: Niemeyer, 1994.

Kearney, Richard. *The Wake of the Imagination*. London: Routledge, 1988.

Kegler, Adelheid. "Der Schlaf der Seele: Night's Pore in Torments. Die Verschmelzung Traditioneller und Schwedenborgianischer Denkstrukturen in MacDonald's *Lilith*." *Inklings: Jahrbuch* 13 (1995) 137–58.

———. "George MacDonald oder die Resakralisierung des Wissens." *Inklings: Jahrbuch* 2 (1984) 85–110.

———. "Silent House: MacDonald, Brontë and Silence Within the Soul." In *The Victorian Fantasists: Essays on Culture, Society and Belief in the Mythopoeic Fiction of the Victorian Age*, edited by Kath Filmer, 104–32. London: Macmillan, 1991.
Kegler, Karl. "Eine Stadt aus Kristall." *Inklings: Jahrbuch* 13 (1995) 75–89.
Klauck, Hans-Josef. *Allegorie und Allegorese in Synoptischen Gleichnistexten*. Neutestamentliche Abhandlungen 13. Münster: Aschendorff, 1978.
Knoepflmacher, U. C. Introduction to *The Complete Fairy Tales*, by George MacDonald, vii–xx. New York: Penguin, 1999.
Kreglinger, Gisela H. "George MacDonald." In *The Tolkien Encyclopedia: Scholarship and Critical Assessment*, edited by Michael D. C. Drout, 399–400. London: Routledge, 2006.
———. "George MacDonald's Christian Fiction: Parables, Imagination and Dreams." PhD diss., University of St. Andrews, 2008.
Kremer, Detlef. *Romantik*. Stuttgart: Metzler, 2003.
Kruger, Steven F. *Dreaming in the Middle Ages*. Cambridge Studies in Medieval Literature. Cambridge: Cambridge University Press, 1992.
Lakoff, George, and Mark Johnson. *Metaphors We Live By*. Chicago: University of Chicago Press, 1980.
Leupould, Ulrich S., editor. *Luther's Works*. Vol. 53. Philadelphia: Fortress, 1965.
Lewis, C. S. *The Allegory of Love*. London: Oxford University Press, 1938.
———. *George MacDonald: an Anthology*. London: Centenary, 1946.
———. "The Vision of John Bunyan." In *The Pilgrims' Progress: A Casebook*, edited by Roger Sharrock, 195–203. London: Macmillan, 1976.
Lewis, W. H., editor. *Letters of C. S. Lewis*. London: Bles, 1966.
Lincoln, Andrew, and A. J. M Wedderburn. *The Theology of the Later Pauline Letters*. Cambridge: Cambridge University Press, 1993.
Louth, Andrew. *Discerning the Mystery*. Oxford: Clarendon, 1983.
Lubac, Henri de. *Medieval Exegesis*. Translated by Mark Sebanc. 3 vols. Edinburgh: T. & T. Clark, 1998.
MacDonald, George. *Adela Cathcart*. Whitethorn, CA: Johannesen, 2000.
———. *Alec Forbes of Howglen*. Whitethorn, CA: Johannesen, 1990.
———. *Annals of a Quiet Neighbourhood*. London: Paul, Trench, Trübner, 1893.
———. *At the Back of the North Wind*. Glasgow: Blackie and Son, 1871.
———. *The Complete Fairytales*. New York: Penguin, 1999.
———. *David Elginbrod*. London: Hurst & Blackett, 1871.
———. "Diary of an Old Soul." In *Rampolli*, 183–302. Whitethorn, CA: Johannesen, 1995.
———. *A Dish of Orts*. Whitethorn, CA: Johannesen, 1996.
———. *Donal Grant*. Whitethorn, CA: Johannesen, 1991.
———. *England's Antiphon*. Whitethorn, CA: Johannesen, 1996.
———. *The Hope of the Gospel / Miracles of our Lord*. Whitethorn, CA: Johannesen, 2000.
———. *Lilith: First and Final*. Whitethorn, CA: Johannesen, 1998.
———. *Paul Faber, Surgeon*. Whitethorn, CA: Johannesen, 1992.
———. *Phantastes*. Grand Rapids: Eerdmans, 2000.
———. *The Poetical Works of George MacDonald*. 2 vols. London: Chatto & Windus, 1911.
———. *The Princess and Curdie*. London: Blackie & Son, 1900.
———. "The Princess and the Goblin." *Good Words for the Young*, 1871, 1–14.

———. *Rampolli*. Whitethorn, CA: Johannesen, 1995.
———. *Ronald Bannerman's Boyhood*. Whitethorn, CA: Johannesen, 1993.
———. *Salted with Fire*. Whitethorn, CA: Johannesen, 1996.
———. *The Seaboard Parish*. Whitethorn, CA: Johannesen, 1995.
———. *Twelve of the Spiritual Songs of Novalis Done into English by George MacDonald*. Huntly Library Archives, 1851.
———. *Unspoken Sermons*. Whitethorn: Johannesen, 1990.
MacDonald, Greville. *George MacDonald and His Wife*. Whitethorn, CA: Johannesen, 1998.
MacDonald, Ronald. "George MacDonald." In *From a Northern Window*, 55–113. London: Nisbet, 1911.
MacNeice, Louis. *Varieties of Parable*. Cambridge: Cambridge University Press, 1965.
Manlove, Colin. *Christian Fantasy*. London: Macmillan, 1992.
———. *Modern Fantasy: Five Studies*. Cambridge: Cambridge University Press, 1975.
Marcus, Joel. *The Way of the Lord: Christological Exegesis of the Old Testament in the Gospel of Mark*. Louisville: Westminster John Knox, 1992.
Marshall, Cynthia. "Allegory, Orthodoxy, Ambivalence: MacDonald's 'The Day Boy and the Night Girl.'" *Children's Literature* 16 (1988) 57–75.
Martin, Tim. "A Checklist of Biblical Allusions in Lilith." *North Wind*, 14 (1995) 75–78.
McGillis, Roderick. "The Fantastic Imagination: The Prose Romances of George MacDonald." PhD diss., University of Reading, 1973.
———. "Phantastes and Lilith: Femininity and Freedom." In *The Gold Thread*, 31–55. Edinburgh: Edinburgh University Press, 1990.
McInnes, Jeff. "Shadows and Chivalry: Pain, Suffering, Evil and Goodness in the Works of George MacDonald and C. S. Lewis." PhD diss., St. Andrews University, 2004.
Mendelson, Michael. "George MacDonald's *Lilith* and the Conventions of Ascent." *Studies in Scottish Literature* 20 (1985) 197–218.
Morris, Jeremy. *F. D. Maurice and the Crisis of Christian Authority*. Oxford: Oxford University Press, 2005.
Novalis. *Die Christenheit oder Europa*. Stuttgart: Reclam, 1984.
———. *Henry von Ofterdingen*. Translated by Palmer Hilty. New York: Ungar, 1964.
———. *Novalis: Das Dichterische Werk, Tagebücher und Briefe*. Vol. 1 of *Novalis Werke*, edited by Hans-Joachim Mähl and Richard Samuel. München: Hanser, 1978.
———. *Novalis: Das Philosophisch-Theoretische Werk*. Vol. 2 of *Novalis Werke*, edited by Hans-Joachim Mähl and Richard Samuel. München: Hanser, 1978.
Pagaard, Timothy Lowell. "Parable in the Fiction of George MacDonald." MA thesis, University of California, 1987.
Pelikan, Jaroslav. *Christian Doctrine and Modern Culture (since 1700)*. Vol. 5 of *The Christian Tradition*. Chicago: University of Chicago Press, 1989.
Pennington, John. "Thematic and Structural Subversion in the Fairytales and Fantasies of George MacDonald." PhD diss., Purdue University, 1987.
Perkins, Mary Ann. "Religious Thinker." In *The Cambridge Companion to Coleridge*, edited by Lucy Newlyn, 187–99. Cambridge: Cambridge University Press, 2002.
Pfefferkorn, Kristin. *Novalis: A Romantic's Theory of Language and Poetry*. New Haven: Yale University Press, 1988.
Polanyi, Michael. "The Creative Imagination." *Chemical & Engineering News* 44 (1966) 85–94.

Preus, James Samuel. *From Shadow to Promise: Old Testament Interpretation from Augustine to the Young Luther*. Cambridge, MA: Harvard University Press, 1969.

Prickett, Stephen. "F. D. Maurice: the Man Who Re-wrote the Book." *North Wind* 21 (2002) 1–13.

———. "'The Living Educts of the Imagination': Coleridge on Religious Language." In *Romanticism and Religion the Tradition of Coleridge and Wordsworth in the Victorian Church*, 9–33. Cambridge: Cambridge University Press, 1976.

———. *Romanticism and Religion: The Tradition of Wordsworth and Coleridge in the Victorian Church*. Cambridge: Cambridge University Press, 1976.

———. "The Two Worlds of George MacDonald." In *For the Childlike: George MacDonald's Fantasies For Children*, edited by Roderick McGillis, 17–30. Metuchen: Scarecrow, 1992.

———. *Victorian Fantasy*. Waco: Baylor University Press, 2005.

———. *Words and the Word: Language, Poetics and Biblical Interpretation*. Cambridge: Cambridge University Press, 1986.

Raeper, William. *George MacDonald: Novelist and Victorian Visionary*. Tring, UK: Lion, 1987.

Reardon, Bernard. *Religious Thoughts in the Nineteenth Century*. Cambridge: Cambridge University Press, 1966.

Reed-Nancarrow, Paula Elizabeth. "Remythologizing the Bible: Fantasy and the Revelatory Hermeneutic of George MacDonald." PhD diss., University of Minnesota, 1988.

Reis, Richard H. *George MacDonald*. New York: Twayne, 1972.

Richards, I. A. *Coleridge on the Imagination*. London: Routledge, 1968.

Ricoeur, Paul. "Biblical Hermeneutics." *Semeia* 4 (1975) 26–148.

Riga, Frank P. *The Platonic Imagery of George MacDonald and C. S. Lewis: The Allegory of the Cave Transfigured*. Metuchen, NJ: Scarecrow, 1992.

Robb, David. *God's Fiction*. Vol. 4. Eureka, CA: Sunrise, 1987.

Roder, Florian. *Novalis: Die Verwandlung des Menschen*. Stuttgart: Urachhaus, 1992.

Ruskin, John. *Time and Tide and Other Writings*. London: Dent & Sons, 1936.

Sadler, Glenn Edward. *An Expression of Character: The Letters of George MacDonald*. Grand Rapids: Eerdmans, 1994.

Schottroff, Luise. *The Parables of Jesus*. Minneapolis: Fortress, 2006.

Schulz, Gerhard. "Novalis (Friedrich von Hardenberg)." In *Deutsche Dichter: Romantik, Biedermeier und Vormärz*, edited by Frank Rainer Max Gunter Grimm. Deutsche Dichter. Stuttgart: Reclam, 1989.

Scott, A. J. *Discourses*. London: Macmillan, 1866.

———. *On the Academical Study of a Vernacular Literature*. London: Walton & Maberly, 1848.

Scott, Bernard Brandon. *Hear Then the Parable: A Commentary on the Parables of Jesus*. Minneapolis: Fortress, 1989.

Sepasgosarin, Wilhelmine Maria. *Der Tod als Romantisierendes Prinzip des Lebens*. Frankfurt: Lang, 1991.

Shippey, T. A. *The Road to Middle-Earth*. London: Allen & Unwin, 1982.

Smalley, Beryl. *The Study of the Bible in the Middle Ages*. Oxford: Clarendon, 1941.

Snodgrass, Klyne R. "From Allegorizing to Allegorizing: A History of the Interpretation of the Parables of Jesus." In *The Challenge of Jesus' Parables*, edited by Richard N. Longenecker, 3–29. Grand Rapids: Eerdmans, 2000.

———. *Stories with Intent: A Comprehensive Guide to the Parables of Jesus*. Grand Rapids: Eerdmans, 2008.
Soskice, Janet Martin. *Metaphor and Religious Language*. Oxford: Clarendon, 1985.
Soto, Fernando. "Kore Motifs in the Princess Books: Mythic Threads Between Irenes and Eirinys." In *George MacDonald: Literary Heritage and Heirs*, edited by Roderick McGillis, 65–82. Wayne, PA: Zossima, 2007.
———. "Mirrors in MacDonald's *Phantates*: A Reflexive Structure." *North Wind* 23 (2004) 27–47.
Spina, Giorgio. "Contrapositions, Correspondences and Symmetries in George MacDonald's Fiction." *Inklings: Jahrbuch für Literatur und Aesthetik* 13 (1995) 27–45.
Steiner, George. *Language and Silence: Essays 1958–1966*. London: Faber & Faber, 1985.
Stern, Frank. *A Rabbi Looks at Jesus' Parables*. New York: Rowman & Littlefield, 2005.
Störig, Hans Joachim. *Kleine Weltgeschichte Der Philosophie*. Stuttgart: Kohlhammer, 1990.
Strauss, David Friedrich. *The Life of Jesus Critically Examined*. Edited by Peter C. Hodgson. Translated by George Eliot. Philadelphia: Fortress, 1972.
Swartley, W. *Israel's Scripture Traditions and the Synoptic Gospels*. Peabody, MA: Hendrickson, 1994.
Swiatecka, Jadwiga. *The Idea of the Symbol*. Cambridge: Cambridge University Press, 1980.
Tennyson, Alfred. *In Memoriam*. London: Macmillan, 1905.
Thiselton, Anthony. *The Two Horizons*. Exeter: Paternoster, 1980.
Tolkien, J. R. R. *The Monster and the Critics and Other Essays*. London: Allen & Unwin, 1983.
———. "On Fairy-Stories." In *Tree and Leaf*, 9–73. London: Allen & Unwin, 1964.
Tulloch, John. *Movements of Religious Thought in Britain During the Nineteenth Century*. London: Longmans, Green, 1885.
Turner, Frank Miller. *Between Science and Religion*. New Haven: Yale University Press, 1974.
Vanhoozer, Kevin J. *Biblical Narrative in the Philosophy of Paul Ricoeur: A Study in Hermeneutics and Theology*. Cambridge: Cambridge University Press, 1990.
Warnock, Mary. *Imagination*. London: Faber & Faber, 1976.
Wellek, René. *A History of Modern Criticism: 1750–1950*. Vol. 1. London: Cape, 1955.
Wheeler, Michael. *Death and the Future Life in Victorian Literature and Theology*. Cambridge: Cambridge University Press, 1990.
Whitman, Jon. *Allegory: The Dynamics of an Ancient and Medieval Technique*. Oxford: Clarendon, 1987.
Williams, Rowan. *The Wound of Knowledge*. Cambridge, MA: Cowley, 1990.
Wink, Walter. *The Bible in Human Transformation: Toward a New Paradigm for Biblical Study*. Philadelphia: Fortress, 1973.
Wolff, Robert Lee. *The Golden Key: A Study of the Fiction of George MacDonald*. New Haven: Yale University Press, 1961.
Woodworth, Arthur. *Christian Socialism in England*. London: Swan Sonnenschein, 1903.
Wordsworth, William. "Preface." In vol. 1 of *Poems: 1815*. Oxford: Woodstock, 1989.

Wordsworth, Jonathan. "'The Infinite I Am': Coleridge and the Ascent of Being." In *Coleridge's Imagination*, edited by Richard Gravil, Lucy Newlyn, and Nicolas Roe, 22–52. Cambridge: Cambridge University Press, 1985.

Wright, N. T. *Jesus and the Victory of God*. Vol. 2 of *Christian Origins and the Question of God*. Minneapolis: Fortress, 1997.

Zipes, Jack. *Fairy Tales and the Art of Subversion*. New York: Routledge, 1988.

Author Index

Aiura, Reiko, 141, 144, 146, 162
Ankeny, Rebecca, 155, 166
Aquinas, Thomas. *See* Thomas Aquinas.
Aristotle, 18–19, 21–22, 37
Auden, W. H., 170
Augustine, 34–35, 46
Bacon, Francis, 114
Bailey, Kenneth, 18, 32, 45, 53, 55–56
Balthasar, Hans Urs von, 74
Bannermann, James, 109
Barbour, Ian, 31
Barfield, Owen, 61, 88–89
Bauckham, Richard, 51–52, 57
Baumgarten, Alexander Gottlieb, 37
Baur, F. D., 37, 115
Bede, 35
Bengel, Johann Albrecht, 37
Bergmann, Frank, 195
Berlin, Isaiah, 80–82
Best, Ernest, 175, 187
Biser, Eugen, 71, 74
Black, Max, 30–31
Blake, William, 164, 180, 200
Boccaccio, 41
Bohm, David, 91
Boyle, Robert, 114
Broome, F. Hal, 176, 181, 184
Brown, Nicola, 98, 200–201
Browning, Robert, 158
Buber, Martin, 96
Bulloch, James, 103, 109, 115
Bunyan, John, 38, 41, 48, 56, 149, 167
Burns, Robert, 12

Calvin, John, 7
Carlyle, Thomas, 105
Cavaliero, Glen, 170
Chadwick, Owen, 104, 108, 112–13, 115
characters, fictional
   Anderson, Annie, 7, 10
   Anodos, 91, 121, 130, 142, 177
   Armstrong, Ralf, 10, 158
   Blatherwick, James, 130, 163, 184
   Curdie, 114, 130, 146
   Diamond, 132, 134, 138, 163–64
   Elginbrod, David, 9
   Elginbrod, Janet, 9
   Elginbrod, Margret, 105
   Falconer, Robert, 130, 163
   Forbes, Alec, 130
   Gibbie, Sir, 10
   Grant, Donal, 117
   Grant, Janet, 9–10
   Grant, Robert, 10
   Hum-Drum, 118–19
   Irene, 9, 163
   Isy, 163
   Keck, Kopy, 118–19
   Lilith, 132, 144, 146, 163, 174, 176, 185, 187–90, 194, 197–98
   Macbeth, Lady, 85, 100
   Makemnoit, Princess, 118
   Mara, 174, 176, 185, 198
   McLear, John, 9
   McLear, Margret, 130
   Mossy, 160
   North Wind, 126, 132, 138, 163–64

Author Index

Nycteris, 9
Odysseus, 34
Photogen, 9
Raven, Mr., 172–75, 177–78, 181–97, 202, 204, 211
Sclater, Reverent Clement, 130, 163
St. John, Mary, 163
Sutherland, Hugh, 130
Tangle, 140–41, 144, 160
Vane, Mr., 64, 67, 70, 98, 114, 121, 130, 132, 138, 163, 169, 171–75, 177–78, 181–90, 192–99, 201–6
Chaucer, Daniel, 26, 38
Cheyne, Alec, 103
Coleridge, Samuel Taylor, 2–3, 19, 38, 77–78, 82–101, 104–11, 115–16, 128, 130–31, 145, 151–53, 180, 209
Copleston, Frederick, 80–81, 84, 86
Cosslett, Tess, 116
Crossan, John Dominic, 18, 32, 38, 51, 54
Dante Alighieri, 2, 11, 38, 56, 99, 114, 148, 167, 183, 203–4
Darwin, Charles, x, 111, 114
Davies, Sir John, 88, 90
Davis, Philip, 98, 114, 119–20, 164, 178
Dawson, John David, 35
De Wette, Wilhelm Martin Leberecht, 37
Dearborn, Kerry, 4–11, 89, 100, 124–27, 131–32, 164–65, 172
Docherty, John, 194
Dodd, C. H., 17–18, 32
Drummond, Andrew, 103, 109, 115
Dunn, James, 191
Edwards, Mark, 34–35, 41
Eichhorn, Albert, 37
Eliot, George, 98, 111–12, 116, 177
Engel, Manfred, 64–68, 70
Engell, James, 87–88
Erlemann, Kurt, 33
Ernesti, Johann August, 37
Erskine, Thomas, 8, 11, 144
Evans, Marian. *See* Eliot, George.
Ferrier, J. F., 119

Feuerbach, Ludwig, 98, 112
Fichte, Johann Gottlieb, 79, 86
Fishbane, Michael, 36
Fitzgerald, John Anster, 201
Fletcher, Angus, 22, 39, 41
Flusser, David, 15
Flynn, Joseph, 140, 145, 152
Fouqué, Friedrich, 97
Frei, Hans, 112
Frör, Kurt, 34–37
Frye, Northrop, 39–40
Gabler, Johann Philipp, 37
Gerold, Thomas, 4–5, 8, 117, 125–29, 131, 133, 165, 172
Goethe, Johann Wolfgang von, 2, 5, 38, 56, 105, 158, 173
Goodwin, Charles, 113
Green, J. H., 108
Greeves, Arthur, 60
Gregory the Great, 35
Gunton, Colin, 28–30, 54
Haldane, Robert, 103
Hardenberg, Friedrich von. *See* Novalis.
Harding, Anthony, 104
Hardy, Thomas, 180
Hart, Trevor, 7, 51–52, 57, 79–81, 86–87
Hays, Richard, 56–57
Hayward, Deirdre Christine, 67–68, 70, 72, 76
Hegel, Georg Wilhelm Friedrich, 98, 112
Hein, Rolland, 5–6, 11, 105, 114, 131, 133, 155, 169, 172–73, 177, 179
Heine, Heinrich, 5
Helmholtz, Anna Augusta, 86
Herbert, George, 2, 148, 155
Herder, Johann Gottfried von, 37, 65
Herzog, William, 18, 33, 45–46, 48
Heschel, Abraham, 25
Hobbes, Thomas, 19, 28
Hobbis, Faith Mary, 181, 194, 202
Hoffmann, E. T. A, 195
Holmes, Richard, 86
Homer, 33–34
Honig, Edwin, 39
Hooper, Walter, 43, 60, 149, 181

Horrocks, Don, 8, 161
Hugh of St. Victor, 35
Hume, David, 119
Jackson, Bernard, 55
Jeffrey Johnson, Kirstin, 12
Jeremias, Joachim, 15, 17–18, 32, 49, 53
Jerome, 35
Jesus, ix–xii, 1–3, 7–8, 10, 13–18, 32–34, 37, 43, 45, 47–49, 51, 53–58, 68, 71, 73–76, 91, 105, 109, 112, 121–23, 125, 127–29, 131–33, 135, 137–38, 140–48, 151–52, 154–56, 160–63, 166–67, 169, 171, 173–75, 178, 182–84, 188, 190–93, 196–97, 207–8, 210–11
John the Baptist, 175
Johnson, Mark, 19, 24–27, 30, 134
Jones, Peter, 8
Jowett, Benjamin, 115
Jülicher, Adolf, 17–19, 32, 37, 46, 48–49
Jüngel, Eberhard, 19, 21–22
Kafka, Franz, 58
Kant, Immanuel, 77–80, 83, 86–87, 92, 100, 119
Kasperowski, Ira, 66
Kearney, Richard, 81, 83, 89
Kegler, Adelheid, 136, 165, 196, 198, 203–204
Kegler, Karl, 203
Kingsley, Charles, 8, 105
Klauck, Hans Joachim, 33, 39, 56–57, 134, 153
Knoepflmacher, U. C., 119
Kremer, Detlef, 134
Kruger, Steven F., 69
Lakoff, George, 19, 24–27, 30, 134
Leupould, Ulrich S., 11
Lessing, Gotthold, 37, 41, 108
Lewis, C. S., 2, 4, 6, 39–40, 43, 46, 60, 99, 125, 149, 157, 170–71, 181
Lightfoot, J. B., 115
Lincoln, Andrew, 186–87, 190
Locke, John, 19, 28
Louth, Andrew, 39
Lubac, Henri de, 35–36
Ludlow, J. M., 8

Luther, Martin, 5, 11, 37
MacDonald, George, ix-x, xii, 1–14, 19, 26–27, 31, 40, 43–44, 47–48, 56–62, 64–73, 75, 77–78, 82, 84–86, 90–111, 114, 116–81, 183–205, 207–12
MacDonald, Greville, 5–6, 9, 11–12, 105, 147, 164, 168
MacDonald, Ronald, 12–13, 212
MacKay, George, 10
MacNeice, Louis, 1, 173
Manlove, Colin, 179
Marcus, Joel, 175
Marshall, Cynthia, 136, 149
Martin, Tim, 173
Mary Magdalene, 43
Maurice, F. D., 8, 11, 105, 137
McGillis, Roderick, 139, 172, 180–81, 195, 203–4
McInnes, Jeff, 179
McLeod Campbell, John, 8
Mendelson, Michael, 198
Milton, John, 2, 5, 12, 38–39, 56, 118, 148, 164
Moltman, Jürgen, 202
Morris, Jeremy, 137
Muratori, Ludwig Anton, 65
Newman, John Henry, 178
Novalis, 3, 5, 11–12, 19, 56, 60–77, 85, 122, 134, 140–41, 170, 179, 196, 198–200, 202–4, 209–11
Numenius, 34
Origen, 34–36
Pagaard, Timothy Lowell, 42
Paul, Jean, 65
Pelikan, Jaroslav, 161
Pennington, John, 162
Perkins, Mary Ann, 89
Perrault, Charles, 118
Pfefferkorn, Kristin, 64, 76
Philo of Alexandria, 34
Poe, Edgar Allan, 182
Polanyi, Michael, 94
Porphyry, 34
Powell, James, 105
Preus, James Samuel, 37
Prickett, Stephen, 84, 89, 105, 136, 143, 145, 150, 170, 179, 181, 192, 203

Ptolemy, 114
Quintilian, 18
Raeper, William, 5–6, 9, 11–12, 125, 181
Reardon, Bernard, 115
Reed-Nancarrow, Paula Elizabeth, 125, 147, 161
Reimarus, Hermann Samuel, 37
Reis, Richard, 168
Richards, I. A., 21, 87
Richerz, Georg Hermann, 65
Ricoeur, Paul, 20, 51–52
Riga, Frank P., 136
Robb, David, 85, 172, 176, 179
Roder, Florian, 73–74, 134
Ruskin, John, 11, 104
Sadler, Glenn Edward, 8–9, 11–12, 90
Sattaur, Jennifer, 172
Schelling, Friedrich Wilhelm Joseph, 78–83, 86–87, 89–92, 94
Schiller, Friedrich, 5
Schleiermacher, Friedrich, 37
Schottroff, Luise, 18, 34, 45–46
Schulz, Gerhard, 71
Scott, A. J., 11–12
Scott, Bernard Brandon, 33, 52
Scott, Sir Walter, 10, 12, 113
Semler, Johann, 37
Sepasgosarin, Wilhelmine Maria, 70, 72
Shakespeare, William, 2, 12, 39, 56, 97, 100, 110, 145, 147, 153–54
Shelley, Percy Bysshe, 12
Shippey, T. A., 45
Silverstris, Bernard, 38
Smalley, Beryl, 36–37
Smith, Page, 114
Snodgrass, Klyne R., 17–18
Sophia (mythical figure), 74
Sophie (Novalis's fiancée), 73–75
Soskice, Janet, 18–25, 28–29, 31–32, 139, 143
Soto, Fernando, 139
Spenser, Edmund, 38
Spina, Giorgio, 75
Steiner, George, 58
Stern, Frank, 18
Störig, Hans Joachim, 80–81, 90
Strauss, David, *ix*, 111–12
Swartley, W., 175
Swedenborg, Emanuel, 200
Swiatecka, Jadwiga, 99, 110, 155
Tennyson, Alfred Lord, 12, 97, 113–14, 158
Thiselton, Anthony, 54
Thomas Aquinas, 37
Thoreau, Henry David, 199
Tieck, Ludwig, 11, 61
Tolkien, J. R. R., 2, 4, 43–45, 172
Tulloch, John, 109–10
Turner, Frank Miller, 113
Vanhoozer, Kevin J., 20
Warnock, Mary, 78–81, 84, 86–87, 89
Wedderburn, A. J. M., 186–87, 190
Wellek, René, 38, 86
Wheeler, Michael, 164, 180, 182–83, 189
Whitman, Jon, 33–34, 38, 40
Williams, Rowan, 212
Wink, Walter, 54
Wittgenstein, Ludwig von, 28
Wolff, Christian, 64–65, 75, 203
Woodworth, Arthur, 8
Wordsworth, Jonathan, 82–83
Wordsworth, William, 91, 121, 131–33
Wright, N. T., 45
Zipes, Jack, 162

Scripture Index

Genesis
	34, 56, 103, 113, 144, 163, 173
40–41	41
41	34

Exodus
3:14	84
12:15	52
12:19	52
34:25	52

Leviticus
2:11	52
6:17	52
7:13	52
10:12	52
23:17	52

Numbers
21:8	144

Ruth
1:20	176

2 Samuel
12:1–19	15

Job
14:13–15	133

Psalms
9:17	7
23	56
42	142
78:2	1, 141
119:105	154, 198

Proverbs
9:1	141

Ecclesiastes
7:1–5	176

Song of Songs
	35, 73
3:12	35

Isaiah
5	34, 49
5:1–7	15
63:16	53

Ezekiel
	34
17	15, 34
17:1–8	15
17:3	53
17:12–21	15
17:22–24	15
17:22	53
17:23	53

Ezekiel (cont.)

19:1–9	15
19:10–14	15

Hosea

7:4	52

Amos

4:5	52

Matthew

10:16	144
11:28	174
13	52
13:34–35	1
13:35	141
16:6	52
16:11	52
16:18	160
18:23–35	50
18:23–27	51
20	53
20:1–15	51
21–22	53
23:37	51

Mark

	175, 182, 193
1:3	175
4	15, 34
4:1–9	15
4:13–20	15
6:8	175
8–10	175
8:15	52
8:21	175
8:27–33	175
9	176
9:33–37	175
9:34	175
9:42	176
9:43	176
10:24	175
10:52	175
12:1–12	10, 15–16
12:1–2	49
12:14	175

Luke

9:61	174
10	16, 45–46, 51
11:9	174
12:1	52
12:37	51
13	52
13:34	51
15	16, 51, 53, 56
15:18	48
16	16, 53
17	51
18	45, 51–52
18:2	48
18:4	48
18:9–14	54
20:38	133

John

	153, 184
1:1–4	106
1:3	131
4	142
14	205
14:6	133
16	205

Romans

	179, 190
5	190
6	170, 181, 185, 190–1
6:1–13	190–1
6:2	191
6:20	176
13:4	185

1 Corinthians

3:18	174
5:6–8	52
13:9–13	138
13:12–13	205

2 Corinthians

3:18	137–8, 143

Galatians

4:21–31	34
4:31—5:1	193
5:9	52

Ephesians

	179, 185–90
1:7	187
1:19–21	187
2	186
2:1–10	186–7
2:1–5	186
2:1	185
2:2	185
2:3	185
2:5	185
4	185
4:14	178
4:22	170, 187
4:24	187
5	186
5:8	195
5:14–15	186
5:14	185–6, 195
5:22	185
6:17	185

1 Timothy

2:14	176
2:15	185

Hebrews

	16, 143, 145
4:12	144
11:1	152
12:29	153

Revelation

	173
1:16	185
2:12	185
3	202
3:5	202
3:18	202
4:4	202
6	164
11	43

Subject Index

abstraction, *x-xi*, 78, 88, 107–9, 128
Adela Cathcart (MacDonald), 10, 61, 85, 118, 120, 148–49, 156–59, 166
aesthetics, 10, 17–18, 62, 68, 74, 77, 79, 121
Aids to Reflection (Coleridge), 89, 107–8, 145, 180
Alec Forbes of Howglen (MacDonald), 7, 10, 130
allegory, 3, 17–18, 22, 30, 32–51, 53–57, 68, 92, 102, 135–36, 148–50, 156, 170–72, 174, 176–77, 181, 208, 210
allusion(s), biblical, 10, 55, 83, 173–74, 176, 178, 183, 185
anagogy, 36–37
analogy, 27–30
anthropology, theological, 4, 128
Apocrypha, 107, 117
Aristotle, 18–19, 21–22, 37
art(s), 6, 10–12, 59, 76–77, 81–82, 85–88, 91, 94, 101, 131–32, 150, 167–68, 209
At the Back of the North Wind (MacDonald), 69, 126, 130, 132, 134, 138, 155, 163–64
atonement, 3, 6–7, 124, 127
authority (biblical), *x*, 107–11, 116, 152–53

baptism, 120, 155, 170, 190–91
beauty, 68, 90–91, 96, 98, 121, 131–32, 163–64, 168

Beowulf, 44–45
Bible, *x–xii*, 2, 9–10, 35–38, 63, 103–17, 122–25, 129, 139, 144, 151–55, 165–66, 173–76, 178, 185, 197, 207–8, 210–11. *See also* Scripture.
Biographia Literaria (Coleridge), 82–84, 86, 88–92, 99

Calvinism, 6–8, 124–25, 131, 144, 163, 172
"Castle: A Parable, The" (MacDonald), 10, 149
Celtic tradition, 10–11
Christian Socialist Movement, 8
Christology, 123–27, 156, 166, 196
Church of England, 8
clergy, 158–59, 184. *See also* minister, priest, sexton.
cognition, 2–3, 78–79, 86–87, 93, 100–101, 139, 152, 209
Confessions of an Inquiring Spirit (Coleridge), 83, 104–9
consciousness, 24, 27, 56, 61, 80–83, 86–87, 90–91, 93, 96, 98–101, 201, 209
creation, *ix–x*, 2–3, 7–8, 35, 38, 53, 79–81, 83–86, 93, 95, 97, 99–100, 102–3, 113, 123–24, 126–28, 131–35, 137, 141–42, 147, 150, 155–56, 166, 210
creativity, 2, 22, 31, 68, 77, 83–101, 209
crisis of faith, 3, 103, 108, 111–16

231

Critique of Judgment (Kant), 78
Critique of Pure Reason (Kant), 78

David Elginbrod (MacDonald), 9, 61, 85, 104–5, 130
"Day Boy and the Night Girl, The" (MacDonald), 9, 72, 121–22, 160
death, 2–3, 61, 63, 72–76, 120, 123, 127, 129–30, 164–65, 169–70, 174–75, 177–99, 203–5, 209, 211–12
depravity, 3, 6, 124, 144
depression, 25, 74
Diary of an Old Soul (MacDonald), 125
dictation (theory of biblical inspiration), 104, 106
discipleship, 1, 175
Dish of Orts (MacDonald), 61
disobedience, 168, 176, 185, 198. See also obedience.
Divine Comedy (Dante), 38, 99, 148, 167, 183
Donal Grant (MacDonald), 117
dreams, 34, 62–70, 72, 74–76, 98, 113–14, 163–64, 169–70, 179, 195, 199–205, 209–11

education, 8–9
election, 6
empiricism/empiricists, 19, 65, 69, 78, 119–21, 136, 169, 177, 195, 198, 200, 202
England's Antiphon (MacDonald), 5, 97, 105, 131, 133, 135, 139, 144, 147–49, 155, 165
Enlightenment, 64–65, 71, 99, 103, 195
epistemology, 28, 87, 95
eschatology, 17–18, 36, 62–63, 66, 69–70, 180, 200, 202–5, 211
Essays and Reviews (1861), 111, 114–16, 200
Essence of Christianity (Feuerbach), 98, 112
Eucharist, 120, 155, 197
evolution, *x*, 114

evil, 52, 85, 100, 113, 132, 151, 168, 179, 181, 185, 187, 189–90, 203
exegesis, 39, 153
experience, religious/spiritual, 71, 74–75, 108–9, 116, 125, 152, 166, 169, 176, 195, 198, 200
experience, sensory, 78–79, 87, 93

Faerie Queene (Spenser), 38–39
fairy-stories/fairytales, 4, 10, 13, 39, 44, 59, 62, 66–68, 72–73, 97, 101, 103, 107, 117–21, 149, 156, 159, 162, 166–67, 207, 212
fancy, 92, 97–98
fantastic/fantasy, 10, 13, 39, 67, 71, 97, 149–50, 162, 166–68, 170–71, 205, 207, 210, 212
fear, 6, 98, 176, 196
femininity, 9, 126. See also women.
figurative speech/language, 15, 19, 22, 24–25, 30, 36, 96, 110, 139, 178, 207
fiction, 2–5, 9, 13–14, 46–48, 58–59, 156–57, 160–62, 167–69, 171, 211–12
forgiveness, 53, 57, 188, 197–98
fourfold interpretation, 36–38
fundamentalism (religious), 103–4
funeral, 160, 182, 191–93, 211

genre, 5, 17, 39–40, 42, 50, 58, 66–68, 77, 97, 110, 120, 161, 167, 170–71, 195, 205, 207, 211
geology, ix, 103, 111–18
German Higher Criticism. See higher criticism/historical criticism.
"Golden Age"/"Golden Future", 62–63, 66, 200
"Golden Key, The" (MacDonald), 61, 140, 144, 160, 163, 203
gospel, 1, 8, 12–13, 43, 110, 115, 145, 162, 165, 168, 172–73, 184, 196, 206, 211
Gospel(s), 9, 16–18, 34–35, 45, 106, 112, 130, 153, 160, 175, 182–84, 192–93
grief, 74–75, 149, 176, 193. See also sorrow.

Heinrich von Ofterdingen (Novalis), 60–62, 65–66, 69–70, 73–74, 76
hermeneutics, 18, 37–38
higher criticism/historical criticism, ix–x, 3, 104–5, 111–12, 115–16, 123, 208
"History of Photogen and Nycteris, The" (MacDonald). *See* "Day Boy and the Night Girl, The" (MacDonald)
holiness, 8, 60, 126
Hope of the Gospel, The (MacDonald), 105, 125, 127–28, 132, 134, 140, 155, 176, 192
Hymns to the Night (Novalis), 61–63, 70–77, 122, 141, 195–96, 200, 209

imagination, ix–x, xii, 2–5, 10, 13–14, 31, 47, 57, 62–67, 70, 77–101, 105, 113, 129, 133, 137, 142, 147–50, 156–57, 168, 201, 205, 209–10, 212
Incarnation, xi–xii, 43, 81, 110, 131–32, 135–36
Industrial Revolution, 136
industrialization, 8
intertextuality, 55–56
Idealism, 3, 65–66, 70, 77–84, 86–92, 95, 100–101, 119, 209
inerrancy (biblical), 103, 116
infallibility (biblical), 103–4, 106, 111, 151, 153
Inklings, 2, 4
inspiration (biblical), 103–4, 106–11, 115–16, 151, 153. *See also* dictation theory, subjective theory, verbal theory
intellect, 64, 78, 85, 93, 99, 105, 107–8, 122, 139, 152, 157, 160–61, 177
interpretation, 3, 17–19, 31–39, 45–46, 50, 92, 97, 103, 106–10, 115, 138–39, 149, 153, 162, 165, 169, 172–73, 207, 211

Jane Eyre, 189
Kabala, 176

Kingdom of God, 1, 6, 16–18, 47–59, 133, 135, 141, 143, 153, 156, 161, 165–66, 171, 188, 199, 207–8, 211
Kunstmärchen, 59, 167, 170, 195
language, x, 14, 17–18, 20, 23–26, 59, 94, 122–24, 134, 136, 139, 145, 152, 156, 158, 161–62, 165, 166, 169, 173, 189–90, 202, 208
erotic, 72–73
figurative, 36
literal, 19, 27–29, 145, 157
liturgical, 197
metaphorical, 19, 22–23, 28–29, 157, 208
of Scripture, 1–2, 210
paradoxical, 188
philosophy of, 13
poetic, 11, 13, 58, 67
positivistic accounts of, 28
religious/theological, 20, 23, 58, 108, 137–38, 194
symbolic, 137

lectio divina, 129
legalism, 6
legend, 44, 112, 176
Life of Jesus (David Strauss), ix, 111–12, 116
"Light Princess, The" (MacDonald), 103, 117–21, 163, 177, 179
Lilith (MacDonald), 2, 3, 10, 13–14, 43, 59, 61–62, 64, 67, 70–71, 77, 98, 101, 114, 121, 130, 132, 137–39, 142, 144–46, 149, 160, 163, 167, 168–206, 209–11
Lion the Witch and the Wardrobe, The (Lewis), 43–45, 171
literalism (in biblical interpretation), 36, 104, 106
literature, 4–5, 9–11, 15, 33, 38–40, 148–49, 154, 164, 211
logic, 68, 91, 99, 139, 161
Lord of the Rings, The (Tolkien), 2, 44–45, 172
love, 6–8, 26, 53, 57, 72–77, 113, 120, 122, 125–27, 131–32, 142, 182, 186–87, 196

Malcolm (MacDonald), 114
Marquis of Lossie, The (MacDonald), 61
Mary Marston (MacDonald), 114
materialism, 100, 118–20
metaphor, 3, 17–33, 36, 38–41, 43, 45, 47, 50–57, 70, 72, 92, 94, 114, 119, 122, 125, 133–34, 136, 139, 143, 145, 153, 162, 169–72, 176–81, 183, 185–96, 198–99, 202, 204–6, 208, 210–11
metaphysics, 35, 65, 74, 79, 81, 86, 94, 114, 117–21, 142, 177
metonymy, 41
Middle Ages/medieval period, 35–39, 66, 69, 73–74, 149
mind, 24, 27, 34, 63–64, 78–95, 106, 122, 125, 129–30, 134, 139, 143, 145, 148, 154–55, 201
minister, 12, 204
miracles, 104–5, 112, 149
Missionar Kirk, 6–7
models (conceptual), 30–32, 40
moon, 106, 146, 154, 197–98, 202
mystery, *ix*, 3, 10, 23–24, 27, 35, 37, 58, 73, 75–76, 81, 128, 136–37, 140, 156, 169, 188, 191–92, 194–95, 197–98, 204–5, 208–9, 211
mysticism, 35–36, 71–75, 82, 122, 139
myth, 39, 44, 76, 112, 170–71
mythopoeic, 42, 170

natural theology, 108, 113, 115–16
nature, 27, 44, 64–65, 80–82, 86–87, 89–95, 111–14, 131–32, 134–35, 139, 153, 155
New Hermeneutics, 18, 38
night, 9, 43, 71–76, 121–22, 160, 169–70, 179, 195–99, 202, 206, 209–11
nihilism, 194

obedience, 117, 125, 127, 129, 133, 168, 190–91, 205. *See also* disobedience.

parables/parabolic speech, *x*, 1, 3, 10, 13–19, 32–34, 36–39, 41, 45–59, 68, 77, 91, 94, 101–2, 112, 121, 123, 131, 135, 141, 143–44, 148, 150, 152–53, 155–63, 165–67, 169–73, 177–78, 188–89, 193–96, 205, 207–11
  of the Good Samaritan, 16, 45–46, 49, 51, 163, 171
  of the Humble Servant, 51
  of the Laborers in the Vineyard, 16, 53
  of the Leaven, 16, 52, 55, 143–45
  of the Lion, 15
  of the Lost Coin, 51
  of the Lost Sheep, 51
  of the Mustard Seed, 15–16, 53, 55
  of the New Wine, 48
  of the Pearl, 16
  of the Pharisee and Tax Collector, 45, 51, 54
  of the Prodigal Son, 7, 10, 16, 45, 47, 49, 53, 55, 163
  of the Rich Man and Lazarus, 47
  of the Sower, 15, 34
  of the Treasure, 16
  of the Two Eagles and the Vine, 15, 34
  of the Unforgiving Servant, 52
  of the Unjust Judge, 52, 155
  of the Unjust Steward, 16, 47
  of the Unmerciful Servant, 47, 50, 52
  of the Unshrunk Cloth, 48
  of the Vine, 15
  of the Vineyard, 15
  of the Weeds, 34
  of the Wicked Tenants, 10, 15–16, 45–47, 49–50, 55
  of the Wise and Foolish Maidens, 47
Paradise Lost (Milton), 38, 164
paradox, 54, 75, 89, 169, 181, 188
participation, *x*, *xii*, 2, 4, 50, 56–57, 76, 128, 152, 157–61, 166, 169, 186–88, 191–92, 194, 198, 204, 210–11

pastoral ministry, *ix*, 1-2, 5, 7-8, 10-12, 14, 47, 56, 58, 156, 161-63, 166-68, 189, 205, 207, 209, 211
penal substitution, 3
personification, 9, 38, 41, 164, 187-88
Phantastes (MacDonald), 2, 14, 61-62, 67-68, 90-91, 96, 105, 121-22, 130, 139, 142-43, 146, 157, 168
Pilgrim's Progress (Bunyan), 38-39, 41-44, 46, 48, 50, 149, 167, 175
Platonism, 34, 136, 203
pneumatology, 129. *See also* Spirit.
poems/poetry/poetics, *ix-xi*, 1-5, 9-11, 13, 15, 22, 26-27, 39, 44, 58-59, 61-62, 65-70, 72, 76-77, 81, 84, 87-98, 101, 113-14, 121-22, 126, 131-34, 136-37, 139-41, 145, 147-49, 157-58, 162, 166, 180, 182, 199-200, 209-10
Poetics (Aristotle), 19
poverty, 8, 12
preaching, 5, 7, 12, 106, 184
predestination, 6-7
Presbyterian, 9
priest, 2, 46, 49, 76-77, 159, 166, 180, 184-85, 193-94, 209, 211. *See also* clergy, minister, sexton.
Prince of the Power of the Air, 185, 187
Princess and Curdie, The (MacDonald), 2, 9, 114, 126, 130, 137, 146
Princess and the Goblin, The (MacDonald), 2, 9, 126, 163
prose, 1, 22, 63, 66-67, 145-46, 157, 162
Protestant(ism), 5-6, 116
proverbs, 15-16
Puritan(s), 8

rabbis/rabbinic, 15, 34
Rampolli (MacDonald), 61, 63, 72-73, 75, 122, 141
rationalism, 28, 177. *See also* reason.
"Raven, The" (poem), 182
reason, 34, 64, 68, 71-72, 78, 91, 195. *See also* rationalism.

redemption, 7, 72, 85, 100-101, 126, 187, 195, 197
Reformation, Protestant, 37, 66
reformed (theology, church, etc.), 3, 5-7
revelation, *xi*, 1-2, 47, 54-55, 58-59, 62-66, 69-71, 75, 84, 96, 98, 102, 106, 111, 115-17, 123-35, 146-48, 151-62, 166, 196, 198, 200, 202, 208, 210
resurrection, 2-3, 43, 61, 63, 72-73, 75-76, 112, 170, 175, 179-80, 182-83, 186-88, 191-92, 194-99, 203-5, 209, 211-12
rhetoric, 19
Robert Falconer (MacDonald), 6, 8, 10-11, 130, 163
Romanticism, 2-3, 5, 13, 19, 37-39, 60, 64, 66-68, 72, 74, 76-78, 81-82, 86, 113, 132, 134, 145, 195, 200, 203, 208
Ronald Bannerman's Boyhood (MacDonald), 136

sacraments, *xi*, 155, 197. *See also* baptism, Eucharist.
Salted with Fire (MacDonald), 9, 130, 163, 184
scholasticism, 6-7, 37, 124
science, *ix-x*, 3, 11, 28, 30-31, 65-66, 91, 93-94, 102-4, 112-22, 124, 137, 141-42, 177, 199, 201-2, 208-9
Scotland, 5-9, 11, 115
Scottish Evangelicalism, 103
Scripture, *x-xi*, 1-2, 4, 9-10, 35-37, 56-57, 102-11, 115-17, 123, 126, 129, 131, 135-36, 139-40, 142, 145-48, 150-56, 174, 186, 197, 200, 208, 210. *See also* Bible.
Seaboard Parish, The (MacDonald), 61, 128-29
Secession, 6
sensus allegoricus, 36
sensus anagogicus, 36
sensus historicus, 36
sensus litterali, 36
sensus moralis, 36

sensus tropologicus, 36
sermons, *ix*, 5, 7, 13, 122, 125–26, 130–31, 133, 140–41, 145, 152–53, 175, 192–93, 197
sexton, 182, 184–85, 191–92, 197, 211
shock, 1, 2, 27, 30, 45, 47–48, 51–55, 57–58, 101, 161–62, 166, 208–10
sin, 15, 43, 46, 52, 57, 71, 143–44, 170, 176, 185–94, 196, 198, 204
Sir Gibbie (MacDonald), 9–10, 130, 155, 163
skepticism, *x*, 6, 64, 69, 103, 111
sleep, 64, 67, 72–73, 118, 137, 169–70, 174, 179–80, 182, 184–88, 190, 192, 196, 198–99, 203–5
sorrow, 117, 169, 175–76, 182, 198. *See also* grief.
sovereignty (of God), 6–7
Spirit (Holy, of God, of Christ, etc.), *xii*, 107–8, 110, 125, 128–29, 138, 151
spiritual formation/growth/development/transformation, 2–3, 10, 42, 77, 102, 105, 108, 114, 138, 146, 156, 163, 171, 176, 184, 194–95
"Spiritual Songs" (Novalis), 11–12, 61, 70
story/stories, *ix–xii*, 1–3, 5, 15–16, 34, 38, 40–59, 62–63, 68–69, 73, 77, 85, 101–2, 104, 112, 117–18, 120–23, 126, 130–31, 135, 141, 146–49, 151, 156–67, 169, 171–74, 176–77, 181, 185, 187, 194, 196–97, 199, 207–8, 210, 212
subconscious/unconscious, 70, 81, 86–87, 98–99, 101, 209
subjective theory (of biblical inspiration), 107, 109, 111. *See also* dictation, verbal theory.
suffering, 12, 72, 75–77, 130, 165, 176, 193, 195–98
supernatural, *ix*, 63–66, 68, 200–202
symbol, 3, 38–39, 62, 67, 70–71, 73–74, 88, 102, 120, 122, 130, 132–50, 152–53, 155–57, 159–66, 171, 179, 181, 185, 199, 209–10

synecdoche, 41
temptation, 42–43, 144, 160
theology, spiritual, 5–6, 211–12
There and Back (MacDonald), 10
Thomas Wingfold (MacDonald), 114
transcendence, 23, 66, 78, 83–84, 117, 132, 200
tropology, 36–37
truth, *x–xii*, 1, 9, 28, 34, 36, 44, 47, 64, 69–70, 76, 96–98, 100–101, 104, 106–9, 111, 115–17, 120, 122, 124–25, 128, 130, 133, 139, 141–43, 147–48, 151–52, 154–62, 165, 175, 194, 205, 208–10

Unspoken Sermons (MacDonald), 117, 120, 122, 124–43, 147, 151–54, 161–62, 165, 175, 179, 197
urbanization, 8, 114

verbal theory (of biblical inspiration), 103–4, 106, 109–11, 116, 151. *See also* dictation, subjective theory.
Vicar's Daughter, The (MacDonald), 114
Victorian Age, *ix*, 1–6, 8, 98, 102–4, 106, 108, 111–17, 119–20, 123, 144, 151, 157, 164–65, 169, 173–83, 189, 191, 193, 200–201, 208, 211
vocation, 12, 184, 211

Wisdom of Solomon, 107, 117
women, 6, 9, 51, 126, 185. *See also* femininity.
word(s), *xi–xii*, 21–22, 24, 27–30, 34, 41, 51–52, 67, 104–6, 108–11, 120, 124, 129, 134, 139, 141, 144–45, 147–48, 150–52, 154, 157–59, 172–73, 185, 190, 198

www.ingramcontent.com/pod-product-compliance
Lightning Source LLC
Chambersburg PA
CBHW051053230426
43667CB00013B/2280